PENGUIN BOOKS

A TUSCAN CHILDHOOD

Kinta Beevor was born in 1911 at Northbourne in East Kent. After her father joined up in the First World War her mother, Lina Waterfield, took Kinta and her brother out to Florence, where she started the British Institute. Kinta's childhood was spent at Poggio Gherardo and at her parent's castle at Aulla. She returned to England, married and had three sons. She lived at Eastry, close to where she was born, but she still returned to Italy each year. Kinta Beevor died in August 1995.

FROM REVIEWS OF *A Tuscan Childhood*

'Kinta Beevor's distinctive contribution is in her detailed and unsentimental account of the peasant life of the time, its surrounding, its labours and its joys, and in her ability to convey the remembered happiness of a childhood spent in the freedom of two exceptionally beautiful houses amid some of the most delectable countryside in the world' – Isabel Colegate in *The Times Literary Supplement*

'A delightful memoir' – *Marie Claire*

'Its unpretentiousness and authenticity, and above all the sincerity of the writer' affection for an Italy now long lost, make it an attractive and engaging read' – *Spectator*

KINTA BEEVOR

A Tuscan Childhood

PENGUIN BOOKS

PENGUIN BOOKS

Published by the Penguin Group
Penguin Books Ltd, 27 Wrights Lane, London W8 5TZ, England
Penguin Books USA Inc., 375 Hudson Street, New York, New York 10014, USA
Penguin Books Australia Ltd, Ringwood, Victoria, Australia
Penguin Books Canada Ltd, 10 Alcorn Avenue, Toronto, Ontario, Canada M4V 3B2
Penguin Books (NZ) Ltd, 182–190 Wairau Road, Auckland 10, New Zealand

Penguin Books Ltd, Registered Offices: Harmondsworth, Middlesex, England

First published by Viking 1993
Published in Penguin Books 1995
7 9 10 8 6

To my grandchildren

CONTENTS

LIST OF PLATES

Section I

La Fortezza della Brunella

The Return from the Ride. Charles Furse's portrait of Aubrey and Lina after their marriage (*The Tate Gallery*)

Aubrey Waterfield before his marriage to Lina Duff Gordon

Lina and Aubrey working on the ramparts, with Gordon in the wheelbarrow

A picnic in the Lunigiana hills before the First World War: Gordon, Lina, Mariannina and Ulisse the Wise

Three pictures by Aubrey Waterfield: Ramponi, Adelina and Montàn

One of Aubrey's paintings of the Carraras from above the Lagastrello campsite

Aubrey working on one of his frescoes of local landscapes in the *salone* at the castle

The Carraras seen from the window made by Fiore the stonemason

View of the castle from a distance

Aunt Janet supervising the *vendemmia* at Poggio before the First World War

Loading the grapes on to an ox-cart

Agostino in the kitchen at Poggio Gherardo during the First World War

Beppe the gardener

Pippo. The fresco of the beloved poodle of the Gherardi family

Poggio's main entrance from the edge of the *bosco*

Section II

CHAPTER ONE

The Garden in the Sky

'There it is!' said my mother pointing out of the carriage window. The curve of the track as it followed the contours of the hills along the river Magra gave us a glimpse up the valley. The castle stood revealed on a distant spur that overlooked the confluence of two rivers. In between, wooded hills sloped in on either side like scenery in a toy theatre. This landscape of steep hills covered in chestnut trees, with mountains in the background, was typical of the Lunigiana, the north-western frontier of Tuscany. Beyond the Apennines lay Parma, and to the west of the Magra lay Genoese Liguria.

Those who saw the Fortezza della Brunella for the first time had mixed feelings. As the word fortress implied it was a massive military structure, with square towers at each corner and huge walls like the base of a ziggurat, yet I could see why my mother still tended to refer to it as 'the castle'. It had a certain majesty up on its rock above the river. For my father, who had fallen in love with it at first sight in 1896, this extraordinary choice for a dwelling place promised an enchanted world far from English formality.

Yet this was my first sight of the castle. It was the late summer of 1916. I was five and my brother John was seven.

My father was away at the war and my mother had decided to bring John and me over from Florence where we were living with our great-aunt, Janet Ross. Following Italy's declaration of war on the Allied side, a small detachment of soldiers had been sent to the castle to watch for Austrian aircraft, and my mother wanted to check that all was well.

At Aulla station, she greeted several people and found the driver of a pony-trap who was willing to drive us up to the castle. On the narrow carriage-drive, his *barroccino* rattled and creaked and lurched and jarred alarmingly, for this serpentine route up the steep hillside had been hewn from volcanic rock. At each of the hairpin bends the thin little horse had to circle sideways, pivoting the cart on its own axis.

John and I kept glancing back and forth, from the red-brown rock with its strange igneous streaks on one side to the drop down the very steep slope on the other. We wondered how many carriages and carts had toppled over. In those days there were only a few ilex trees to halt a very stony descent. Later, the outcrops of volcanic rock were softened or concealed by a whole wood of ilexes planted by my father, as well as cypresses and umbrella pines grown from seeds that he brought back from the island of Elba where they were famous for the straightness of their trunks. There were no olive trees to be seen in either of the flanking valleys because of the river mists.

It was a relief to reach the top of the ridge on which the castle stood hidden by more ilex trees and some stone pines. But this first sight of our parents' home at close quarters came as a shock. From the train coming up the Magra valley there had been that distant glimpse of a toy fortress, but now we found ourselves facing massive ivy-covered walls and towers across a deep dry moat. The effect was overwhelmingly powerful.

John and I climbed down from the trap feeling very subdued. We gazed up at the ramparts high above us. The place looked as if it had been abandoned under an enchanter's spell. I became conscious of the noise of the cicadas throbbing in the heat and the smell of baked earth and pine needles. We walked cautiously to the edge of the moat while my mother paid the driver.

The entrance door was reached by a brick bridge that spanned the moat like a miniature viaduct. Although fixed, it was always known as the drawbridge. When my mother led us across John and I clung to her, hardly daring to look down into the moat's scrub-concealed depths over twenty feet below. Looking up produced a similar sensation, for the square corner tower was nearly sixty feet high.

We found ourselves in a dark, cell-like room with small square windows set deep in the thick walls. It was cool, almost cold after the heat outside. There was a damp smell of whitewash. As our eyes grew accustomed to the gloom, we saw that we were entering a tunnel with smooth walls but a rough, cave-like ceiling which showed that it had been cut through solid rock. Up one side a staircase ascended to the top of the tower; when we passed, our movement disturbed some of the bats who emitted virtually inaudible squeaks of alarm.

We saw daylight at the end of the corridor and came out into a courtyard not much wider than an alley and cobbled with round stones brought up from the river-bed. Even in the height of summer it had a cool, mossy smell. We discovered that the L-shaped courtyard divided the living quarters from the cisterns and old dungeons. They lay behind the uneven stone wall on the left that seemed to reach to the sky.

As soon as we crossed and entered the door to the hall, the frightening impression of the castle's exterior vanished. The hall, with the double doors of the *portone* open on to the terrace, was flooded with sunlight. John and I ran from room to room, our voices and footsteps echoing under the high, vaulted ceilings. Even the fireplaces carved from grey *pietra serena* reached far above our heads. I felt as if I had shrunk, like Alice. My mother pointed out a shield carved into the stone. It depicted a lion rampant looking understandably anguished in a thicket of thorns. This, apparently, was the coat of arms of the Malaspinas, the family that had ruled these valleys since the eleventh century.

The embrasures leading to the french windows showed the sixteen-foot width of the walls. We went out on to the balcony to look down at the town. A train was emerging from the tunnel on the far side of the valley. We began to count the carriages as it crossed the bridge over the river. It seemed endless.

'We're going upstairs to see the garden now,' said my mother. We followed her. The idea of a garden high above our heads diverted our attention from the number of carriages. She led the way up a dark, perilous staircase at the end of the courtyard. We kept close to the wall. As we emerged again into the daylight we saw vines above us on a pergola.

John and I immediately ran off to explore, ignoring her cries to be careful. We peered through some trellis down into the narrow courtyard from which we had just come – it was indeed a long way down – then we rushed from tower to tower, where we gazed at the valleys far below with astonishment and delight. We also raced round the sentry's walk. This followed the outside edge of the terracotta-tiled roof over the living quarters. But our greatest delight was my father's garden in the sky.

At the centre stood a fantastic rose-covered *tempietto* of white trellis-work with a dome in the middle and a pinnacle on either side. My father's design must have been inspired by the Brighton Pavilion. As a backdrop, it had the most extraordinary aspect of all: an avenue of mature ilex trees extending between the two towers.

Underneath the dome was a sunken marble *vasca*, six foot square and five feet deep, which formed a pool with water-lilies and goldfish. And from this focal point a broad grass walk advanced with flower-beds on each side, edged by miniature box hedges, straight towards the greatest view of all – the four main peaks of the Carrara mountains, or Apuan Alps, as they are officially known.

We were still too young then to appreciate the full beauty of this roof-garden. That came later. It was the sheer improbability of the place that appealed to us so much.

Next we explored the towers. Despite all the warnings about dangerous staircases, we slipped from one to another. We wondered whether a secret chamber lay hidden behind one of the walls. At Fyvie Castle in Scotland, my grandfather and his cousin, Cosmo Duff Gordon, had hung towels over every accessible window-sill in the Meldrum tower; then they had gone outside and pinpointed a secret chamber from the one casement left unmarked. But all we found at Aulla were bare, crudely fashioned rooms lit only by daylight from an embrasure. In one of them we came across the bedding rolls of the soldiers posted there to watch for aircraft. This was the first sign of occupation: the soldiers had treated everything with the greatest care. We found my mother talking to them and their corporal. As true Italians, they made a great fuss of John and me and allowed us to try on their hats.

My mother took us back down to the Albergo d'Italia where we stayed for the next few nights, spending each day up at the castle. John and I continued our explorations. There was only one place that retained its power to inspire fear: a subterranean magazine where men of the garrison, massacred by the Spaniards, were said to have been buried.

Before our return to Florence, my mother organized a good lunch for the soldiers to thank them for taking such good care of the castle and the roof-garden. With their emotions warmed by red wine, they acclaimed her as *la madre dei soldati italiani*. They seemed to believe that she somehow had the power to keep them there, far away from the fighting on the Austrian front. On our departure, John and I said goodbye to our new friends and to the castle itself. We were not to see it again until the war was over.

John and I longed to know more about the history of the place and how my father had found it. Luckily, the following year, he was transferred from the Somme to the Italian front where, as an Italian speaker, he served on Lord Cavan's staff. As soon as he was allowed some leave, which was spent on the coast at Forte dei Marmi, we were able to ask him directly.

'Well, the thing to understand,' he told us, 'is that Aulla stands at a very important and strategic place. The main valleys of the Lunigiana join there and it covers the route over the mountains to Parma and Milan – that's the Cisa Pass that Hannibal was supposed to have used – and also the road from Genoa coming over the Bracco Pass.

'There used to be a castle down below the hill close to the river, guarding the ancient abbey of San Caprasio, built by Adalberto of Tuscany in the ninth century – over a thousand years ago. But that castle was pulled down before the Fortezza della Brunella was built. From the Middle Ages the Lunigiana was ruled by the Malaspina family, who eventually became Dukes of Massa Carrara.'

'Isn't that their coat of arms on the fireplace in the *salone*?' John asked. 'The lion with a crown on its head, standing up in the thorn bush?'

'That's right. There were two branches of the family. One had a lion rampant with flowers, so it was known as the Malaspina *fiorita*, and the other had a lion in a thicket of thorns, so it was called the Malaspina *spinosa*. Anyway, a great Genoese admiral and soldier called Adamo Centurione took over, having ousted a *condottiere*, or warlord, known as Giovanni delle Bande Nere – John of the Black Bands. As you might imagine, with mercenary bands and warlords, those were very violent times.'

'Did they have cannons?' John asked. 'We found a cannon-ball in the moat, which we showed to Ramponi.'

'They might well have done, but the cannon-ball you found was probably later. In the eighteenth century Spanish troops besieged the castle, which up to then had been impregnable, so when they finally captured it there was great rejoicing in Madrid and a *Te Deum* was sung in celebration. In fact they managed to penetrate the defences only when a traitor led them up a secret path under cover of a river mist early one morning. The whole garrison was massacred.'

'Yes,' said John, 'and they are all buried in the magazine.' Like most small boys, he took a macabre satisfaction in such details.

'The Spaniards,' my father went on, 'had struck such fear into the Italians that even to this day mothers tell their children that if they are naughty the Spaniards will take them away. Funnily enough there's even a Tuscan saying that goes "*E meglio stare al bosco e mangiar pinoli, che stare in castello con gli spagnoli.*" It means: "Better to live in the woods and eat pine nuts than in a castle with the Spaniards."

'But the most important thing about the Spaniards in this case,' he went on, 'is that after capturing the castle, they hauled their guns up to the roof over the dungeons and cisterns to cover the two valleys. And to absorb the recoil when the cannons fired, they put earth down, and this showed me that it was possible to make a garden up there.'

John then asked about the holes in the towers, and heard that they were for pouring boiling oil on any attackers who crossed the moat. 'But please, *Babbo*,' I broke in impatiently, 'I want to hear how *you* discovered the castle.'

And so my father told us the strange story of how he had come to this place. In 1896, when an undergraduate at Oxford, he had been staying at the castle of Portofino, which belonged to the English consul, Monty Brown. Brown collected Savona vases, yet his fame as a lover of ancient objects spread before him to such an extent that he was offered castles as well. Popular legend credited him with buying sixteen of them, mostly in inaccessible places. The Fortezza della Brunella was said to be so wild that one member of the house party even claimed that it had moufflons, a rare species of wild sheep, grazing upon its roof.

The mildly eccentric Brown had bought the castle at Aulla for little more than the price of one of his maiolica jars, and despite carrying out a good deal of necessary work he had never spent a night there. A fellow guest suggested to my father that they should pass that way, for he had argued at dinner, in one of his sudden passions, that no seaside place like Portofino could ever be typical of a country.

When my father and his companion reached Aulla, they found that Monty Brown had made the castle habitable with a roof over the living quarters. He had also allowed the railway company, then building the new line to Parma, to quarry stone in return for building a carriage-drive up to the castle, which we had ascended that first day. Brown, who had refused any payment for the quarrying, ended up with the best of the bargain. The railway company had not imagined quite how unyielding the volcanic hillside would be.

The carriage-drive was the only visible improvement. Brown did not want to make any alterations or repairs to the exterior of the castle itself. Even the ivy growing thick upon its sloping walls was left untouched.

My father instantly fell in love with its wild beauty and wonderful views. They never left his thoughts. Seven years later, he took my mother to see his dream castle for the first time at the end of their honeymoon. He wanted to show it to her at its best, which meant waiting for the evening light. So, after lunch at the vine-covered Albergo d'Italia, he took her up the valley of the Aulella in a hired pony-trap and they swam in one of its deep green pools. (Years later I discovered that they had bathed naked. It was hard to imagine one's parents doing such things, especially in those days.)

Once the bright sunlight had turned to the apricot glow of early evening, he led the way to the track that zigzags up the side of the fortress hill between ilex trees and patches of violets and cyclamen. They reached the terrace between the two south-eastern towers and, with an ancient iron key more than a foot long, let themselves in through the huge double doors of the *portone*.

The locals were frightened of the castle: they claimed to

Lina Duff Gordon in her travelling-hat (*Aubrey Waterfield*)

see unexplained lights up there and ghost stories had been lovingly elaborated around the massacred garrison. Nobody dared go near the place after dark. Even by day, rumours of huge serpents in the overgrown moat kept people away. In the minds of those superstitious townsfolk who had watched my parents set off up the hill, the stage must have seemed set for one of those Gothic tales in which an innocent English couple with romantic tastes move into a haunted building, having pooh-poohed all warnings.

The sound of the giant door creaking open reverberated in the empty hall. My father took my mother through the ground floor rooms, then up a perilous stairway in one of the towers, and on to the roof. From there they looked down three hundred feet to the Aulella river with its stony shallows and deep green pools, like the one in which they had bathed a few hours earlier.

The peaks of the Carraras beyond remained lit by the setting sun while dusk fell rapidly in the valleys. The cry of falcons gave way to the squeak of bats wheeling and swooping overhead. Then, in the distance, the Angelus rang from the Benedictine bell tower of San Caprasio down by the river Magra. It was a gentle, clear chime.

My mother remained silent, entranced by the beauty, but her silence distressed my father. Eventually he could stand it no longer. 'But Lina, don't you like my castle?'

'Oh yes, Aubrey,' she answered, roused from her reverie. 'I was just wondering how long it would take for two camp-beds to arrive from the Army & Navy Stores.'

Although my parents immediately applied to Monty Brown by telegraph for a lease on the castle, they did not begin to live there until two years later when they returned to Italy. They came via Bergamo, then famous for its old furniture market, where they purchased eighteenth-century pieces of substantial proportions so that they would not look dwarfed in the large rooms. A quantity of huge cupboards, tables, sideboards, chests of drawers and chairs cost them very little because in those days antique furniture was sold in poor repair and generally despised as second-hand.

My parents began life in the castle with their two camp-beds and a packing-case as a table until the furniture arrived. It was an eerie sensation to lie awake in this empty fortress, watching fantastic shadows from the huge fireplace weaving on the high, semi-vaulted ceiling and listening to owls hooting outside. My mother silently prayed that the ghosts of the massacred garrison would guard, not threaten them. But no phantom, either benevolent or malevolent, made an appearance.

My mother later admitted that she was very frightened during their first nights of occupation, but at the time she made light of it to the Aullese townsfolk who were so eager to hear about their nocturnal impressions and proffer advice on almost every subject. When the furniture from Bergamo finally arrived, those who helped the carters negotiate the hairpin corners on the drive and carry it into the castle looked at it dubiously.

'We have heard that English people like old things,' they told my parents. 'But Orfeo down in the town has such beautiful furniture, all quite new and polished. You can see your face in it. And there are iron bedsteads, too, with a coloured picture of the Madonna at the head. But, of course, signori, you could choose any other saint you please.'

It was often said of my parents that they had all the luxuries of life but none of the necessities. They lived in a castle and later inherited the fourteenth-century villa of Poggio Gherardo outside Florence, yet they seldom had money for those things that their relations considered the basis of civilized life.

Poggio Gherardo belonged to my great-aunt, Janet Ross, a character invariably described as formidable. As my mother's guardian, she had vigorously opposed her 'imprudent' marriage to Aubrey Waterfield. She believed that a young girl like Lina Duff Gordon, brought up in considerable style in London and at Fyvie (until my spendthrift grandfather was forced to sell it), was far too delicate to survive as the wife of an impecunious painter in an abandoned mountain fortress. Aunt Janet promptly sent Davide, her steward, to inspect the Fortezza della Brunella. On his return to Florence, he confirmed her worst prejudices by pronouncing it 'a place not fit for Christians'.

Aubrey, my father, was almost as dedicated to gardens as he was to his painting, so he looked forward to landscaping their surroundings once the necessary work inside and out had been accomplished. His vision was grandiose, but his luck was even greater. He did not have to assemble a workforce: individuals turned up offering their services, and seldom has such a haphazard process of selection turned out so happily.

Montàn, the first *contadino* or peasant farmer at the castle, could remember from his own childhood – it must have been in the 1840s – the carriage of the last Duke of Modena passing through the little town on the way to his summer palace. Montàn was typical of the Lunigianese; staunch, yet open-minded.

Even before my father had time to spread the word that he needed a stonemason, Ulisse and his son, Archimede, turned up to propose themselves. Ulisse, known locally as Ulisse the Wise, had already worked on the internal restoration for Monty Brown. Their team was completed by Emilio Christiani, a local carpenter, and Bagòn, a carter with huge cavalry moustaches, who used to drive his wagon and mules down to the river-bed to fetch sand and stones, either for repairs, or for use in paths and steps.

My father, with Ulisse and Archimede, began to repoint loose stonework on the outer walls. Using ropes strapped to a primitive harness and a pulley, either Ulisse or Archimede moved up and down the walls like an abseiler. Meanwhile, Bagòn, down in the moat, mixed the mortar for them, stirring in soot from the old fireplaces to conceal the restoration.

When my father wrote to Monty Brown to tell him that the roof over the living quarters leaked, he received no satisfaction except the unusual present of a gazelle, which arrived by train. The gazelle was not sent as an obscure joke – a replacement for the mythical moufflons on the roof – but because Mervyn Herbert, the undergraduate son of a neighbour in Portofino, had bought it from a sailor in Genoa, and his mother did not know what to do with it when he went back to Oxford.

The gazelle was given winter quarters in the moat with a hut and a fat woolly sheep for warmth and company, but it promptly attacked this stable companion with its sharp little horns; my mother, never very handy with a needle and knowing little of animals, showed great courage sewing up the poor sheep's lacerated flanks. She even made the gazelle a jacket for the cold months, but the unfortunate creature was later stoned to death by boys from the village when my parents were away.

The programme of repairs took longer than my father had expected. My eldest brother Gordon, born in 1902, was brought out to Italy two years later by his English nanny and my father's mother who took the extraordinary living conditions in their stride. There is a photograph of Gordon seated in a wicker howdah attached to the back of a donkey while the work went on, and another of him being given a ride in a wheelbarrow by my father while my mother unconvincingly wields a hoe for the camera. As her unsuitable garb indicates, she was no Vita Sackville-West. Once the walls were finally repaired, my father was able to embark on his dream: the garden on the roof of the castle.

My father and Ulisse fixed a stout pole with a pulley to one of the square towers, and hauled wicker baskets full of soil up to the ramparts to add to the earth already put there by the Spaniards. Over the next few years, they planted the avenue of ilexes, the vines, flowers, the miniature box hedges and a hedge of rosemary. They also installed the deep, square fish-pool of Carrara marble. Emilio then built, to my father's design, the pavilion of trellis with its grand cupola. When all was finally done, they contemplated their work with a satisfaction akin to that described in the first chapter of Genesis. 'And I, Ulisse,' said the stonemason nodding his head in slow emphasis, 'I say that the *fortezza* is a paradise.'

The roof-garden was the centre of this paradise. It formed the focus of our whole life at the castle, when we returned after the First World War. It was then full summer, and by late morning, when the heat became stifling, we would go up to the roof to take advantage of the midday breeze funnelled up the Magra valley from the sea. The wind would start gently, then gather strength until we heard a door which somebody had forgotten to close banging in the distance. We either sat under the trellis pavilion or stretched out on the grass in the avenue of ilex trees, whose leaves rustled in the wind. The mingled scent from flowers and box and rosemary bushes was enough to make one's head swim. Staring up between the trees at the sky, I felt my body floating on a different plane.

I never grew bored of that magical garden in the sky. It was so peaceful that its bellicose past of massacred garrisons and Spanish cannon seemed too improbable to turn into a serious image. The rampart walls had small irises growing out of the top. Lizards basked immobile on stone spotted with saffron-coloured lichen. When they finally moved, they would advance in a sudden rush of activity, then freeze again as if in a game of Grandmother's Footsteps. If John and I came too close, they would flick over the edge of the parapet or into some crevice which looked too narrow to admit even a beetle. From the parapet we watched the hovering and diving of a pair of kestrels, which nested high on the outside of one of the walls. We also kept a lookout for *mormore*, a sort of squirrel, which ran along the vine pergolas in search of grapes. *Mormore* were not natives of Italy, but were supposed to have come down from Germany in the Middle Ages on wagon-trains.

There were scorpions on the roof, but their sting, although painful, was not as serious as that of their African cousins. My mother's pet jay, however, died from eating one. My mother and father were given many animals beside the gazelle and the jay. They used to arrive in embarrassing quantities, as if everyone believed that the castle had to be filled with captured wildlife. They refused a pair of eaglets taken from a nest high in the Carraras, but felt obliged to accept some of the other presents. A peasant boy proudly brought a leveret, which grew into a fine semi-house-trained hare with magnificent ears. It lolloped everywhere, for few doors were ever closed, and sometimes at night it jumped on to my parents' bed, startling them. Finally it killed itself in a characteristically mad rush of activity by leaping from the parapet on the roof.

John and I also used to watch the forest fires in the chestnut woods through a huge pair of naval binoculars missing one eye-piece. We feared for the people who lived on the hillside, but Ramponi, the *contadino* who came to help Montàn, assured us that everyone would be organizing themselves to fight the fires. He probably did not know this and was just trying to calm us, but we never doubted his word about anything. It was a relief the next morning to see that the black scars on the hillside were not so great as we had feared under all the smoke.

At dusk, we would come up again to watch the sunset on the Carraras, particularly on the main peak, the Pizzo d'Uccello, or bird's beak, which rises to nearly six thousand feet. From an apricot gold in the low-angled sunlight, the mountain tops changed to purple, the colour of a Florentine iris, then they became a blue-black silhouette against the evening sky. As darkness fell earlier in the valley, lights appeared in the town below. Lastly, the extended halo along the western hilltops beyond the Magra disappeared and we began to see the stars.

We would have dinner up in the roof-garden under a persimmon tree next to the trellis pavilion. My father had erected a pulley with a long rope so that food, plates and *fiaschi* of both wine and drinking-water could be hauled up in a large basket from the courtyard outside the kitchen. My father summoned guests to table and warned the kitchen of the basket's descent by blowing on a conch shell, like the local mountain shepherds. This marine horn – its tip filed off to provide a mouthpiece – gave out a long, deep, eerie sound, more like a whale calling under the ocean than a musical instrument.

We dined by the light of candles on *zuppa di verdura* and *ripieni* (stuffed vegetables), followed by freshly picked figs and peaches. John and I, by then ten and eight, were considered old enough for 'baptized' wine; wine mixed with water. As a special treat, we were allowed to cut up a peach, put the pieces in our glasses and top them up with red wine and sugar. Afterwards we sat without talking, weightless in the soft night air, listening to the cicadas and tree frogs, breathing in the scent of the tobacco-plants and watching the fireflies. Only the sound of a train in the valley below reminded us of the real world.

On hot nights, the whole family slept on the roof in old naval hammocks of thick, hard canvas, which we padded with cotton quilts. John and I slung ours away from our parents, either between the trees of the avenue or under the trellis pavilion. To our great surprise, our father – fearing the link between moonlight and madness – forbade us to sleep out when the moon was full. We had to pitch a tent instead.

But the moon fascinated us. It rose over the Carraras and relit the mountains, hills, valleys and rivers in such a different guise that it seemed to turn this familiar scene into a magical landscape – the sort of transformation you see only in dreams. Moonlight made the surface of the two rivers shine with an unnatural brightness, and the water became black again only beyond their confluence, on its way down between the hills to the sea.

As I lay in my hammock in the avenue, I could gaze out at the silvered peaks of the Carraras between the dark masses of ilex and listen to the nightingales. But however much I wanted to stay awake and look at the mountains or up at the stars, sleep came over me before I was aware of it.

Early in the mornings, John and I would awake to yet another strange world, this time lightly shrouded in mist. After rolling out of the hammocks, we stripped naked and jumped into the cool, deep water of the marble *vasca* – a plunge that must have terrified the goldfish. After clambering out, we ran round the roof, still naked, to dry off. Our parents, we usually found, had got up before us and disappeared, my mother to her typewriter and my father to paint in the early morning light.

Almost always late, John and I would race down for breakfast on the vine-shaded terrace just outside the *portone*. From the roof, we had caught the smell of coffee and the toasted maize bread, which we would spread with white unsalted butter and Mariannina's apricot jam. We would then return to the top of one of the towers to gaze at the strange images caused by the river mists. A single umbrella pine would be visible, standing alone as if on a tiny island in a sea of cloud. Gradually, more trees appeared, then, as the sun strengthened, the hillsides across the Aulella began to emerge above the nebulous flood that filled the valley below.

By eight o'clock, only odd patches of mist lingered. The sun had pierced and broken the spell, ending the blanket of eerie silence that had concealed the awakening valley. Sounds drifted up again from the railway: the hand-cranked chime of the level-crossing bell, then the stationmaster's toot on a miniature trumpet and, finally, the slow, earnest chuffing of the steam engine, straining against the weight of the carriages behind. From the corner tower over the town, unseen and with an invincible, god-like sensation, we watched the train, small as a toy, in the valley below.

CHAPTER TWO

Exploring

In those years at the castle just after the First World War, John and I led a life unusually free of supervision for those days. My eldest brother Gordon was away at school in England, and our parents left us to our own devices. Their views on child-rearing were a curious mixture of the reactionary and the progressive. They subscribed to the Edwardian belief that children, like racehorses, were the product of their blood-lines. Good breeding spoke for itself. Any unsatisfactory offspring from sound stock could therefore be explained only as a throw-back. This conveniently deterministic theory allowed them to ignore the rearing of their own children and also to disclaim responsibility for the results.

They were probably no more heartless than their contemporaries. They certainly loved tall thin John, who had been very delicate as a baby. A skin condition meant that he had to be rubbed regularly with a special ointment. John used to tell people that all babies were made with ointment, but God had run out of it when he was made, and that was why he had to be given it on earth. My parents indulged his fantasies. He created an imaginary baby daughter called Inky and they often asked after her. But John evidently became tired of the question because one day he suddenly answered that she had gone. 'What do you mean "gone"?' asked my mother.

'She went down the plug-hole in the bath,' he replied, and went on with what he was doing.

My parents' far-sightedness had saved Gordon when he caught polio, for they kept him flat on a bed and engaged a masseuse to exercise the muscles constantly so that they never became wasted. As a result he was just about the only polio victim accepted for commando training in the Second World War. They were also advanced in the way they approved of John and me swimming and running around naked. They even forced us to go barefoot everywhere to strengthen our feet.

John, despite his day-dreaming and lack of robustness, was adventurous and I followed him with all the admiration of a younger sibling. Others teased him as 'Little-Johnnie-head-in-air', yet I lost my fear of heights scrambling up walls after him. We spoke little together, but we did not need to say much. Our circumstances made us close. We felt right only when we were together. The worst wrench came later in Florence, when John was sent to join Mary Berenson's informal little school at I Tatti and I was excluded.

During the long days spent out of doors, the sun turned our skin brown and our fair hair pale gold. Our feet were as tough as those of the peasant boys. Running through the dry grass and wild thyme, our bare feet striking the ground unseen, felt like leaping through the shallows at the seaside. The crickets fell silent at our approach, and then exploded out of the desiccated undergrowth around us like flying shrimps.

★

Gordon as a boy (*Aubrey Waterfield*)

Almost every day we went to see Ramponi on the castle's little farm that lay on the far side of the ridge from Aulla. It was a small *podere*, or farm, fairly typical of the poorer areas of Tuscany – only a few hectares with vines, maize, chickens and a 'working cow' used for ploughing as well as milk.

Montàn, already quite an old man when my parents arrived, had been helped by Vincente Ramponi. Ramponi then took over entirely and, ever since, had been one of the kindest and most important figures in our lives. A few years younger than my father, Ramponi was a tall man with the proud bearing of a mountaineer and a gentle smile that lit up his long face. He had a straight nose, flowing moustache and large ears. Only when he removed his hat, an almost permanent fixture, did one see that his hair had receded at a relatively early age. Like most *contadini*, he wore a collarless shirt, waistcoat, baggy trousers and heavy hobnailed boots. Yet his bearing and manner were such that even with heavy farmwork he always looked clean.

In the early days there was no house for the *contadino*, so Ramponi used to come on foot each morning from Pomarino, a village on the far bank of the Aulella, a few kilometres upstream. He had to wade the river there to avoid a long walk over the hills, but he never showed any sign of fatigue, and John and I admired his apparently effortless strength. We had heard how, soon after his arrival, my father showed him the wheelbarrow he had brought from England. Ramponi, who had never seen such a contraption before, dutifully filled it with earth, and then, to my father's amazement, bent down, eased the shafts on to his shoulders and lifted the whole load as if the wheelbarrow were a hod. Like any self-respecting *contadino*, he could turn his hand to anything. The grassy terraces of vines grown on pergolas were perfectly kept, their leaves a pale blue-grey after spraying with copper sulphate. The rows of maize were straight and clean of weeds. And Bruna the cow, purchased at the end of the First World War, could not have had a better master.

Throughout most of Tuscany, cows were allowed out only to carry back their own hay. They lived shut up in a dark byre under the peasant's farmhouse. But in the hill country of the Lunigiana, a relatively poor and less intensively farmed region, there were very few of the highly prized and expensive oxen available for ploughing, so a 'working cow' was used instead. John and I used to walk behind Ramponi as he manoeuvred the plough while calling encouragement to Bruna. And later, when he took her back to the entrance room in the corner tower which, since our first arrival, had been turned into a rather unusual byre, he would milk her and fill glasses for us. Bruna's milk tasted warm and sweet, and carried her own special smell.

Whether ploughing, milking or haymaking, Ramponi neither rushed nor tarried. He paced himself and thus achieved far more in the end. His movements, especially the swing of the body when scything, mesmerized us with their grace. Even when he paused from scything to sharpen his blade with the whetstone, another rhythm began.

Through him, we began to acquire some knowledge of peasant life, with its thrift, superstitions, sense of humour and harsh realities. The grey-blue tinge of vine leaves took on a different guise after he told us a terrible story from his village of Pomarino. In one family, a bottle of sulphuric acid, used to make the copper sulphate, was left in a moment of carelessness in the kitchen, where the blind grandmother drank it by mistake and died.

We began to grasp some understanding of the Tuscan

system of *mezzadria* – the equal split of produce between landlord and tenant farmer – when Ramponi came to my father to say that he had used up his half of the wine. My father, who believed in austerity for its own sake, lectured him on the need to ration oneself over the course of the year. Ramponi listened to him politely. '*Ah, si signore,*' he said, nodding when my father had finished. 'You are right in all you say. But if one has only polenta to eat, one needs something to wash it down.' My father pondered this for a moment, then told him to take some of his own share.

There were, of course, many other things that we still did not understand, such as the belief that it was essential to sow maize under a waxing moon. Unlike my father, the Italians put much faith in the good effects of moonlight. They even used the phrase *quando aveva la luna buona* to mean when a man was in a good mood. Yet while field crops were sown according to the phase of the moon, vegetables and herbs in the *orto*, or kitchen garden – peas, potatoes, tomatoes, zucchini, carrots, onions, parsley and basil – were sown by tradition on Easter Saturday.

Maize was known in Tuscany as *granoturco*, Turkish grain, as opposed to *grano frumento*, or wheat grain. The harvest, both for wheat and maize, also had to be perfectly timed, even though, when it was still standing, its fate was entrusted to divine providence – '*Quando il grano è ne' campi, è di Dio e de' Santi*' – 'When the grain is in the fields, it belongs to God and the Saints.'

In most peasant families, it was a woman's job to winnow the freshly harvested ears of wheat; but since Ramponi's wife was in Pomarino, he did the winnowing in his own way on the castle's little farm. He would carry a sack of grain up on to one of the towers and spread a large cloth on the ground.

Then he would wait for a strong breath of wind and shake the grain in batches from a large sieve. I loved to see the chaff blowing away, and followed it with my eyes as it drifted out over the valley into invisibility. Small birds would arrive one by one, cautiously eager for any spoils.

Later, in the autumn, the wives and daughters of the *contadini* from all around would sit outside in the mellow sunlight stripping the parchment-like husks off the maize cobs. Their houses were festooned with maize – a deep copper-red variety as well as the more common buttery gold – spread out in the sun or hung up under the eaves to dry. Every imaginable space was used, for this was also the time of year for drying grapes, peppers, tomatoes and wild mushrooms. Figs were easier. They were impaled on thorn bushes, a sap-like syrup oozing from the wound. It made me think of that sad fairy tale by Oscar Wilde, when the nightingale spears himself on a thorn to turn a rose red.

Some of the maize was used for feeding the hens, and gave the yolks of their eggs a rich colour and taste. The chickens were kept in the moat, where they pecked contentedly among the bushes. At night they lived in a dungeon at the base of one of the corner towers. They entered through the window by a long ladder put up by Ramponi. I was amazed that ungainly Leghorns could be so sure-footed as they made their way up each evening to become the best defended hens in the province.

On Ramponi's advice my father bought a pig, and they built a sty for it opposite the drawbridge entrance. But the pig grew and grew until it became too large to get out of the door. Rather than knock down the wall, it was decided to slaughter and dismember the poor animal *in situ*. In most peasant families, slaughtering the pig was seen as a day of celebration as well as hard work. But there was little celebration on this occasion. Such a job in a very restricted space was not going to be pleasant. My father took John and me off for a long walk to spare us the squealing while Ramponi and a friend completed the task. On our return there was not a trace of the killing: the sty had been hosed down. And when we ran into the castle to inspect the results, we were kept out of the way. Standing on tiptoe in the courtyard, we could see only the tops of several heads in the kitchen, where everyone was still busy. It was such hard work, since almost everything had to be done within the day, that friends from the town had come up to help. We did not stay long. The heavy, slightly sickly smell from all the blood stuck in our throats.

A day or so later, we were amazed to see the sheltered end of the courtyard look like a delicatessen. The huge pig had provided enough Bologna sausage, blood sausage and loin, as well as four magnificent hams – to say nothing of all the stewing pork – to make everyone happy. Every bit of the animal was used for different purposes: meat, blood, bone and skin, even down to a slab of very smelly fat left hanging on a string to grease farm implements.

In later years, the pigsty across the bridge was knocked down and the site used to build a house for Ramponi and his growing family. It was a good position. There was space at the front for a threshing-floor, which looked across the moat beside the drawbridge. To the side there was a fertile outcrop from which one looked down on to the town, and there Ramponi's family dug and planted their own little *orto*, which was close to the house to make watering easier.

As well as doing all the farm work, Ramponi was constantly helping my father plant trees. It was he who cultivated the umbrella pines along the carriage-drive, grown from seeds that my father had brought back from Elba. We often went to search under these trees for fallen pine cones, which had begun to open, like flowers, to release their nuts. These nuts, which we cracked open between stones, contained the slender ivory-coloured *pinoli*. Afterwards we collected the cones in sacks; they were a valuable fuel for winter hearths. My father also allotted us much harder work. In the morning, before the sun became too hot, we had to take turns at the pump on the roof-garden, raising water from the cisterns for his plants.

Water was precious in summer months, and since the garden took priority, there was little enough left even for the odd meagre hip-bath. Often, bearing towel and soap, we tried to persuade my father to accompany us down to the river. If he agreed, we would hang around impatiently as he gathered together his painting materials. When finally ready, we would set off together through the farm on the far side of the ridge from the town and down the terraced hillside. Across the little road up the Aulella valley there was an old peasant woman who allowed us through her little farm beside the river. Sometimes, if she had just been baking, she would give us some fresh hot bread with wild honey.

My father would set up his easel and paint while we played ducks and drakes or swam in one of the Aulella's deep green pools, jumping in from the water-smoothed rocks. Sometimes we had to dive back under the surface again to avoid the sting of horseflies. My mother would come down and join us when she had finished what she was writing, either part of a book on Italy or one of her newspaper articles.

On a number of evenings, as a special treat for us children, Ramponi would bring down a wicker picnic hamper with bread and wine and fruit, including a few lemons from the garden. The main course was waiting in the river.

There were few fishermen in those days and the river teemed with trout. John and I would crouch behind Ramponi, holding our breath as he tickled one. Then, in a sudden movement, he would flick his chosen victim out of the water for us to catch. We tried several times under Ramponi's guidance, but every time we touched the slippery skin, we jumped and the fish escaped.

He would catch us one each, then a few more for his own family. He then wished us '*Buon appetito e buona notte!*' and carried on towards Pomarino, his boots crunching on the stones. As evening fell, we would make a fire on the river-bank, gut the fish – a job I hated – and skewer them on a poplar branch. When the fire burned down to a red glow, we grilled them. My father, leaving the cooking to us, retrieved the *fiasco* of wine from where it lay cooling in the water, and poured himself a glass while watching the effect of the setting sun on the clouds.

Finally, when the lemons were sliced and the fish were ready, we slipped them off their charred skewers on to the plates and began to eat. The flesh, delicately grilled, tasted of the wood fire. My father would allow us both a glass of the castle's dry white wine, whose distinctive taste came from the volcanic rock. As we ate and night fell, we threw the rest of the wood we had collected on to the fire to make a good blaze. John and I watched the reflections of the fire upon the water and looked back at the silhouette of the castle on its spur.

On most days the grown-ups did not have time for such diversions, so John and I roamed at will. We used to venture into the moat down a flight of stone steps that led us under the *salone* windows, so we either had to be very quick, or we crawled to avoid being seen. In the moat, we advanced, well hidden amongst the bay bushes, as far as the drawbridge where the ivy was still so thick – the girth of its main stem was like the trunk of a contorted tree – that we were able, like Beanstalk Jack, to scale the sloping wall to the drawbridge.

I am always astonished, when thinking back, that we came to no harm, either exploring round the castle, or wandering alone in the countryside. We used to walk over the narrow iron railway bridge and through the tunnel in the hill opposite, listening hard for the hooting of a train or the vibration of the rails. I was mainly worried for our disobedient spaniel, Nerino, who would never keep to heel.

Perhaps John looked after me more carefully than I realized, or else my presence held him back. At any rate we always observed local superstitions. When passing the cypress-bordered cemetery, we were careful to touch metal to ward off the evil eye. We were sure never to open an umbrella inside the house, even on the day of a great summer thunderstorm, which nearly brought disaster. It was one of those Lunigiana cloudbursts that my father used to describe as 'God emptying his bath.' Soon after it began, water started to pour down the steps from the roof, making a powerful cascade into the courtyard. Umbrellas were soon discarded as useless and we put on bathing-costumes to fight our way up through the cascade. The outlets round the sentry's walk had become jammed with leaves. This had created a reservoir whose only escape was down the stairs to the courtyard.

Storms in the lower Lunigiana seemed to treat the castle as their focal point, prowling round and round the surrounding hills like wild animals, and roaring at a distance. To go out with an umbrella could be an unnerving experience: the force of the rain would make the handle judder in your grasp. On one occasion, lightning struck the umbrella John was holding and he collapsed with the shock; although unhurt, he was shaken for some time afterwards. And even without lightning, the rain sometimes came down so hard that on hitting the ground it bounced up against your legs. We soon discovered on walks how useful wayside shrines were for shelter.

Our other great friend from those days, and until his death in 1956, was Fiore Pasquino, a stonemason from a mountain village above Licciana, who took over from Ulisse. My parents encountered him on a long walk through the wooded hills of the Taverone valley, searching for *porcini* mushrooms, and fell into conversation.

Fiore, a tall man with an angular face, had recently returned from America. Those decades around the turn of the century had been particularly hard in the Lunigiana – one child in three died before the age of five – and many young men who had never been further than the local town had gone to work abroad. Few had even seen the sea, and most of those who headed on foot for England knew nothing of the Channel barring their way.

Fiore had worked his passage to the United States without speaking a word of the language. On hearing about the gold-fields from fellow Italians, he had abandoned his attempts to set up as a stonemason, and set off to find his fortune. Although he never became rich, he had made enough money by 1905 to send for his wife. Together they set up a boarding-house, and not long afterwards their son Amadeo was born. But like many from the region, Fiore and his wife became homesick for the Apennines and returned.

Fiore had a perfect eye for proportion. Everything he

touched turned out beautifully. He built a stone balcony outside the dining-room windows following a drawing done by my father, and a curving staircase using as his design a postcard of the Bargello in Florence. Justifiably pleased with the balustrade that he built on the narrow terrace below, he asked my father if he could add an inscription. When asked what he had in mind, Fiore shyly brought out a beautiful little terracotta plaque on which he had inscribed some verses from Horace.

In August and September he sometimes took John and me off on mushroom hunts and taught us which were edible and which were poisonous. Tuscans adore horror stories about an acquaintance of some cousin of theirs who eats an unidentified fungus and dies in agony. In Italy, pharmacies still identify mushrooms without charge, but countrymen regard such a service as something for townsfolk. The other favourite scare story told by mushroom hunters and sportsmen is about the danger of vipers; much-maligned beasts who, if all accounts are to be taken seriously, act as the silent avengers of a much-persecuted wildlife.

We learned from Fiore how the *porcini* appeared when the conditions were right in late summer and early autumn, after heavy rain had soaked warm earth – a combination which made 'smoke'. Eight to ten days later, the *porcini* would have grown to their optimum size and most of the population would be out looking for them. Some years could be very poor, mainly due to autumnal droughts, but occasionally they grew in astonishing abundance.

Fiore gave us each a wicker basket of loose weave. This was so that once mushrooms were collected the spoor could escape to fertilize other parts as you moved on. We never found huge quantities, certainly not the quantities claimed by some people we met on our searches, but from what Fiore said Italians invented mushroom stories much as British fishermen. On our return, we watched him slice the mushrooms delicately, then spread the thin segments out on a table or planks of wood to dry in the sun. Afterwards, the dried slices would be hung in muslin or calico bags near the kitchen fireplace or range, ready for use. Each autumn after I married, one of these bags would arrive by post in London with a note of greetings. The last one arrived in the autumn of 1939, shortly after the outbreak of war.

From Fiore we learned about the 'dance of the seasons', and how one should follow the rhythm of the year and its changing produce. One harvest followed another, domestic and wild crops alternating, each stimulating fresh dishes and all producing more than enough for immediate needs, so that the wise could dry or conserve enough to last until the following year. The earth, capable of producing such a perfect variety in the wild – garlic, mushrooms, chestnuts and truffles – possessed its own sacred mystery.

Truffles were the most mysterious of all. They were much rarer in the Lunigiana than in other parts of Tuscany, mainly because it was a region of chestnut woods. (In Umbria truffles could be so plentiful that they even made a liqueur from them, but this dark-brown concoction looked, smelled and tasted more like a primitive hangover cure.) Fiori explained that truffles were likely to be found only in areas where oaks grew, such as in his valley of the Taverone. The ideal combination was a mixture of oak and broom. White truffles, he told us, were usually the size of a child's fist. They could be up to a kilo in weight, but a large part of such a growth is likely to be rotten by the time it is discovered. In Italy, the white truffle is much more *profumato* than the black, and therefore more expensive. Black ones tend to be used most in a galantine, because, like the addition of green pistachio nuts, they provide contrasting colours.

Italians prefer to use dogs rather than pigs, who are so greedy that they can be almost impossible to control once they have scented a truffle. Taking his dog to a likely spot, the truffle hunter spurs him on with cries – '*Dai! Dai! Cerca!*' – similar to those of a *cacciatore* after gamebirds. If the dog finds a black truffle virtually on the surface, he will bring it in his mouth like a retriever, but it will probably be rather damaged. White truffles grow up to fifteen inches down. Almost as soon as the dog begins to scratch, his handler will pull him off in case the truffle is destroyed. The handler will then get down on all fours and sniff for the smell of must, before starting to dig very carefully.

One thing that has not changed since I was a child is the Sunday fusillade. In the autumn, men used to leave their wives to take the children to mass while they went off with gun and game-bag – theoretically in search of pheasant, partridge and even wild boar, but more usually after rock-dove and much smaller birds. Few peasants in the Lunigiana could afford a gun and cartridges, so shooting tended to be the status symbol of those rising into the middle class, such as shopkeepers.

My parents, if they had any illusions, soon discovered quite how unsentimental Italians could be about animals and wildlife. A local *cacciatore* offered them a bunch of blackbirds strung together by the neck as 'an excellent roast'. They promptly delivered a lecture on the shooting of songbirds. He listened so attentively that they rejoiced, thinking they had made a convert. But then he looked up with his eyes opened wide in sudden understanding. '*Ah, sangue della Madonna!*' he exclaimed. 'Then you have no sport in England!'

Such reasoning sorely provoked my father. Yet the English were just as unsentimental in their way. His own regiment, the Northamptonshire Yeomanry, had ridden off to war in 1914 with fighting cocks in wicker cages strapped to their saddles.

John and I first got to know the local peasant farmers through Ramponi. He persuaded my father that we should sell Bruna, before she became too old, and buy another cow. My father entrusted him with the whole business, so on the day of the livestock market outside Aulla, a special event that only took place a few times a year, Ramponi set off with John and me in tow.

I remember the hot, dusty unsurfaced road – what Tuscans call a 'white road' – and kicking stones along our route. Ramponi had given us both a long switch with which to flick Bruna's hindquarters to hurry her along. As we came closer to where the market was held we encountered more and more *contadini* and their families headed in the same direction. Some carried trussed chickens upside down, others led several pigs, each attached by a rope to one leg.

The market was too loud and confusing to recall the sale of Bruna and the purchase of the new cow. I think she was called Bruna too: it was a very popular name in the surrounding valleys. Ramponi took some time to find his middleman, or *sensale*. The job of the *sensale* was to conduct the bargaining, then, when a deal was struck, he joined the hands of the two parties for the contractual shake before receiving his modest fee. Afterwards, the men had a glass of wine to celebrate. Seeing friends and catching up on news and gossip was undoubtedly one of the main points of the day.

Aulla's position made it the natural centre for the Lunigiana valleys in all their diversity. This was perhaps best expressed by the variety of men's hats. There were Livorno hats made from finely plaited straw, the narrow-brimmed black felt hats of the Tuscan peasant and the much larger-brimmed hats of mountain shepherds, more like artists' fedoras in the manner of Aristide Briand. There was even the odd townsman lifting his boater every now and then to show off his pomaded hair.

John and I wandered round looking at everything. There were stalls selling tools, terracotta pots of all sizes and shapes, clasp-knives and *zoccoli* – the local version of clogs, with thick wooden soles and a broad strap of leather across like a sandal. Other stalls sold wine or coffee by the glass. It was a very serious market, we decided. A man's fair.

The noise of the livestock – the regular lowing of cattle, the odd squeal of pigs, the bleating of goats and sheep – became oppressive after a time, and there were few amusements for children once we had seen everything. I became so tired by the end of the afternoon that Ramponi had to carry me part of the way home.

CHAPTER THREE

The Castle Kitchen

Soon after our parents moved into the castle, a young widow, self-possessed and intelligent, had approached my mother down in the town to propose herself as cook. 'Signora,' she said, 'it was destined that I should serve you.' She then explained that as soon as she had heard that English people had moved into the *fortezza*, she had gone on a pilgrimage to the shrine of the Madonna of the valley to pray for guidance. Afterwards, a dream about a dog had, for some inexplicable reason, given her the final assurance that her instinct was right from everyone's point of view.

Mariannina, although small, held herself proudly. She had a well-shaped face and neck, which were accentuated by her flawless olive skin and shining mass of dark hair coiled on top of her head. Mariannina originally came from near Carrara. This made her a foreigner in the eyes of the people of Aulla where she had been working for a local official and his wife as cook, housemaid and wet-nurse for a salary of £7 a year. The Aullese found it hard to believe that she should volunteer to work in the *fortezza* – a place the whole town knew to be haunted. A few months later, her younger sister Adelina also came to the castle to join the household.

It was much more surprising that Adelina did not take fright at the thought of ghosts since she was very superstitious and even feared natural phenomena such as thunderstorms. She also found it hard to grasp unfamiliar ideas. She thought that the British Isles must be in perpetual danger of being washed away, mainly because her idea of islands was based on the sandbanks of the Magra river, which vanished when heavy rain swelled the torrent. Not only was she ingenuous; she also had unpredictable enthusiasms, suddenly breaking into a little dance or rhapsody. Once, after seeing King Victor Emmanuel surrounded by magnificently mounted cuirassiers, her sense of fairy-tale drama led her to believe that all these handsome cavalrymen were kings too.

Adelina required constant praise. 'You must come and see how I have cleaned the *sala*,' she would say, summoning my mother. 'It shines like a looking-glass – enough to dazzle you.' She was so pleased with her work that it seemed churlish to point out all the things she had missed. But my mother was as fond of Adelina with all her naïve idiosyncrasies as she was grateful for the more self-contained Mariannina.

Finding servants was not easy, even though the Lunigiana was one of the poorest parts of Tuscany. Among peasant families in those days, to go out to work for others was regarded as degrading for a woman. She would not be allowed to cook – the employer usually reserved that for herself – and so would be used purely for menial tasks. Female servants were generally restricted to innocent outcasts from a family with too many mouths too feed. They might be unmarried daughters who could not find a husband, or widows ill-treated by their late husband's family and not accepted back by their own. One might have expected such harsh conditions to produce downtrodden servants, but the idea never seemed to occur to them. In fact all those roles so often assumed in England before the war, from the self-importance of a butler or cook, to the faintly ironic servility of a valet or chauffeur, were unimaginable in the Lunigiana.

Unless shy or withdrawn by nature, all the Italian servants I knew were disarmingly straightforward. They were friendly without being familiar, if only because the Tuscan's instinctive respect for others prevented such a thing. Any jealousies they might have harboured sprang from their own families and not, as in England, from some servants'-hall pecking order. The fact that servants, except those belonging to grand establishments, wore no uniform made a great difference: instead, they tended to indulge a love of bright colours. And in Tuscany, those with fine voices enlivened their work and their surroundings by singing *stornelli*, which were lively ballads, and *rispetti*, which were allusive, often melancholy, love songs. *Stornelli* could even be used in an operatic argument or running exchange of insults – a process that even had its own verb, *stornellare*. The brief *rispetti*, usually of six to ten lines, were descendants of the courtly songs of the Middle Ages. This excerpt from a popular one gives an idea of their highly ornamental style:

> *La luna s'è venuta a lamentare,*
> *Inde la faccia del divino Amore;*
> *Dice che in cielo non ci vuol più stare;*
> *Che tolto gliel' avete lo splendore.*

> The moon has come to make her lamentation
> Before the face of the God of Love.
> No more in the sky, can she maintain her station
> Because you have taken all her splendour.

Occasionally, a stuffy visitor on his first visit to Italy could be left agape at an Italian servant's lack of ceremony; but for most English, the escape from the hidebound formality and false deference of home contributed greatly to their spontaneous love for Tuscany. On one occasion, when my mother was seated in the *salone* talking to a distinguished old Englishman, Adelina burst into the room, ran its whole length past them, and flung open the shutters in the deep embrasure to yell a forgotten item to a boy on his way down the steep hill to carry out an errand in the town.

As well as possessing a great sense of the dramatic, Adelina saw herself as an artist. She used to come singing into the dining-room to lay the cloth and would spend a long time decorating the table with sprigs of bay or box, and flowers and fruit depending on the season. Every now and again she would step back and, with her head on one side, observe the effect.

Once the family was seated in the cool, still dining-room, shuttered against sun and the midday wind, she would carry in a mound of macaroni on a brass salver held high on an upturned hand, as if she were bringing in the head of John the Baptist. When my father painted her in this pose, he suggested that she hold the salver empty so that it would be less tiring. 'But signore,' Adelina protested, 'that would not be right!' She insisted on loading it with items from the kitchen so that she would hold as in real life. When the family was alone, Adelina was just as likely to laugh at any jokes or join in the conversation while she served at table, as to observe that the English were mad to want fresh plates and knives and forks with each course. On the other hand, when guests were present, she was mortified that my parents always served *fiaschi* filled from the cask like everyone else, and did not bother to provide bottled wine to impress them. 'But we could make a good display spending little,' she would say afterwards, trying to persuade my father – '*Figuriamo di molto e spendiamo poco.*'

She was also very disappointed that my mother wore simple, everyday clothes on excursions down into the town: a long tweed skirt in winter and linen in summer. On a public occasion, such as a local christening, Adelina begged her without success to wear an evening gown and jewels – *per far bella figura*. For Adelina, the final straw of English perversity was that my mother, who refused to dress up for public show, would change for dinner alone with her husband – she in silk shirt and long velvet skirt and he in his smoking-jacket.

Even the admirable Mariannina had her foibles. My mother was baffled by her fatalism. If something could not be found, she would say with a shrug: 'Ah, signora, it must have been taken by the spirits of the *fortezza*.' My mother was also exasperated by her habit of appropriating items for a particular task – whether stirring the soup with a silver paper-knife, stoking the fire with one of my father's walking-sticks or taking a beautiful porcelain bowl for the chicken-feed. The last straw, at which point my mother more or less gave up, came when she saw her best Gordon plaid being used to cover the uncooked loaves of risen dough and keep them warm.

Before Fiore built us our own brick oven, Mariannina used to take the loaves on a large wooden tray down the steep mule-track to the bakery in the town. As a true country-woman, she carried almost everything on her head, from a suitcase to a bundle of washing, her whole body marvellously erect, her hips swaying in forward movements. But for my mother, watching from an upstairs window, the sight of the tray covered in Gordon tartan zigzagging gracefully down the hill between the ilex trees inspired less than generous feelings.

Domestic life was, at any rate, never dull. In fact the unexpected – whether irritating or delightful – tended to become the rule rather than the exception. Once my mother returned to the kitchen, where she was making jam with the wild strawberries that we used to pick in great quantities, to find the baker and village tailor there with their guitars to serenade her.

The main annual event for women in a Tuscan household was spring-cleaning to prepare for the priest when he came to bestow his Easter blessing. In its way it was as important as the grape harvest was for the men. Everything was attended to, including the refilling of mattresses with sheep's wool. The Lunigiana was fortunate to have good grazing for flocks. In many places mattresses were filled with the previous autumn's crop of dried maize leaves, a stuffing that crackled fiercely whenever you moved in bed.

Adelina prepared herself suitably for the event. She tied a yellow kerchief round her head, borrowed one of my father's large painting aprons and pinned up her skirts on one side. She rolled up the matting and carried it on her head to the terrace where she spread it in the sun and cleaned it with a damp cloth. Sunshine was a vital part of the cleaning process: heavy rain was seen as an ill omen for the household as well as a misfortune on the day.

Buckets of water were thrown over stone or tiled floors – a traditional practice which, in more conventionally built homes, led to rotting timbers – then Adelina, with a broom made of millet stalks, swept the water towards the french windows and out through a little hole in the stone balcony.

Before the age of washing-machines, the *bucato*, or laundry, was the pride of every housewife. All the household linen was well lathered on a marble slab with a dark green brick of soap made from olive residue, then pressed into an immense terracotta pot called a *conca*, the sort in which lemon trees are planted. This stood by the hooded fireplace in the kitchen. A rough linen cloth was spread over the washing and wood ashes strewn thickly on top. Boiling water was then slowly poured over the clothes from the cauldron, which hung from a thick chain over the fire. The boiling water, percolating through, ran out through the hole at the bottom of the *conca*. When the water finally appeared clear, the *bucato* was done and all stains should have disappeared.

The damp washing was then carried in baskets to the river where it was rinsed and stretched out to dry on the stones of the river-bed. It was a wonderful scene, with cheerful groups of women, skirts rolled up round their hips, standing out in the stream, swinging their washing to and fro and slapping it on the water with scarcely an interruption to the banter and laughter. When all was done, they lifted the heavy baskets on to their heads, and set off home majestic as carnival queens with outsize crowns. Adelina, true to form, did not hesitate to tell everyone on her return how Signora so-and-so had admired the whiteness of our linen.

Mariannina's rule over the kitchen was gentle, yet imperceptibly firm. Nothing ever flustered her; she never hurried, yet she never wasted a moment. Casual visitors – whether the postman, a passing tradesman or Fiore – all found themselves with a bowl of peas to shell or potatoes to peel while they chatted with her, a glass of wine at their elbow. As children we too were always drawn to her kitchen when we were not out roaming the fields and hillsides. It was our favourite refuge; cavernous and welcoming, with delicious smells.

Mariannina, when she saw us standing hopefully in the door, would warn us that lunch was still a long time away. Time, in that clockless world, went by the railway timetable as expressed by toots and bells in the valley below. Instead of saying, 'But it's not yet one o'clock,' Mariannina would tell us: 'The train from Milan has not yet arrived.'

Since hunger was a sign of health, and thus something to be encouraged, she never sent us away. As a true Italian, she showed a natural affection far removed from the cold British notion that 'children should be seen and not heard'. She would give us bread dipped in wine with sugar on it, or bread rubbed with garlic, then covered in olive oil and salt.

The local bread, especially that *fatto in casa*, tasted like no other. Each loaf was like a huge round hill. When cutting it, people held it lengthways against the chest and sawed at it with a clasp-knife. It had a thick, strong crust dusted with flour and its flesh was a sandy colour from the mixture of wheat and maize flour – *farina gialla*. Made from unsalted dough, it went hard but never mouldy, and could therefore be used for at least a week in soups or other dishes to give them body. Old maize bread never really lost its taste, and could serve instead of toast under slices of tomato with basil as a simple but delicious antipasto.

The bread oven built by Fiore was sited across the drawbridge, near Ramponi's house at the top of the footpath down to the town. Ovens were seldom built inside a house because of the heat in summer. Brushwood was used to create

John as a boy (*Aubrey Waterfield*)

a quick, violent fire; the moment it had burnt itself out, the ashes were pushed to one side, and the loaves were slid in on a long wooden shovel before being dislodged with a flick of the wrist.

In those days, just after the First World War, the kitchen was the best place in which to get to know the region. And the herbs and vegetables, still smelling of the warm volcanic earth, could start a love of Tuscan cooking that would last a lifetime. For the servants, as well as their friends and relations who dropped in on visits, the kitchen was not simply a place of work but the centre for their favourite subject of conversation. Everyone, men and women alike, compared recipes. When somebody talked of a particular dish, another might say that a cousin of theirs who had married a Piedmontese prepared it a slightly different way. They would argue the relative merits, go away and experiment, and discuss it again the next time.

The cooking of the Lunigiana, while essentially Tuscan, reflects its geographical reality as a border region and its history of 'armies, pilgrims and merchants' passing through. Surrounded by Genoese Liguria, Parma and Reggio nell'-Emilia, it has borrowed what it likes: *pesto* with pine nuts in the Genoese style; the curing of hams and the preparation of sausage and *coppa* from Parma (the *pecorino* cheeses from up the valleys also bore a strong affinity to Parmesan); and the local favourite of *panigacci* – a form of unleavened maize bread cooked between iron dishes and eaten with *pesto* – from Emilia.

The basis of life sixty years ago was *la cucina povera*, peasant cooking, which made the best use of home-grown raw materials – maize flour for polenta, semolina for gnocchi, onions and beans for soups, fresh vegetables from the *orto* for stuffing and tomatoes for sauces, while the wild mushrooms, herbs, nettles and particular grasses gathered from hillsides went into *torte* (flans) and even *tortelloni*. But almost every meal depended upon that ancient trinity of bread, olive oil and wine.

Polenta, a pale golden colour from the flour of Indian corn, formed the solid staple of winter months when no fresh vegetables were available. Cut into strips, it was eaten fried in olive oil, baked with Parmesan or served with a sauce and a little meat if available, such as goat, garlic salami or *zampone* – a pig's trotter made into sausage. So central was polenta to the diet of the northern Italian that southerners used to call them *polentoni*. Tuscans were also called the bean-eaters, because the *fagioli* gathered in the summer, then dried, shelled and sacked up for the winter, provided the bulk of their protein, usually in the form of minestrone.

Beef was almost unheard of, unless an old animal had been killed, and veal was a rare luxury. Often the tougher bits were boiled, making a consommé, then the meat was served with *salsa verde*, a green sauce made from very finely chopped parsley, onion and capers with oil and sometimes an anchovy. Any pieces of meat left over were minced, then augmented with egg, breadcrumbs, parsley and basil or other herbs in season, and used to make *ripieni* – stuffed vegetables, such as tomatoes, onions, aubergines, zucchini, or lightly boiled cabbage leaves made into a parcel.

Most fresh meat came from chickens, pigeons and rabbits, which were cheap to raise. One of my favourite dishes, which both Mariannina and Adelina cooked superbly, was a *bomba di riso* of squabs or fledgling pigeons. For this you line a bowl with partly cooked rice mixed with egg, then fill the remaining cavity with young pigeon breasts in a mushroom sauce with chicken livers. It is a dish you do not often find today, but as soon as you mention it, people suddenly remember the taste from their youth with a reawakened longing.

I never really liked eating rabbit, not because I thought of the animal as a cuddly pet, but because I was exasperated by Adelina – whose lack of scientific reliability was all too apparent even to us children – insisting that it contained lots of iron and so was especially good for *padroncini*, or little masters and mistresses.

Tuscans have deeply held beliefs about the effects of food, some of which are no doubt true, while others are fanciful. Figs, they say, are bad for you at night. You will avoid illnesses of the liver if you use only the very purest olive oil. Red chilli is good for stomach trouble. A tea made from fennel seeds helps soothe a baby's colic. Eating raw garlic keeps mosquitoes away, and also, one might add, other species from vampires to Lotharios.

Another range of sayings I remember concerned the preparation of food. Basil should be torn, not cut with metal, otherwise it loses its taste as well as its goodness. Parmesan should never be grated because the friction cooks it. And each cooking utensil – knife, cutting-board or pan – should be used for one purpose only so that flavours do not mix.

Variations in the cooking of the Lunigiana are, like in other areas, dictated by the seasons, but certain foods are clearly associated with specific feast days. For the Aullesi, one of the most important annual events, the Feast of San Severo on the first Saturday of September, is even known by the name of the dish – the *Festa della Capra*. For this celebration of that local favourite, kid and polenta, the meat is slowly brought to the boil. The water that is produced, known as the *selvatico* — the wild element — is thrown away. The purified *capra*, a very lean meat, is then cooked in oil with *soffritto* — lightly fried onions, celery and dry sausage with herbs — capers and *mortadella di Maiale*. Meanwhile, a sauce for the kid and the polenta is prepared consisting of tomatoes, onions, carrots, celery and white wine.

The calendar ran roughly as follows. In Carnival, exotically stuffed *tortelloni* were popular; and a surprisingly unfestive choice at this time was boiled chickpeas. The onset of Lent was a penance that sat easier on the poor who could seldom afford to eat meat. And since fresh fish was also too expensive, the diet of peasant families changed little, except for the addition of *zuppa di magro* — or Lenten soup. It was also a time when people remembered the story of the '*zuppa dei poveri*'. A poor man arrives at the door of a house and asks the wife if he could have some water for his soup. She peers into the saucepan he is holding and sees only a stone.

'What?' she exclaims. 'Soup made with just a stone and some water?'

'Well, signora,' says the man, 'it is true that it would taste better with a carrot as well.'

'But soup made with just a stone and a carrot . . .'

'Well, it would be better with a potato if you happen to have one to spare.' And so on.

Easter was a time for peasant families to kill a chicken, either to prepare *pollo in umido* or *pollo al cacciatore* served with carrots and shallots cooked whole. Chicken in those days, thoroughly free-range and fed on maize, had a deliciously gamy taste. But the paramount importance of the chicken for producing eggs was borne out by the year-round popularity of *frittate* — cold omelettes — and quiche-like *torte.* We were always given onion *frittate* in a picnic basket. And fairly often appearing on the table would be an onion tart, known as *la barbuta*, or 'the bearded woman', because the fine slices of vegetables were supposed to look like hair; or a *torta* of spinach cooked in the bread oven, or even, in the spring, a *torta* made with nettles when they were still young and fresh.

The centre-piece of Aullese Christmas fare was usually a capon, but most of the other dishes were very different to British tradition. The first course was often *tortelli* stuffed with ricotta and wild herbs or mushrooms, followed by a *torta di verdura* – a rich quiche with pumpkin, leeks, spinach, beet, onion, nettles and borage.

The seriousness of the whole enterprise, above all when preparing for a feast day, was not to be underestimated. Tasting was not just a formality; Mariannina's expression was genuinely preoccupied until reassured both by the taste and, after a loaded silence, by the after-taste. Only then would she pronounce her work satisfactory.

Much later, when all was eaten and the copper saucepans cleaned, polished and hung up, Mariannina would sit down in the large kitchen chair and take out her embroidery. This was the best time to beg her to tell us fairy tales. In a typically Tuscan way, most of them involved delicious food produced by magic as well as the more conventional rewards of great riches, or marriage to a prince or princess.

CHAPTER FOUR

❧

Market Theatre in Aulla

For Mariannina, as for any Tuscan, the first step in the preparation of the day's meals was seeing which vegetables were ready in the *orto*. Only then would she consider what produce was fresh and reasonably priced – either in the market, or available from travelling vendors. Anything not grown at home was automatically regarded with suspicion, so selection was as important as the cooking itself.

Vendors used to turn up unannounced with frequent irregularity. Coming down to breakfast, we would often find a peasant woman seated upon the hall steps, surrounded by scrawny chickens with their legs tied together. She would pinch the poor fowls to show how fat they were while Mariannina or my mother bargained. Others arrived with sacks of chestnuts or baskets of apples, eggs or home-made cheeses.

On one occasion, Mariannina opened the door of the *salone* and shepherded in a live turkey as if announcing a rather shy guest. The turkey stalked haughtily around the room and eventually came to a halt, contemplating the fire in fascination. Mariannina wanted my mother's agreement on the price before concluding such a major purchase. They decided to buy him. He would be quartered outside by the magazine and fed on maize and acorns in preparation for Christmas.

Our turkey, an apparently tame and complacent creature, took on the habits of a domestic pet, wandering in through the *portone*, up the steps to the hall and even to the kitchen. His imprisonment was incomparably more civilized than that of most large birds destined for the pot. In many farmhouses the capon or cock being fattened up for Christmas was kept in a wicker cage near the kitchen fire. Yet perhaps our turkey suddenly perceived his fate on one of his perambulations, for one day this hitherto willing prisoner jumped from the outer wall into the ilex wood below, softening his fall with an energetic flapping of stubby wings.

Ramponi, who had spotted the escape, was certain that such a slow bird could not elude him. He delayed his pursuit until he had finished what he was doing. But this proved a severe miscalculation for which Mariannina never forgave him – or indeed herself, since she had been the one who had persuaded my mother to buy the bird in the first place. She and Adelina had long discussions afterwards about whose pot the turkey had disappeared into, but their speculation on his fate only increased their frustration.

The temptation for both travelling vendors and stallholders in the town to get the better of the English – to be *furbo*, or cunning – with stones in the bottom of the sack or other such devices, was often too great for them to resist. In those days, when the *libra sterlina* was still on the gold standard, English travellers and residents were automatically assumed to be milords and charged accordingly, which meant at least double the price demanded from Italians.

Local friends would laugh at my mother's disappointment after a particularly nice vendor turned out to have been dishonest in a transaction. 'Never trust your neighbour,' they would tell her. 'Your neighbour does not expect it.' Life was a process of cheat and be cheated, a circle of rough justice. Peasant women who could neither read nor write were constantly tricked by shopkeepers in the town, and they in turn would get their own back from anyone they thought could afford it.

The only weighing machine anyone trusted was the one at the railway station, and many people used to rush there to check their purchases. It was Signora Fortunata, the wife of a local merchant, who eventually mustered the courage to turn the butcher's scales upside down. She tore off the weights that were concealed on the underside and lectured him so loudly that a crowd gathered, peering in at doors and windows to watch him quiver under her magisterial tongue-lashing.

In a small town like Aulla, shopping and social life were closely linked. The local inhabitants were of course keenly interested in the price as well as the quality of the food on offer, yet the market itself provided the main source of excitement. This meeting-place, inevitably the main centre for gossip, was above all a stage for declamatory theatre and dialogue – a public contest in which the bargaining reputation of both stallholder and housewife was at stake.

Bargaining was an immensely serious business, a matter of state; yet for many it was also the most exciting part of the day, and a subject for endless discussion afterwards. But once the duel, however acrimonious, had run its course, it was suddenly resolved. The purchaser, extracting the money from a purse hung round the neck, maintained a watchful eye in case a different article to the one she had chosen was placed in her basket or bag, then the whole encounter was concluded with nods and smiles and mutual compliments. My mother, although a writer with no natural interest in housekeeping, was fascinated by the game that was played out there each day, but she found it very hard to follow Mariannina's advice to be constantly on guard.

Aulla market started early, usually around five in the morning. The noises of assembly – the creak and rattle of handcarts, the cries of greeting and raillery between peasant women coming in from the two valleys – mingled and, if the river mist was not heavy, drifted up to the castle. The little town's more prosperous matrons, each one closely followed by a maid bearing large baskets, would make their appearance later, but not too late. As if to emphasize the dignity of their position, they would not show any sign of pleasure at the colourful and lively scene but would circle the stalls with pronounced disdain as they eyed them for bargains.

Alongside the proper stalls with tables and awnings, peasant women squatted in the shade of huge umbrellas with hefty baskets in front of them filled with eggs, or vegetables from their own *orto* or, if they were shepherds' wives, heavy, round *pecorino* cheeses.

I loved to accompany Adelina when she went down to the market, if only because of the variety of produce and its colours. In summer it was like looking through a kaleidoscope – the red, yellow and green of peppers, the glossy purple of aubergines, and the orange of persimmons. Even the less garish produce – cardoons, cabbages, spinach, strings of onion and plaits of garlic – were all displayed to attract the eye. And the whole time one would hear the singsong cries of the vendors – '*O signori, la mia bella verdura*' – chanted in what sounded like the proud lament of an opera without music.

La Fortezza on the hill

The fish stall fascinated me most, with its red and grey mullet, crayfish, prawns, cuttlefish and whiting laid out on glistening marble slabs. Every so often, when no customers were in the way, a young lad threw a bucket of water over them to keep them cool and fresh-looking in the heat. Inland, fish was expensive – except in the unappetizing form of *baccalà*, or dry salt cod – so any member of the household returning from La Spezia would bring some fresh fish back from the large market there. On days when Mariannina had asked somebody to do this, she would go out on to the dining-room balcony to watch for the train from La Spezia. If a handkerchief was waved energetically from a carriage window as the train drew into the station, she knew that all was well and that she would not have to prepare an alternative meal at the last moment.

When there was a feast day Adelina used to take us down to the town. She took great care with her appearance – she was a clever dressmaker, whether refashioning an old dress of my mother or making her own. I was fascinated by what she could achieve with a length of material from one of the bolts of cotton print that came from Genoa. Dresses were generously cut, full-skirted and down to the ankle, and a shawl or scarf was worn round the neck, ready to be draped over the head when entering church.

Once mass was over in the church of San Caprasio, the day was for seeing – the crowds, the stalls, the sideshows and the spectacles – and for being seen – either in the general *passegiata*, or showing off a new dress by dancing in the Piazza Fontana to the music of a concertina. In the background, as if to confuse the dancers, the town's brass band, in which Ulisse played a trumpet until his death, could be heard going through its repertoire – mainly excerpts from Verdi and Rossini.

In a way, a feast day was rather like market day, but the stalls were designed, as was the occasion itself, for pleasure, not daily needs. They sold ribbons and materials for dressmaking, cheap gewgaws, or delicacies to be consumed on the spot such as chestnut cake, sticky as marrons glacés and cut into segments with a wire.

Vendors walked round offering unusual wares, from large grasshoppers in crudely fashioned little cages to patent medicines. Other men, standing by baskets of pears, figs and other fruit, loudly declaimed their virtue, then, having selected a fine specimen, proceeded to eat it with a conspicuous display of relish.

The local letter-writer did not miss the opportunity to set up his tent: he increased his charge when asked to compose love-letters, and there was a further supplement for verses. Meanwhile, fortune-telling crones spun wildly optimistic predictions for love-sick girls. Small crowds gathered round travelling organ-grinders, jugglers, tightrope walkers and acrobats or *saltimbanchi*. All the sounds competed: the brass band, the hubbub of voices and the hurdy-gurdy of the merry-go-round, on which we had as many rides as possible.

The feast day of San Caprasio, the patron saint of Aulla, on 1 June was one of the high points of the year. It finished with a religious procession following the statue of the Virgin, borne by relays of perspiring volunteers. At Corpus Christi, also in early summer, flowers were scattered in the road and attached to lampposts. On such occasions the procession round town, with an embroidered canopy held over the priest who carried the chalice and host, ended with a blessing outside the railway station.

Religion, in a small community like Aulla, was down-to-earth and personal. God seemed to be addressed like an understanding yet feared head of the family from whom favours were constantly sought. There was an innate flexibility that Protestants never seemed to understand. Even anticlericals, like the amiable Ulisse, still went to church and accompanied religious processions out of respect for ancient custom. And while devout Catholic wives insisted on remaining chaste during Lent – the birth rate dropped sharply in the month before Christmas – they were more pragmatic on the question of food. One Ash Wednesday, for example, an aunt of Mariannina's, who had made a large quantity of ravioli stuffed with meat for Carnival, found only a small proportion had been consumed. 'What am I to do?' she demanded. 'Here we are in Lent and we should not be eating meat in any form. But it would be such a *peccato* to throw them away.' (The word *peccato* conveniently means a sin as well as a shame.)

'I agree,' said Mariannina. 'But let's look at it this way. The real sin is what comes out of the mouth, and not so much what goes in.'

Mariannina had good grounds for believing that gossip was a greater sin. Like all small towns, Aulla had its coterie of women with nothing better to do than speculate, with sanctimonious *frissons*, on the sins of others. And Mariannina, both a 'foreigner' from Carrara and an attractive widow, was a favourite target.

Mariannina was intelligent, and despite her Madonna-like air of calm she had a quick tongue, which disconcerted her rivals. The stories told about her were recounted with ill-concealed relish. 'That widow has a lover,' my mother was told in one shop. 'A man who is going to be married next week. It is certain there will be a scandal.'

The accusation of stealing the fiancé of a girl from the town was based on the fact that the man, a childhood friend of Mariannina's, had happened to remark, quite accurately, that she had beautiful eyes, and had given a pair of boots to one of her two young sons who had been lodged with her family near Carrara. She, in return, had bought him a box of thin Tuscan cigars at the local fair. Unfortunately, the *fidanzata* had got hold of these cigars, confronted Mariannina in a screaming match in the piazza and thrown the cigars into the sewage drain. Mariannina's protestations of innocence to the rapidly gathered band of onlookers were laughed at and she burst into angry tears at the injustice of it all.

For good measure, the false accusations against Mariannina and Adelina included petty embezzlement. When my mother went down to Aulla with them, one on each side, the gossips apparently used to joke: 'Here comes Christ between the thieves.' Yet Mariannina was scrupulous in her accounts, and my mother, who felt obliged to carry out some spot checks if only to clear her cook's name, took every opportunity to confirm this in the town. It did little good. The sceptics nodded knowingly when she told them: it was just further proof that Mariannina was cleverer in these matters than her naïve English *padrona*. When my mother had gone, they would again talk of Mariannina's cunning and tap the sides of their noses significantly.

In those days, gossip in a small community could produce an alarming intensity of feeling. A woman would put salt in the doorway of another woman whom she suspected of giving her the evil eye. And woe betide the reputation of a recently married girl who gave birth prematurely. Her child would be known as a *bambino a sette mese* – a seven-month baby – on the immediate assumption that it had been conceived before the marriage.

Self-appointed guardians of public morals did not disappear until long after the Second World War. Maria Balestracci, a young Aullese who went with us to England for a time in the late 1930s, bought the most modest bathing dress available in London; it came down to her knees. But when, on her return to Aulla, she wore it to swim in the river, an old woman strode over to her aunt's house to denounce her behaviour as a scandal.

A more friendly form of gossip was exchanged round the fountain; a square marble column in the Piazza Cavour. Women chatted there as they held their copper ewers under the brass spout that issued from a Bacchic mask. Since the cisterns up at the castle were assumed to be full of dead snakes and scorpions, Adelina had to fetch the drinking-water and we helped her, when old and strong enough. She taught me how to roll a circlet of cloth to go on the crown of the head, then bend the knees, lift the heavy ewer on to the head and rise in one slow movement without spilling any water. It was surprising to find how effectively the line of the back and neck acted as a load-bearing column and how much easier it was to carry a heavy weight this way than in your arms.

For men, the centres of gossip were the barber's shop and the wine shop, where they gambled for small stakes. They played Scoppa, which required the traditional Mediterranean pack of forty cards with four suits – coins, goblets, swords and clubs (cavemen's clubs, not the conventional trefoil) – each running from one to seven plus a jack, queen and king. Others sat outside the Albergo d'Italia under its vine-covered pergola and watched the comings and goings at Zappoli's stables on the far side of the Piazza Vittorio Emanuele.

The family whose fortunes and conduct were discussed most was the Barrachini. The old man was a true potentate, being the largest wholesaler in the whole of the Lunigiana. His house was the most imposing in Aulla, with rustication up to the *piano nobile*, balustrades and festoons. Its *nouveau-riche* splendour earned it the ironic title of Palazzo Barrachini.

The older part of the town – from the Piazza Cavour, its arch surmounted with a swallow-tailed battlement from Ghibelline times, down to the real *palazzo* of the Dukes of Modena – was naturally far more attractive than the pompous nineteenth-century architecture round the railway station. The streets, sloping gently towards the river and the church of San Caprasio, were cobbled with round stones from the river while the houses, their stucco flaking and their shutters peeling, huddled intimately together above the canvas awnings of shops.

Linguistically, Aulla was supposed to have been the last outpost of Tuscany, yet Aullese contained many words and phrases that would have sounded foreign to a Florentine overhearing a private conversation, such as *pevero* for pepper and *savon* for soap. Everybody learned the *lingua latina* in school and spoke it to strangers, or on more formal occasions. The local *lingua vulgare* was used only amongst themselves.

In Pontremoli, the next town up the Magra valley towards Parma, they spoke an Emilian dialect. In Podenzana, the fortified village and castle visible high above the west bank of the river, they spoke a Ligurian dialect, while the inhabitants of Bibola, the other fortified village which looked down on the town from across the Aulella, had their own distinct quirks of speech. No wonder each village was called a *paese*, for it was a country all to itself. A local rhyme on the subject of the Lunigiana's many different dialects ran as follows:

Quando 'l Signore: fesct la Lunigiana
'd sabdo, jev la bisaccia vota;
gh' er armasso sasci, tramontana
e, cento dialetti, da 'n filarn 'n boca.

When the Lord made the Lunigiana
On a Saturday, his sack was empty;
Only stones and the north wind remained,
And a hundred dialects to fill the mouth.

The differences between neighbouring villages extended to more than just dialect. For example, Bibola had its own game, played by children and adults alike, called *la mora*, which was rather like the ancient Chinese game of Scissors, Paper, Stone. At a given signal, the players would suddenly show a certain number of fingers and call out what they thought would be the total number of fingers displayed by all the players. But the main game was *bocce*, a version of bowls on beaten earth or, in more Mediterranean terms, a flightless pétanque.

Rivalries between towns and villages could be deep-seated, even centuries old. The Aullesi firmly believed that Santo Stefano di Magra downstream had been a nest of brigands from the beginning of time. And no doubt the Stefanesi had long held equally unsympathetic views about Aulla, whose more advantageous position must have provoked great jealousy.

Aulla was not only the market town for the surrounding valleys; it was also a necessary centre of craftsmanship, from marble masons turning blocks of the local Carrara stone into tables, washing slabs and gravestones, to watchmakers, cobblers and carpenters. Most were wonderful craftsmen, inventive and with a good eye, but many did not live up to their promises. One had to bear constantly in mind the Tuscan proverb: 'Between saying and doing there is an ocean.'

Fundamentally, the Italian wants to give pleasure. '*Ma sì, signora*,' he will say with a radiant smile. Unlike most English workmen, he will enter into a project with enthusiasm, almost as if it were an adventure. A job is never done by a simple call and verbal explanation. There has to be a preliminary visit of inspection, a walk round the problem nodding knowingly, and a drink or two afterwards to discuss it further. A lack of machinery or the right tool will not produce a dubious shaking of the head, that way of demonstrating with pessimistic satisfaction that a job is impossible. The Italian will scratch his head thoughtfully and find an ingenious solution. Mutual congratulations are in order, and a further appointment will be made. Everything will be completed then – *senz' altro* – without fail.

But if a project did not disappear into the ocean between the saying and the doing, it seldom turned out quite as expected. Even the wonderful Ulisse always trusted his eye – he despised accurate measurements as unartistic – so sometimes a wall was a little out of line. If my father pointed this out, he would reply: '*Già, già*, it may be so, but it will have more a look of *antichità*.' And at the suggestion that the wall should be rebuilt, he would look sad and remark that it would be a day lost, as if the signore should feel personally responsible.

My father became used to Italian artisans agreeing with everything he said and still going their own way. On one occasion, he wanted a round table and asked the local carpenter to make him one, having given him a drawing and all the measurements. But when he went to collect the new table, he found it to be oval. 'But I asked for it to be round.'

The carpenter stared at the table with perplexed

concentration, then looked up. '*Ma è riuscito così*' – 'But it came out like this.' When an Italian shrugs in such a situation it is with his arms half out like the wings of a cormorant, then he allows them to drop back to the body as the final expression of his failure to see your point of view.

Such unanswerable turns of logic were taken to a perfect conclusion when my father went to Feliccini, the watchmaker who was repairing a small clock of his. Feliccini could not find it and after he had hunted and hunted for many minutes my father suggested that it might be easier if each item were given a ticket with a number. '*Ma signore!*' the watchmaker exclaimed in horror at such an idea. '*S'immagine la confusione!*'

Having the last word is a skill that extends beyond Tuscany. My mother, before the First World War, accompanied Bernard Berenson on some of his journeys round Italy in search of forgotten masterpieces in wayside churches. In one little church, Berenson was offended when a beggar approached them for alms near the altar as they examined a Virgin and Child. He gave the man a lecture, saying it was unseemly to beg for money in the House of God. '*Si signore*,' replied the beggar, 'you are quite right. I shall wait for you outside.'

CHAPTER FIVE

Upper Bohemia in the Lunigiana

Before the First World War, my father had enjoyed painting informal portraits, but people began to disappear from his work. He concentrated on still life and landscape. His most striking pictures captured not just the terrain of the Lunigiana but its skyscape too, with its dramatic contrasts of sunlight and storm-cloud. They seemed to represent the turbulence underlying my parents' marriage and all our lives.

My father was exasperated by interruptions, whether the arrival of unexpected guests or my mother's sudden forays around Italy. In 1921, the year before the Fascists' March on Rome, J. L. Garvin, the editor of the *Observer*, asked my mother to be the paper's Italian correspondent. Without telling my father she accepted and promptly took up the work with gusto. Politics and the conversation of learned men like Bernard Berenson and Gaetano Salvemini, the historian, fascinated her. She had little time for other women and even less for children.

Indoors, my brother John and I crept round so as not to disturb her at her typewriter or my father in his studio. Sometimes he would roar that whispers were far more distracting than normal speech, but we knew that he preferred total silence. His concentration was impressive. He would work for hours, with only the odd break when he stopped to make tea in a blue enamel teapot on a Primus stove.

Standing by his easel, with his eyes narrowed and a spare brush held between his lips, he would be utterly absorbed by his subject, whether a still life of dried maize cobs and pine cones in a bowl, or flowers that had to be captured before they wilted in the heat, or the mountainous terrain constantly changing with the light and cloud. However long we waited for a good moment to speak to him, he would fail to notice our presence. Yet that childish urgency to tell a parent something would be distracted by his fixed gaze. Following his eyes, we too would watch the pattern of shadows moving across the hillsides.

My mother was equally unapproachable. The door of her study was left open, yet the typewriter's metallic chatter excluded one far more than if the entrance had been physically barred. And there was no hope of obtaining her assistance if my father had vetoed an idea. Like a number of people whose childhoods had been lonely, she was self-absorbed and would do almost anything to avoid a confrontation. Unfortunately, she had married into a family famous for its rows: Nackington House, where the Waterfields lived near Canterbury, was known as Nagington Hall. My father had a habit of erupting with terrible irrational rages. And despite a good sense of humour and all his attempts to be kind, a natural austerity convinced him that compliments corrupted people, especially children, so we received little encouragement.

The memory of the battle with Aunt Janet over my parents' engagement remained a running sore and the trace of its poison spoiled the bohemian idyll. My father could not forgive Aunt Janet's opposition to his marrying her niece and ward. He had, not unnaturally, taken this as a personal affront. It created a resentment that touched his professional self-esteem as well, since Aunt Janet (and also, I suspect, my mother) clearly did not think him capable of earning a living.

He never displayed any arrogance or conceit about his painting, but like all artists he minded desperately how others saw his work. D. H. Lawrence, who used to come up from Fiascherino to stay at the castle, sent a letter of praise that made him 'blush', but then Lawrence wrote to Cynthia Asquith that 'the artist gentleman painted in the manner of various definite gentleman artists – their ghosts haunted his canvases like the ghosts of old dead soldiers in his castle hall'. Kenneth Clark, on the other hand, described him as the most underrated painter of his generation.

My father certainly made no effort to be rated, for he loathed and despised the commercial end of painting. The only exhibition held during his lifetime was in Oxford with the pictures priced very low to encourage undergraduates who wanted to decorate their rooms or start collecting while young. Gallery owners he considered to be charlatans or crooks. Painters, he argued, would be far happier and more productive if they relied on patrons, as in the past, rather than putting their trust in this new breed of leech. In the art world, only figures like Henry Tonks, his professor at the Slade where he had been a contemporary of Augustus John, retained his full respect.

By moving to the castle, my father felt he had escaped the coteries and snide art criticism of London. In a letter to his mother he wrote that there was 'no one to dig you up to see how you are growing'. He steadfastly refused exhibitions – perversely bearing out Aunt Janet's scepticism over his ability to earn a living. Yet his escape to the castle was most certainly not motivated by idleness, for his output was prodigious. Unfortunately, he was such a fearsome perfectionist that many of his pictures were cast aside half-finished.

His rejection of the gallery circuit was perhaps best demonstrated by the amount of time he devoted to frescoes. He decorated the walls of the main bedroom to make it look like a loggia with pillars and arches looking out on to orange trees and blue sky. But his most ambitious scheme was downstairs. The vaulted ceilings at the castle, especially those in the high white *salone*, formed lunettes that begged to be painted. I am sure he must have dreamed of their possibilities the first time he saw the castle. In the *salone* he began to paint the mountain villages of the Lunigiana, set in their landscapes of gorge and wooded crag. Each lunette became a *trompe-l'oeil* window with the appearance of slim marble columns on either side. For this John and I were recruited for several hours, work on each occasion, marbling paper in a hip-bath on the floor. Tragically, only one of these frescoes survived the German army's occupation of the castle in the Second World War, and then in a terribly dilapidated state.

It did not help that my parents' lives and interests, although superficially similar, were in fact so incompatible. My mother, who was devoted to her husband, agreed with a smile when asked towards the end of her life whether she might not have been better suited as the wife of a diplomat than that of a painter. At Aulla she could hardly have been further from the centre of political events and debate, and she leaped at every chance to rush off to follow a story for the *Observer*. My father sometimes accompanied her, since he contributed articles to the *Manchester Guardian* until the Fascist regime threatened to expel him. These were dangerous times. On one famous occasion – it led to diplomatic exchanges and questions in Parliament – my parents were arrested together at Molinella when investigating the Fascists' destruction of agricultural cooperatives.

The problem of leaving behind two children during these expeditions was arbitrarily resolved. Since Mariannina had by this time left to look after her mother and be with her own two sons, John and I were handed over at short notice to Adelina. My mother had made her our nanny without considering for a moment whether she was suitable.

Adelina had a little house of her own down in the town, where we would be left. My mother had never stepped inside it, so she had no idea of what life was like for us there. The only lavatory, unless one used the cow byre like Adelina's nieces, was a privy whose hell-hole gave me bad dreams about falling into its noxious depths. I felt abandoned in a terrifying prison.

Sometimes Adelina would take us down to Carrara to see the rest of her family. Once, when I was six years old, it was decided that we should accompany her to the popular resort of Viareggio for several days with her two nieces, twins called Primina and Secondina. At Viareggio I witnessed a scene that so angered and distressed me that I have never forgotten it. A poor family arrived at the beach. They could not afford one of the bathing cabins, so they changed into their costumes with great care under towels on waste-ground behind the cabins. They left their clothes neatly folded and went into the sea to swim. A pair of *carabinieri* in their black uniforms and bicorn hats arrived and threw all the family's clothes into the sea.

Next day, having built a sandcastle, I went down to the

water's edge to fill my bucket. On my return, I was so anxious not to spill the contents that I did not realize I was walking at a tangent and I soon found myself lost on the crowded beach. I could not identify our umbrella, for they all looked alike, and there was no sign of Adelina. I wandered inland to the *pineta*, wearing only my petticoat, and sat down on a bench and wept. After what I had seen the day before, I was convinced that the police would arrest me for being improperly dressed. A kind woman took pity and comforted me until Adelina arrived distraught, having also suffered wildly exaggerated fears.

This little holiday continued its nightmare course when we returned to Carrara, for Secondina suddenly died. She was one of the casualties from the epidemic of Spanish influenza that swept Europe at the end of the First World War. I remember being absolutely horrified when I was sent in alone to pay my last respects and saw her lying in the coffin, dressed in her little party frock and the shoes of which she had been so proud, but with a waxy aspect to her face, which made her look like an overgrown doll.

Adelina was not cruel, just very insensitive: a fairly common fault in people with a will-o'-the-wisp imagination. At times, her only interest in me seemed to lie in the challenge of making my hair curl, which to me was just a further indignity and torture. When John was with me, our imprisonment in her frightening little house was not so bad, for we had each other; but after he had been sent off to school, the loneliness was terrible and I gazed up longingly at the castle on its hill and ached for my parents' return. I know emotions are painfully polarized in childhood, but these extremes of happiness and sadness seemed far greater than those of other children.

★

Even during the periods when my mother was not rushing down to Rome or up to Milan, my father felt that he had little peace, for there was an almost constant flow of visitors. Members of the family and friends longed to see the castle, intrigued by 'the slight element of imprudence' – as one of them put it – that my parents had demonstrated by moving there. Painter friends of my father were also attracted by the castle and its surrounding landscape. Rex Whistler loved the place so much that he used to bring other friends along to share his enthusiasm. His little oil sketch of the *salone*, in which he has included himself, shows one of them – the famously eccentric composer Lord Berners – in the window, also painting. On one visit, Whistler designed a Venetian bridge to join the living quarters to the roof-garden. Sadly, my father could not afford to turn this fantasy into reality.

The castle seemed to exert an unusually strong fascination on writers, though not always of a benevolent nature. One or two found the place frightening. E. F. Benson thought of vampires, and Baroness Orczy, a short woman who moved precariously on very high heels, announced that it was a marvellous place but that nothing would induce her to live there even for half a day. D. H. Lawrence who, shortly before the First World War, used to come up from Tellaro, either with Frieda von Richthofen or on his own, had strongly mixed feelings about the place.

We were at the weekend at Aulla with Waterfield [he wrote to Edward Marsh] who has a wonderful castle, in a sort of arena, like the victim, with the Apennines all round. It is a wonderful place, but it gives me the creeps down my back, just as if one sat in a chair down in the middle of the amphitheatre at Verona, and the great banks of stone took no notice, but gathered round.

Design for an enclosed bridge at the castle (*Rex Whistler*)

Then, with a volte-face either typical of him – or a reflection of the changing moods exerted by the Lunigiana weather – Lawrence wrote to Edward Garnett a few days later:

It is a wonderful place; a squat, square castle on a bluff of rock, with all the jagged Apennines prowling round, two rivers creeping out of the fastness to meet at the foot of the fortress, where is a tiny town, then flowing on, red-blazing in the sunset, into the black hills towards the sea. And when one is on the roof, and the dawn comes driving rosy across the mountain tops, it is wonderful. Day seems to stay a little while pale in the valley, then comes the sunset all gorgeous flaming, clashing back to red where the dawn came from, and the eastern peaks are alive and rosy above the gathering dust of the valley. You must come here – it is a wonderful place.

Lawrence's mood of claustrophobia may have surged once again on another occasion for a very different reason. A chemist by the name of Soddy from the dynamite factory at Villafranca turned up at the castle having heard in the town that an English poet was staying. Lawrence was surprised on the roof-garden and cornered on one of the towers. He had no choice but to listen to the verses composed by the dynamite manufacturer or throw himself over the parapet. When the ordeal was over, Lawrence repeated some of the lines to my father. 'The drooping lily's chastity' was the most memorably awful.

As summer approached its height, my father insisted on a general escape from the interruptions caused by guests and the *Observer* telephoning my mother from London. He had two favourite places: down the river Magra to its mouth on the sea, and high up into the Apennines to Lagastrello.

Bocca di Magra consisted of a few fishermen's houses and

an old inn called the Sans Façon, where we stayed. This curious name apparently came about because officers from Napoleon's army used to say, 'Let us go to Bocca without ceremony' – *sans façon*. The only other house nearby was very grand in comparison; it belonged to Count Carlo Andrea Fabbricotti, known as the 'King of Marble' because he owned so many of the Carrara quarries until the Fascist syndicates ruined him.

My father painted, and joined us rowing in the estuary to find new places for picnics and swimming. The river was wide and slow at its mouth. We used to watch fishermen, standing in skiffs and swirling nets around their heads to cast upon the water in biblical fashion. Fishing boats, their sails a rusty orange in colour, anchored in the estuary, and from the shore we could see ships loaded with marble, sailing past to the port of Carrara. The mountains themselves, so different when seen from this angle, faced us from beyond the coastal strip, along which there ran a green canopy of umbrella pines – a line of woodland that used to stretch all the way to Pisa.

But during those summers between the wars, the most important and magical pilgrimage was up into the mountains to Lagastrello. Rather as the British in India retired to the cooler heights of Simla or Kashmir during the great summer heat, my father established the practice of moving up into the Apennines from late July to early September to enjoy the invigorating air and dramatic scenery. Cut off from the telephone and correspondence, he felt that he was at last able to paint without the slightest chance of interruption.

In the early years just after the First World War, we used to set off up the Taverone valley to Comano in horse-drawn buggies with fringes on top, like those in *Oklahoma!* In later years we hired a large, slightly dilapidated and dusty touring-car.

At Comano we would wait for the charcoal burners' mule-train which, having brought their latest load down in the morning, would return empty up to the Lagastrello Pass in the late afternoon. The tents and all our equipment were loaded on to the mules. My mother, who had become lame after a bad fall, rode a horse. The rest of us accompanied the muleteers on foot.

The first time my father ordered a horse, it was brought up ready with a deep mountain-saddle, a less flamboyant version of the sort seen in the Wild West. My mother, who was by then a large woman, looked with sympathy at the small horse, whose ribs showed prominently. 'Are you sure that it will be able to carry me?' she asked its owner.

'But of course it will, signora.'

'But I am really quite heavy.'

'But surely not, signora,' came the obligatory compliment.

'Yes, indeed,' she insisted. 'I weigh at least 150 kilos.' Having rapidly converted her weight from stones into pounds, my mother had forgotten to convert the pounds into kilos. The owner of the horse reeled in horror at the effect that the famous diet of roast beef evidently had on the British frame.

Once all our camping impedimenta, including my father's painting equipment and my mother's bundles of books and typewriter, had been carefully strapped to the mules' pack-saddles and then checked for balance, we set off. At first John and I used to rush on ahead. Panting, we would turn round to watch the mule-train and our parents coming up behind. We were followed by Nerino, our cocker spaniel, who was still in disgrace for having knocked over one of my father's largest canvases in the studio. It fell on the Primus stove he used for making tea and a large hole was burned in it.

As we zigzagged up the hillside, heading for the Lagastrello Pass between Monte Malpasso and Monte Acuto, our minds dulled by the uphill plod and the gentle ringing of the mules' neck-bells that swung with each step, we left the chestnut woods of the valleys far below. Eventually we reached the higher slopes of scrub oak and finally those of the beech, which the charcoal burners used. After a four-hour journey, we unloaded and pitched camp.

Every year we went back to the same spot, which became known as *il campo inglese*. This expanse of grass amid the smooth-trunked young beech trees provided a wonderful view over the valleys to the Carrara mountains beyond, their intersecting slopes of shadow-blue paling into the distance. We had first been brought to this place by Signor Zunini and his wife, who had built a house beside the lake – Lago Paduli – which they had stocked with rainbow trout. With no road in those days, all the building materials and contents of their house had come up by mule.

Ramponi helped set up the military tents bought by my father at the end of the First World War, then returned to his family in Aulla. We each had our own officer's-pattern tent – double canvas, with pockets down the inside in which to stow belongings – and slept on a camp-bed and a palliasse stuffed with leaves. One year I found my improvised mattress moving strangely on the first night, and had to release a field mouse that must have been hiding in a pile of leaves when they were pushed into the sack.

My father set up his painting equipment with relish and my mother sorted through her books, wondering where to start. The most important task, however, was to prepare the cooking area. A sapling with its branches cut to stubs acted as a stand on which to hang the saucepans and pots. A grill left in a nearby hut would be reinstalled, and a trestle-table and ruck-chairs with thick leather straps as armrests were brought out of winter storage to form our open-air dining-room. Later, we had a wood-burning stove, which also stayed up at the hut. It had its own collapsible chimney, hotplates, and a tank from which scalding water could be produced at the turn of a tap. But my father would not allow us hot water for washing. He made sure we scrubbed ourselves properly in freezing water from a nearby spring that rose from under a rock.

Everything we needed was close to hand, like the spring, or was brought to us, either by the charcoal burners and shepherds, or by visitors bearing gifts. Our supplies came up daily with the mule-train on its return journey from Comano, an arrival heralded in the late afternoon by a distant sound of their bells and then the sight of the string of pack-animals silhouetted against the sky as they ascended the spur to our right. We took our sack of flour to Maddalena, the wife of one of the *guardafili* – the men who looked after the high-tension cables that ran down the valley on the far side of the ridge – and for a small sum she baked our bread along with that of her own family. She also sold us all the eggs we needed. Local shepherds provided us with fresh milk and cheese from the flocks of sheep then high up in their summer pastures. Fiore and his son Amadeo would come along the hills from Panicale to visit us on donkeys, their panniers filled with figs and raspberries. From mid-August, if the conditions were right, we would hunt for wild mushrooms together. Signor Zunini often arrived bearing freshly caught rainbow trout from the lake, while his young daughter, Yetta, who was allowed to roam the mountains alone providing she took their two St Bernard dogs as companions, used to bring us wild spinach and herbs from the hillsides. (Her offerings increased when Gordon joined us from school, for she fell in love with him.) With such a variety of manna in this idyllic wilderness, we hardly ever had to resort to our emergency supply of tinned food.

Few of the friends who joined us in our mountain retreat were disturbed by our isolation from the world below. Julian Trevelyan, the lanky artist son of the poet Robert Trevelyan, was going through a Parisian phase of seeing everything in alphabetical shapes. He emerged from his tent one morning and gazed round into the distance at trees, bushes and clouds.

'Ah me!' he said sadly. 'There are no letters today.'

'My dear boy,' erupted my father, 'don't you realize that I come here to get away from all correspondence?'

'Ah, I meant letters in the sky,' said Julian dreamily, and wandered off.

My father knew better where he was with Julian's father, Trevy, who strode across the hillsides, his hair awry and his gold-rimmed spectacles glinting in the sun as he recited poetry. Only the sight of a river or pool would halt his progress, for he could not resist stripping off and plunging in, however cold the water. Trevy's behaviour did much to confirm the locals' conviction that the British must be mad. Yet his fervent enthusiasm for the Lunigiana landscape was hardly a sign of eccentricity. What with the mountain air and the scent of wildflowers and herbs, almost everyone found the effect intoxicating and invigorating at the same time. 'Just like the *very* best Champagne,' as one of our more worldly visitors put it. Others simply danced barefoot on the grass in exhilaration.

The sight of my mother absent-mindedly stirring a pot while

Sketch of Robert Trevelyan (*Aubrey Waterfield*)

far more interested by the book in her hand was a familiar one. She did not share my father's love for these mountains to the same passionate extent – in fact I am sure she longed to be back in touch with political events in the real world – but she concealed such feelings well.

She reacted to the life like a good sport, although an air of faint surprise was all she could muster when we ran up to show her something we had found, such as an unfamiliar flower or a dead bird. Of course, we should have gone to my father, who would have been interested, but he was probably lost in the view, teeth clamped on the handle of a paintbrush. One evening my mother, John and I, accompanied by Nerino, joined him high up on the mountain behind. There we lit a fire and had a picnic supper as he painted, including us in the foreground of his picture.

Away from the grown-ups, our favourite diversion was building dams with rocks and mud to block one of the streams that ran down into the lake. Eventually, the pressure would become so great that the dam would topple and the rush of muddy water would spread a pale brown cloud out on the surface of the lake.

To get to the lake, only a few hundred yards from our camping ground, we passed along the stony track of the Passo del Uomo Morto. The dead man in question was said to have been a famous bandit, killed and buried there beneath a pile of stones. Every traveller was supposed to add one more stone on passing by, otherwise they would be haunted by the bandit's ghost. Just to be on the safe side, I always used to lob a couple of rocks on to the pile from a safe distance.

John and I never tired of wandering amidst the broom, wild thyme, wild mint with its tiny pink flowers and borage with its slightly bigger blue ones. We ate bilberries straight from the bushes and drank from the nearest brook. There were small wild roses, patches of heather and numerous wild flowers whose names we always forgot. We kept an eye out for golden eagles, hares and mountain foxes. But we also had to be careful. Thick mountain mists could materialize without warning and it was easy, mistaking one spur for another, to find ourselves in the wrong valley.

One of the most beautiful sounds was the hollow tinkle of sheep's bells. Some of the shepherds still carried conch shells like the one my father had at the castle instead of a dinner bell. They also used Homeric laughter, a juddering cry that carried over astonishing distances. The Greek resonances in these mountains extended even to the shepherds' names – Archimede, Oreste, Aristide and Parise. Parise was our greatest friend. His arrival at our camping ground was announced by the sound of galloping hooves, because he used to catch one of the racehorses put out to graze on the lower pastures and 'borrow' it for the day.

Cut off from his family, mountain shepherds like Parise lived in dry-stone huts assembled from rocks on the hillside. He slept on a criss-cross of branches over which was thrown a palliasse like ours. The hut always smelled of woodsmoke, for he had to heat the sheep's milk to make *pecorino*, taking care that no foreign bodies fell in. (Women making their own *pecorino* at home feared soot falling down the chimney at this crucial moment, for it would spoil the final taste.) Making each *pecorino* cheese was a long process. As the milk and rennet heated, the resulting fatty mass was skimmed off and poured into round wooden moulds. As the cheese set, the liquid was squeezed from it with weights loaded on top.

In many Tuscan farmhouses, freshly made cheeses were put on a shelf suspended by rope so that mice could not get at them. The shepherds also made *ricotta* with the whey – which in the Lunigiana they called *acqua rimasta* – from the *pecorino*. They added a little milk and a little vinegar, and then reheated it (*ricotta* means recooked), which brought a white substance floating to the top. This was strained off, pressed together in a coating of beech leaves and laid on twigs whose ends were then bent round and tied to make a cage that hung from the roof. The last of the liquid then dripped out and the *ricotta* would set. The *ricotta*, when served, still bore the faint, fossil-like imprint of the beech leaves.

The charcoal burners welcomed John and me in their camp where they too showed us their method of work. First they constructed a sort of wigwam with branches, having placed kindling wood at the bottom. They coated the outside with turf, then dropped a burning brand down the hole in the top to ignite the kindling at the base. When it was alight they sealed the top with more turf and the wood slowly cooked over several days.

Having made such friends with the shepherds and the charcoal burners, I was surprised to hear later that the daughters of a peasant family well-established in a *podere* were sometimes forbidden to associate with charcoal burners or shepherds, who were seen as nomadic and semi-savage, even as thieves. This veto was apparently applied even more firmly in the case of fishermen from the coast who, for some reason (perhaps a suspicion that they cavorted with mermaids), were considered deeply immoral. But Tuscan proverbs always warned against marrying outside your own community: '*Chi di lontano si va a maritare, sarà ingannato o vuol ingannare*' – 'Those who go to marry far afield will be deceived, or else they want to deceive others.'

The *guardafili* on the other side of the ridge knew their part of the mountain even better than the shepherds and charcoal burners. One year my father fell ill with rheumatic fever when his bedding, left out to air, had become damp in the evening dew. His condition deteriorated so much over forty-eight hours that Signor Zunini decided he must be taken down to the valley. The *guardafili* volunteered as a team to carry the improvised litter down the Taverone valley. In places the route down was precipitous, and at times we had to cross the fierce torrent, stepping from boulder to boulder over the roaring water. However gentle the *guardafili* tried to be on this perilous descent, I could see the acute pain on my father's face. I have seldom been so relieved as when we reached the valley.

Up at Lagastrello we became very conscious of the seasons. From one day to the next, usually at the very end of August or early in September, there would be a change in the weather that heralded the start of autumn. The charcoal burners would work harder than ever, knowing that they had only a couple of months more before the first snows arrived: they had to earn enough to survive until the following spring. Meanwhile, shepherds would start to assemble their flocks before taking them down to winter pasture. Within a week or so, the chestnut woods below turned a soft yellow.

The inhabitants of the mountain villages would soon be out collecting sackfuls of glossy chestnuts. For them, the chestnut harvest was as important as the maize harvest in the valleys. Only the big round nuts were sold to confectioners. The smaller ones were laid on racks in huts, sometimes even in a room of the house, and slowly dried for a long time over a fire laid on the beaten earth floor. The drying process also cracked the shells, making them easy to peel, and the kernels were ready for grinding into flour to make another variety of polenta, and even bread. During the near-starvation of the Second World War years, bread made from chestnut flour was to become the basic diet of northern Tuscany.

Well before the last of the chestnuts were gathered in the valleys below, we had to return to Aulla. My mother would have left much earlier, called away, in spite of all my father's objections, by a message from London relayed up the mountains. By September he was more magnanimous. He looked forward to his studio where he could reappraise his pictures from the mountains and finish them; or, if dissatisfied, add them to the stack of rejects.

Of all the contradictions in the bohemian life of the castle, the most far-reaching event took place some years later, when I was sixteen. At a lunch at the British embassy, on one of her journalistic excursions to Rome, my mother was seated next to Captain Bevan, the naval attaché. He mentioned that Admiral Sir Ernle Chatfield, commander-in-chief of the Mediterranean Fleet, was about to pay a courtesy visit to the Italian naval base of La Spezia in his flagship, the battleship HMS *Queen Elizabeth*. My mother immediately said that the admiral should visit them at the castle, since it was less than twenty kilometres away, and stay to lunch. Captain Bevan, who had not envisaged how informal life at the castle might be, took her at her word and incorporated the visit into his programme.

My mother's return to Aulla was delayed, and my father, who had heard nothing of all this, received a telegram from Bevan saying how much Admiral Chatfield *and* all his officers were looking forward to the lunch in their honour so kindly suggested by Mrs Waterfield. His explosion was memorable (although less than might have been expected because, for all his love of Tuscan solitude, he missed English male company). He immediately summoned Adelina and they began planning. My mother, on her arrival that night, was taken aback to discover the size of the planned party.

Abandoning all thought of painting for the next couple of days, my father set to work with Ramponi. Together they erected two flag-poles on separate towers. One flew the Italian royal tricolour with the arms of the House of Savoy in the middle, and the other flew the Union Jack. On the morning of the lunch, the long table in the *salone* was covered with starched linen sheets. Adelina insisted on decorating it herself with irises from the roof-garden, despite the pressure of work in the kitchen.

The menu had been quickly decided. We were going to start with *tortellini* made from *pasta fatta in casa* and stuffed with *ricotta* and fresh herbs, the finished product heavily sprinkled with Parmesan. These could be prepared the day before. The main course would consist of a roast of veal *alla giardiniere*, finely sliced and served on a large platter with a sauce of wild mushrooms and chicken livers, surrounded by a variety of colourful vegetables – little carrots, shallots and French beans. This would be followed by the local *pecorino* cheese served with pears and, finally, Adelina's speciality of *zabaglione*.

Whatever the air of confusion, everything was more or less under control by the morning of the visit. Volunteers had turned up, and visitors found themselves dragooned. This was what brought Vittorio Chiodetti into our lives. To say that the thirteen-year-old Vittorio arrived bearing a telegram and stayed for fifty years is hardly an exaggeration.

Vittorio, having placed the envelope on the kitchen table, left on his return journey. He was some way down the mule-track when Adelina hurried to the balcony outside the dining-room window. She had found she was short of bread. '*O, Vittorio!*' she yelled after him in a voice that would have carried all the way down to the Piazza Cavour. '*Portami su del pan!*'

When he eventually tramped back up to the castle with the bread, Adelina eyed him up and down. She needed somebody else to help serve, and although he was small and slight for his age, he was far from clumsy. Even at this early age, Vittorio was clearly an exceptional person. He had a face of great intelligence above a curiously prominent Adam's apple, and his air of polite reserve seemed to underline a reluctance to waste words. The fresh white kitchen apron she tried on him was so large that he looked lost in it until a large reef was taken in and secured with the tapes tied round his body. I saw him standing there looking very self-conscious in this extraordinary rig, and my heart sank as I thought of Captain Bevan.

Captain Bevan arrived ahead of the other guests to check arrangements. A stickler for protocol, he was clearly very concerned to find that the castle was not the sort of grand establishment he had visualized: he quite obviously feared that the party was not appropriate for a commander-in-chief. To cap his discomfort, he noticed, just as the officers from the *Queen Elizabeth* arrived, that the Union Jack hoisted by Ramponi was flying upside down. It was too late to do anything. My father then appeared to greet the admiral, immaculate in clean linen suit and stiff collar but without a tie, which he had forgotten because he had been so pre-occupied with last-minute arrangements. Fortunately, he did

La Fortezza della Brunella

The Return from the Ride. Charles Furse's portrait of Aubrey and Lina after their marriage, with Lina wearing her going-away dress

Above, left: Aubrey Waterfield before his marriage to Lina Duff Gordon
Above, right: Not quite Sissinghurst in Tuscany. Lina and Aubrey working on the ramparts, with Gordon in the wheelbarrow

A picnic in the Lunigiana hills before the First World War: Gordon, Lina, Mariannina and Ulisse the Wise

Three pictures by Aubrey Waterfield: Ramponi digging on the castle hillside *(above, left)*, Adelina with her tray *(above, right)*, and Montàn – the man who had seen the last Duke of Modena ride past, as Aubrey Waterfield told Kinta while she watched him paint *(below)*.

One of Aubrey's paintings of the Carraras from the Lagastrello campsite

Aubrey working on one of his frescoes of local landscapes in the *salone* at the castle

The Carraras seen from the window made by Fiore the stonemason

View of the castle from a distance

Aunt Janet supervising the *vendemmia* at Poggio before the First World War

Loading the grapes on to an ox-cart

Agostino in the kitchen at Poggio Gherardo during the First World War

Beppe the gardener coming up the iris walk that led down to the south gate

Pippo. The fresco of the beloved poodle of the Gherardi family

Poggio's main entrance from the edge of the *bosco*

not understand Bevan's nervous little hand signals and remained unaware of this sartorial *faux pas* throughout lunch.

He need hardly have worried. Admiral Chatfield was delighted by everything: the roof-garden, the view – the Carraras stood proud and clear – and the lunch, which could hardly have been more different to the ponderous fare of a Royal Navy wardroom. Adelina had surpassed herself. As for Vittorio, all my fears had been misplaced. Despite his unfamiliar garb and complete lack of experience, he fulfilled his role as a waiter to perfection, placing a piece of bread on each side plate with a fork as if he had worked for years at the Ritz. Only Adelina found cause for dissatisfaction in the arrangements: my father had again insisted on serving the castle wine straight from raffia-covered *fiaschi*. She was, however, mollified by the fact that some delicious dry white wine from the nearby Cinqueterre was served as a counterpoint to her acclaimed *zabaglione*.

After lunch, the admiral asked my father if he might see his studio. It was then that my father, while showing him his latest painting, reached up, without thinking, to tighten his tie. On discovering its absence, he roared with laughter and apologized to the admiral, who took one glance and replied that he had never noticed. I could not see Captain Bevan at this moment, but by then he could hardly conceal his astonishment that the visit had been such a success in spite of all his fears.

The day was, for us, far more significant for that other event – the arrival of Vittorio. Within a few years he was running everything with such quiet efficiency that life without him became unimaginable. One morning my father heard him answering the telephone in English. We discovered that he had learned it from reading the old copies of *The*

Times that Adelina spread on the kitchen table. But his qualities of wisdom and honesty were to impress others in circumstances that were incomparably more important. During the war, after he had been drafted into an Alpini battalion ordered to the Russian front, his colonel, knowing that most of them would perish, found an excuse to post him back to Italy. Thanks to the kind colonel and later to other miracles, he survived the war.

CHAPTER SIX

Aunt Janet and Poggio Gherardo

The other centre of our life in Italy was Aunt Janet's property of Poggio Gherardo. This ancient castellated villa, surrounded by its three small farms with their vineyards and olive groves, overlooked Florence from the Fiesole hillside. The formality of its establishment bore little relation to life at Aulla.

John and I came to know the place well. Not only did we spend the First World War there until the soldiers had left the castle, but on many occasions we returned in the 1920s, and sometimes my mother left us there with Aunt Janet. My father, on the other hand, usually found a good reason to stay at Aulla where he had his studio and his freedom. The old animosity with his wife's guardian had never healed.

Aunt Janet was a handsome and erect *grande dame* of about eighty. Her penetrating eyes and startling black eyebrows were quite sufficient, when raised, to bring malefactors and innocents alike to heel. Her white hair was coiled up into a bun on top of the rear part of her head, giving it the profile of a doge's cap. As if to complete this archaic and magisterial impression, she used to wear long white cashmere dresses, all beautifully made to the same pattern, with silver filigree buttons and a silver-edged black leather belt from which hung a chatelaine of keys and a large gold watch. During thunderstorms, she would stand on the terrace with this watch in her hand and time the difference between the flash and the crack of thunder. She was greatly attached to the watch for family reasons. When her grandmother, Sarah Austin, was on her way to her wedding, a rejected suitor had run beside the carriage and thrown it through the window on to her lap.

I never quite understood why friends of all ages – whether Bernard Berenson at sixty or Kenneth Clark at twenty – addressed her as Aunt Janet when they were not related at all. Perhaps it was because she had assumed the rank of Great-Aunt-General and they had fallen into step, half-dragooned and half-amused.

Visitors with a letter of introduction would be invited to tea on Sundays. Until we were old enough to be allowed to join the company, John and I could only peek in at the Sunday-afternoon proceedings from round the door. The major-domo, Davide, in white gloves and white coat, served tea and passed round plates of delicious little *langue de chat* biscuits made by Agostino, the chef.

Aunt Janet's fearsome reputation was considerable. It had grown in the telling ever since she was said to have horse-whipped Ouida in the streets of Florence for libelling her in the novel *Friendship*. Ouida, infatuated with the Marchese della Stufa, had convinced herself that Janet Ross must have seduced him away from her. The only copy of the novel that gained entry to Poggio Gherardo had been hung in the lavatory, shorn of its binding and ready for use. Years later, when a journalist arrived unannounced to ask her about Ouida, she simply said: 'And who was Ouida?' The man was shown out.

Aunt Janet did not hide her feelings about people. She had

sworn enemies on one side and, on the other, friends to whom she was fiercely loyal. New acquaintances were left in no doubt, for her likes or dislikes were instant and often arbitrary. Even Virginia Woolf emerged smarting from Sunday tea at Poggio, having felt 'patronised' by the 'formidable Mrs Ross'. One Englishman, clutching his letter of introduction, came all the way up from his hotel in Florence, only to find his nerve fail after ringing the bell: he ran away just before the servant appeared. But those who were not intimidated and who met her favour were treated with a brisk approval that often concealed real affection.

Some of Aunt Janet's public intolerance was due to the fact that she found herself regarded as an ancient monument on the list of items that had to be seen in and around Florence. People would pay calls assuming that she had nothing better to do than receive them. Whenever one of these less welcome visitors started to ask about all the people she had known in her youth, she was apt to retort: 'Read my books.' And if they had on 'their sitting breeches' – as she used to say of those who showed little sign of leaving – she would not conceal her impatience to return to her desk or her farms.

Her upbringing had indeed been out of the ordinary. As the daughter of Lucie Duff Gordon, she had been surrounded by her parents' friends – Thackeray, Dickens, Macaulay, Tennyson, Caroline Norton and Thomas Carlyle – and their conversation had provided a large part of her education. Later, George Meredith and Eastlake appear to have been in love with her, yet this fearless young horsewoman suddenly announced that she had decided to marry Henry Ross because he rode so well out hunting. She was unreflective as well as unromantic. In later life she reread the letters and poems Meredith had sent her, and exclaimed, 'How extraordinary! I think my poet must have been in love with me.' And when speaking of the act of conception that produced her only child, she is supposed to have said, 'I must have been drugged!' She enjoyed being provocative in other ways. The three great bores in Italian history, she used to proclaim, were Saint Francis, Dante and Savonarola. And, probably to tease my mother, she sometimes called me Carpathia.

'No, *Zia*,' my mother would reply firmly. 'Her name is Carinthia.'

'Oh well, I knew you'd given her the name of some outlandish country.'

When I was presented at Court several years after Aunt Janet's death, and I sank into the obligatory deep curtsy, ostrich feathers and all, I nearly lost my balance on hearing the courtier intone, 'Miss Carpathia Waterfield.' Despite the gravity of the moment, I had to glance round. Fortunately, the courtier bore no resemblance to Aunt Janet. My immediate instinct about reincarnation or transmigration of souls evaporated, but I rose from the curtsy a little unsteadily.

Aunt Janet hated wasting time. If she was not writing or working on the farm accounts at her huge marquetry desk, she was out in the fields picking up olives or helping with the harvest. She remained a creature of habit and self-discipline until the end of her life. Meals were served precisely on time, and after lunch she would smoke half a cigarette, leaving the other half to be smoked after dinner on the terrace looking down on Florence. Her austerity extended even to mattresses stuffed with maize leaves in peasant fashion, because she considered it an economic and hygienic practice. In the old days, guests kept awake by the deafening crackle every time they moved at night had to ask for a conventional replacement, until finally she changed all the mattresses at Poggio save her own.

She was a curious mixture in other ways. She spoke a number of languages including French, German and Arabic. Her knowledge of Italian – both the *lingua latina* and the *lingua vulgare* – was excellent even if she pronounced the words with what Kenneth Clark described as a 'Churchillian defiance of accent'. She deciphered the family letters of the early Medici that had never been published, and wrote a dozen other books. Yet she could not master multiplication, which meant she had to do the farm accounts using an immensely laborious system of adding figures so many times.

She also had astonishing gaps in her knowledge. One day, when Filippo de Filippi, the explorer, arrived at the house unexpectedly, she said, 'Ah, Filippo, you are just the person I want. Now, what is the equator?'

'It is an imaginary line encircling the earth,' he replied with surprise and amusement.

'Imaginary line?' said Aunt Janet scornfully. 'I've never heard of anything so ridiculous.'

Although Aunt Janet played the role of an autocratic old empress in the presence of grown-ups, she was fair and painstaking with children. She thoroughly disapproved of the way my mother took little interest in our upbringing and could leave us with a peasant woman like Adelina. And despite her rumblings of complaint to Mary Berenson about the way we were dumped at Poggio, I think she quite enjoyed our company. She was lonely in that huge house after Uncle Henry died. Joan Haslip and her sister, sent by their mother with a bunch of flowers on her birthday, were astonished by her tears of gratitude.

*

I first knew Poggio during the First World War, when I was young enough to be rather frightened of going to bed in the high-ceilinged, whitewashed room on the ground floor, the window heavily barred in Florentine style. The room smelt of cold stone and camphor mothballs, and in winter the little stove stood no chance against the chill. I used to lie there in bed, not daring to move under the bedclothes, listening to owls hoot from the wood outside. Most intimidating of all was the tall and ancient cupboard of dark wood inlaid with the Medici shield of six balls. It looked the perfect hiding place for an assassin.

Such fears had a certain historical justification. One of these ground-floor bedrooms, whose windows looked out over vineyards and olive groves towards Settignano, had been the scene of a murder. Poggio Gherardo had been a Guelph (pro-Papal) stronghold, and, in a true Romeo-and-Juliet story, the daughter of the house had fallen in love with the son of a Ghibelline (pro-Imperial) neighbour after their eyes had met at mass in the little church of San Martino a Mensola, which lay half a mile below. The girl's brothers, having received word of a meeting at Poggio, lay in wait one night and stabbed the boy to death as he tried to kiss her through the thick grille of bars over the bedroom window. She wasted away in grief. Her ghost was sometimes seen at the window, although not by any of us, and her spirit – very sad rather than frightening – could on occasions still be felt in that part of the house.

Poggio Gherardo provided the setting for the first three days of *The Decameron*, when a group of young Florentines fled the plague of 1348. Boccaccio, who had grown up only a few hundred yards away, described it as: 'a palace on the brow of a hill with a fine and spacious courtyard in the centre, and with loggias and halls and rooms ornamented tastefully with jocund paintings; surrounded with grass plots and marvellous gardens, and with wells of coldest water, and cellars of rare wines, a thing more suited to curious topers than to sober and virtuous women'. Palagio del Poggio, the palace on the hill, became Poggio Gherardo when it passed to the Gherardi family in 1433. Aunt Janet and Henry Ross purchased it in 1888 from three Gherardi contessas, all spinsters and the last of their line.

Although a large fortified house with its square Guelph battlements, Poggio had an open, cheerful atmosphere. The exterior walls were a warm apricot stucco that glowed in the evening sun. Lemon trees in large terracotta pots surrounded the *piazzale* outside the main door.

The hall, cool after the baked air outside, was open and light since it followed two sides of a central courtyard. Doors off the hall, their handles a brass fist holding a baton, were seldom closed. In fact, throughout the house, doors always seemed to be open in all directions. The need for coolness in summer and the Italian sense of space did not permit that English desire for privacy.

Several of the rooms had delightful grisailles and *trompe-l'oeil* (what the Italians call *pare vero*). My favourite depicted Pippo, a poodle adored by the Gherardi family in the eighteenth century: his grave, a classical marble tomb, stood outside, on the edge of the little wood inside the north gate. A *trompe-l'oeil* landscape set in a remarkably life-like, carved gilt frame decorated each of the side walls of the 'Poodle Room'. This was my very unusual nursery. Next door was our bathroom, in what had been the family chapel. Lying back naked in the bath, I found it strange – perhaps more in retrospect than at the time – to gaze up at a ceiling painted with a dove symbolizing the Holy Ghost.

POGGIO GHERARDO - FLORENCE - ITALY

FROM A DECAMERON CODEX TRANSCRIBED FORTY YEARS AFTER THE DEATH OF BOCCACCIO
(NATIONAL LIBRARY - PARIS.)

Decameron codex of Poggio Gherardo

Aunt Janet's study, although one of the smaller rooms in the house, was the centre of authority and organization. Davide came there to receive instructions for the household and outdoor staff; and Agostino to discuss menus. Newcomers, shown in there on arrival, were fascinated by the room's Victorian clutter of pictures and mementoes. It had the look of a shrine dedicated to ancestor worship. A profile of her mother, Lucie Duff Gordon, by Henry Phillips hung on one wall, and when Aunt Janet worked at Lucie's desk, a bust of Alexander Duff Gordon sat at her right elbow. But whatever the quantity of objects and pictures, the room could never have been claustrophobic with its two french windows looking out over the Arno valley. Someone remarked that it was rather like being in the gondola of an airship.

The french windows gave on to a stone balcony shaded by wistaria. On either side, a staircase in the same stone descended to a broad parterre with exotic trees including a medlar, a magnolia, a persimmon and a large camphor tree, whose clusters of tiny blossom scented the air around. Set in under the balcony was a grotto with a pool, inhabited by goldfish with wide chiffon tails. More of these fish, originally brought back from Burma by an admirer of Aunt Janet's, lived in the circular stone basin of the fountain, which formed the centre of the terrace. Aunt Janet used to breed them and give them away to friends. Harold Acton still has some of their descendants at La Pietra. A less fortunate pair was presented to Charles Bell, Keeper of Fine Art at the Ashmolean, to take back to Oxford by train. The journey was hot and slow, and the two goldfish began to gasp in distress, so when the train halted at Pisa, Charles Bell dashed out of the station to buy a bicycle pump. He then spent the rest of the journey pumping away to aerate the water, and they survived the ordeal.

The view from the terrace extended over Poggio's sloping olive groves and across the terracotta roofs of Florence to Giotto's tower and the perfect shape of Brunelleschi's dome. Behind the house stretched the hills of Fiesole and Settignano, with their vineyards and olives and cypresses and ilex woods. These hillsides offered innumerable walks among wild narcissi and anemones and carmine-coloured tulips, their petals ending in long graceful points. The most intriguing walk, to the pinewoods of Vincigliata, led past the ancient and beautiful Medici hunting-lodge of Bagazzano. The isolation of this spot was preserved by its owner, a partially crippled man of letters who used to go up there to escape Florentine society. He had allowed no road to be built beyond the Villa Gamberaia, so he reached his idyllic house on a sledge drawn by white oxen.

Aunt Janet, despite having chosen to live in such a magnificent setting as Poggio Gherardo, was proudly impervious to the scenery around her. Only the practical side of her farms interested her. She considered visitors to Florence who were concerned about the view from their hotel to be quite unreasonable. They should not have come to Florence to sit around gazing in vapid enchantment, she insisted. They should be off studying the city's art and architecture, or reading up its history.

As at Aulla, sounds from the valley drifted up. At Poggio the most memorable were the songs of the *contadini* working in the vineyards and olive groves, the rag collector drawing out the doleful cry '*Cen-ciaio!*' and church bells, either from the campanile of San Martino a Mensola, or those down below in Florence. Their chime was so much more cheerful than the mournful Protestant tolling of the north. Yet many of them originally came from England, either sold off following Henry VIII's dissolution of the monasteries, or exported. English bell foundries were regarded as the best in Europe. So prized were they that towards the end of Queen Elizabeth's reign the Corsini family managed to extract the capital of their bank in the City of London by converting it into church bells. The bells were then loaded on to ships and resold in the Mediterranean; a procedure that enabled them to evade the royal decree forbidding the export of capital. With the money brought to Italy, they purchased large estates in Umbria to add to their very considerable properties in Tuscany. This provided them with an alternative base outside the turbulent uncertainty of Medicean politics. When they became Princes of Sismano, the title was not Florentine: it came from their Umbrian castle.

At the eastern end of Poggio, looking towards the hills of Vallombrosa, there was another terrace, this one in herring-bone brick, surrounded by banquettes of marble mosaic. Shade was provided by a pergola of vines which produced delicious eating grapes called salamanders. Just beyond this terrace lived Aunt Janet's menagerie, in a row of brick-based cages: her magnificent white cockatoo whose favourite cry was 'Agostino! Agostino!' as if summoning the chef; Leone, the large white Maremma sheepdog; and some home-bred wild boar and rabbits raised for the table. There were also pens for her golden and silver pheasants. Very occasionally, one of them would be cooked and served at table on a huge platter in Renaissance style, cloaked in its own skin and feathers.

Below, in a dip just beyond the church of San Martino a Mensola, lay I Tatti with its descending garden flanked by cypresses designed by Cecil Pinsent. The woodland garden on the Poggio side was laid out by my father, and B.B.

always claimed it to be his favourite place for contemplation. I Tatti was close enough for Aunt Janet and Mary Berenson to semaphore to each other from their terraces to confirm lunch or other engagements. Although I was considered too young to join John at the little school Mary Berenson had established for her Stephen and Strachey grandchildren, I was able to join in the games. To B.B.'s horror and exasperation, his wife encouraged us to use his retreat of aesthetic contemplation as an adventure playground. We used to climb over furniture to get round the room without touching the floor and dodge behind statues during Blind Man's Buff. At least I was not responsible for the pool in the hall and the gentle trickle down the stairs which, on one occasion, greeted B.B. and Nicky Mariano on their return from a walk. A rapid investigation upstairs revealed the Stephen children, whose father was a mathematician, testing out Archimedes' principle of water displacement in the bath.

With my mother away (or closeted with her typewriter) and Aunt Janet inspecting the farms, John and I were as free at Poggio as we were at the castle. Adelina, brought over from Aulla as our nanny, spent her time gossiping with the wives of the *contadini*. Later, the friend my mother brought back from East Kent to act as my governess preferred to discuss politics or take singing lessons with a maestro in Florence. Aunt Janet was not pleased by such a lax arrangement. 'That foolish woman,' she wrote in disgust to Mary Berenson, 'goes off to screech for two hours each morning, and actually thinks she has a good voice.'

John and I, left to our own devices, made great friends with Adolfo and Adelcisa, the children of Agostino. Adelcisa and I made dolls, kept a make-believe shop and played at nurses, using the little Red Cross uniform somebody had given me. With the boys we played hide-and-seek, even climbing into the Ali Baba oil jars in the huge cellars that ran under the house. We had competitions catching crickets with our hands or lizards with lassos. Other wildlife – geckos, hummingmoths, hoopoes – we were content to watch.

Our magic kingdom was the *bosco* inside the north gate – the little wood of Aleppo pines and ilex trees where the owls lived. Under the trees the ground was covered with pine needles and the dry, dead, crackling leaves of ilex. The wood was very dark in some places and deceptively lit with patches of sunlight in others. We would hide there, listening to Adelina's exasperated calls for us in the distance. When no grown-ups were about, we would swing from tree to tree. The great challenge was to cross from one side of the wood to the other without letting your feet touch the ground.

We also played at *condottieri*, wondering in excitement mingled with fear whether this would conjure up the ghost of Sir John Hawkwood, who had captured Poggio Gherardo in 1363 with his band of mercenaries, known as the White Company because of the splendour of their armour. (The Italians could not manage the pronunciation of his name and it became corrupted to Giovanni Acuto.) The history of the place made our world of make-believe unusually vivid. We knew all about the great English *condottiere* because Aunt Janet had taken us to the Duomo to see the equestrian fresco of him by Paolo Uccello. Aunt Janet was very proud of Sir John. It was almost as if he had been an ancestor; at the very least he provided an ancient precedent for her occupation of Poggio Gherardo. She certainly regarded him as the first Anglo-Florentine. The inconvenient fact that he had been fighting for the hated Pisans against Florence at that time was overlooked.

One year we really did have something to fear. We were in a corner of the *bosco* when the cicadas suddenly fell silent. All the dogs in the area began to howl. The bell hanging outside the north gate started jangling and was followed by the church bells of San Martino a Mensola and those in the city itself down in the valley. Only then did we feel the vibration of the ground and see the movement of trees and the swaying of stonework. The earthquake seemed to finish as suddenly as it had started. In the palpable silence that followed, everything stood motionless as if this corner of the world had been petrified by an enchanter. Released from the momentary spell, we began to look about us hesitantly. As after a dream, it was impossible to tell how long the experience had lasted, whether minutes or just seconds. I found it hard to believe that everything had returned to normal, but Poggio's castellated tower was uncracked and there was no sign of damage in Florence.

Since I was younger than Johnnie and his schoolfriends, I did not see so much of the other little Anglo-Florentines as he did, first at I Tatti and later when he moved to Miss Penrose's English school. I never even had the chance to see them at the Anglican church – the Holy Trinity in via Lamarmora – because Aunt Janet was a freethinker and my mother a lapsed Catholic. Towards the end of the First World War, however, I was given a compensatory moment of glory when Lady Sybil Cutting decided to hold a children's May Day party at the Villa Medici. I was to be Queen of the May even though the role by rights belonged to her daughter, Iris (later Iris Origo), who was fifteen, the same age as Gordon, my eldest brother.

John and I were driven over in Aunt Janet's horse-drawn

landau by her coachman, Neno, a fat man of great dignity. John wore white ducks and a blue regency jacket and I was dressed like a little bridesmaid in a full dress of broderie anglaise, which was rather prickly. The narrow, hilly roads towards Fiesole had steep sides, either stone-banked or high-walled, which gave a curious echo to the sound of the horses' hooves. The Villa Medici commanded a magnificent view across Florence to San Miniato from its loggia and long terraced parterre of gravel paths, box hedges and statues. Lorenzo de' Medici used the house for entertaining and narrowly avoided assassination there during the Pazzi conspiracy of 1478. Inside there were rooms that had been done up in the eighteenth century in hand-painted Chinese wallpaper showing a profusion of birds and flowers. Others were lined with Lucca silk – pale blue with a tinge of yellow – which Sybil Cutting adored.

I was seated on a throne borne by poles and carried round the garden in state before being crowned Queen of the May with a rather uncomfortable coronet of flowers. Much to their disgust, John and all the other boys had to come and kiss the hand of this six-year-old girl. I was quite bemused by it all.

There then followed a strange choice of game for a children's party, but Sybil Cutting was a strange mother. She called us round a large dish filled with fat raisins that had been soaked in brandy and set alight, and told us to snatch them out and eat them. The whole occasion was, however, most memorable for this first impression of Iris's mother, an imposing Edwardian figure. But the afternoon had one great disappointment. She never fainted.

I had overheard a good deal of gossip about Sybil Cutting, in particular my mother's experience when Sybil had sud-denly collapsed once during dinner at I Tatti. My mother, amazed that everyone else carried on talking as if nothing had happened, rushed round the table to help. Unfortunately, some of Sybil's hair caught in her brooch as she tried to lift her head and, rather reluctantly, another guest had to help disentangle the knot. Others picked up the recumbent figure and laid her on a sofa, then everyone returned to their places and resumed their different conversations as if nothing out of the ordinary had happened. Only afterwards did Mary Berenson explain that Lady Sybil had a habit of fainting – into genuine unconsciousness it must be said – whenever she felt assailed by tedium.

Sybil Cutting was the daughter of the Anglo-Irish Earl of Desart, and the widow of Bayard Cutting, a rich American from an 'Old New York' family straight out of a novel by Edith Wharton. She then married Geoffrey Scott, and together they wrote the single slim masterpiece *The Portrait of Zélide*. Finally, when that marriage broke up, she married Percy Lubbock, another English writer in Tuscany. She liked the idea of a grand Anglo-Florentine literary circuit. Aldous Huxley, although genuinely fond of her, mocked her mercilessly when he cast her as Lilian Aldwinkle in his novel *Those Barren Leaves*. It was in many ways an unfair caricature, for she was a most intelligent woman; but she was breathtakingly self-centred, as Iris knew only too well, and her hypochondria went well beyond the odd fit of fainting.

On one occasion she suffered such an acute attack that both Sir Aldo Castellani, a famous specialist in London as well as personal physician to several royal houses, and Giglioli, the most highly regarded practitioner in Florence, were summoned together to the Villa Medici. The two doctors could hardly have been more different. Castellani had never lost an opportunity to cultivate the air of a court physician, while Giglioli was, on occasions, known to roar with laughter when faced with the sight of a patient looking unusually pitiful.

After coming out from the darkened bedroom, Castellani turned to his rather less deferential colleague in the corridor.

'I have found the bug,' he exclaimed with great satisfaction in English, 'but I cannot put a name to it.'

'Might we not call it the *hum*bug?' was Giglioli's instant retort.

Others in – but not of – the Anglo-Florentine world, which Aldous Huxley acidly described as 'Villadom', included Carlo Placci: a cosmopolitan name-dropper who implied that he had a finger in every political, intellectual and social pie across Europe. If he was not on first name terms with a particular prime minister, then the implication was that the man's future in government was limited. But Placci was clearly well-informed and entertaining, for one saw everybody rush up to talk to him to hear the latest gossip.

An even more improbable character was the writer Vernon Lee, alias Violet Paget, with her cropped hair and men's clothes with stiff collars. She was particularly kind and gave me copies of all her books and, more surprisingly, a loom, as if I were a character in one of her Tuscan fairy tales. Conversation with her, however, was agonizing, for she was old and very deaf. Aunt Janet, for reasons I never entirely understood, loathed her. My father on the other hand liked her enormously, and on his rare visits to Florence he would drive off with her and Sybil Scott in Sybil's large chauffeur-driven Lancia to have a picnic tea in the surrounding hills.

The rest of the English intellectual community in the 1920s

– D. H. Lawrence, Aldous and Maria Huxley and Norman Douglas – steered clear of Villadom on the Settignano–Fiesole hillsides. My parents went to see Lawrence and Frieda again, but they did not renew their friendship of 1913 and 1914. (He was soon to set to work on what he called his 'nice and tender phallic novel' *Lady Chatterley's Lover*, which was printed in Florence in 1928.) And Aldous and Maria Huxley we saw only at the seaside at Forte dei Marmi.

The Huxleys and their friends preferred cheap little *trattorie* such as the Nuova Toscana restaurant in the Piazza Signoria, and speaking Italian with an accent that the real Florentines called *anglo-becero* – *becero* being a sort of cockney accent found on the south bank of the Arno. Yet *anglo-becero* was more usually an inflection that English people, brought up as children in Florence, had picked up from servants. (Harold Acton, whose pronunciation has never been less than fastidious, was of course an exception.) This probably remained uncorrected because their grand Italian friends preferred, whenever possible, to converse in English, but the irony was that a number of *them* had picked up a slight cockney accent from a nanny or governess brought out from London.

As a child, I used to see Florence only on specific outings, usually accompanying Aunt Janet. We would be driven down by Neno in the landau. I loved sitting up straight and surveying the world in a grand style. But sometimes my attention would be mesmerized by the soft folds of jowl that hung down under Aunt Janet's chin, just like on one of her prized white oxen. It quivered when we went over the cobbles, and I felt an overwhelming urge to poke or flick it.

Perhaps because these visits were relatively restricted, I took in the sights and sounds and smells of the city all the more eagerly as we drove into the centre. Passing a market, one saw the usual colourful displays as well as chestnut sellers and fishmongers selling salted white fish – *baccalà* – from barrels lined with brine; porters brought up more produce in large baskets on their heads; donkeys stood patiently until their tails quivered as they prepared to bray; and children and adults alike clustered round a puppet show.

Every aspect of Florentine life could be seen in the streets: a woman sitting in her doorway doing embroidery or plaiting the fine straw in intricate patterns for Leghorn hats; a laundress hurrying past in semi-official uniform, a sort of red-and-black plaid dress; a poor family moving house with all their possessions piled on a handcart; a waiter hurrying back to a trattoria with raffia-covered bottles of Chianti balanced on a round wicker tray on his head; and conscripts on leave, happy without being intoxicated, which, as one English observer acknowledged ruefully, was 'a combination seldom arrived at by northern soldiery'.

There were also exciting smells caught for an instant as we passed – fresh bread from a *panetteria*, the vinegary tang of a wine shop, roasting coffee from a grocer's, new leather from a saddler's – as well as the frequent whiff of drains. From a row of shops one passed to a stretch of four-storey houses, often dilapidated *palazzi* with pitted stucco and once-proud pediments in grey *pietra serena*. When a postman or baker's boy rang a doorbell at one of these tall buildings subdivided into apartments, shutters would be thrown open above, and a woman would lean out to yell '*Chi è?*' Then, to save a long climb, a basket on a cord would be rapidly let down, the letters or bread placed in it, and it would be hauled up again, hand over hand.

The mixture of vehicles all around was noisy, from trams

and Klaxoning automobiles on the main *viale*, to brightly painted little carts known as *calessini* pulled by Sardinian ponies wearing harnesses with bells. Drivers of the larger fiacres used to crack their whips, not to speed up the horses but to clear pedestrians from their paths, as their conveyances of wood and leather creaked and rattled over the cobbles. I have a more leisurely image of them in summer, as they dozed in their carriages waiting for custom while their horses, wearing straw hats with holes for their ears, snuffled around in the bottom of canvas nosebags. One might catch a good whiff of fresh horse dung from time to time, but the remains never lingered for long. Someone would soon run up with a shovel and sack to collect the precious fertilizer for their allotment. Scratch a *cittadino* and you find a *contadino*.

On a street corner I once spotted some urchins teasing a group of seminarists. I could not help laughing as we trotted past, but Aunt Janet, in spite of her freethinking, did not condone disrespect for the clergy. A more solemn frame of mind was conjured up by the sight of the Misericordia, a becowled lay order devoted to the sick and dying, or a priest ringing a handbell on his way to give communion or the last rites. People crossed themselves hurriedly when such people passed – partly, one suspects, as a personal insurance for the future.

At that time just after the First World War, some funerals in Florence still took place at night. This was said to be for sanitary reasons, but in fact it was a tradition dating from medieval plague years. The Procession of the Dead, with the faces of pallbearers hidden by cowls and the glow of flaming torches lighting the walls of ancient *palazzi*, inspired awe, if not terror. By this time, however, the vast majority of funerals took place in daylight, with one of those glass carriages which always made me think of Rose White and Rose Red. They were drawn by four black horses caparisoned in harnesses of black leather with silver ornamentation. The black ostrich feathers fixed upright on their headbands swayed like the plumes of medieval knights. It was very dramatic – indeed, for those who like the idea of saving up for their own funeral, the horse-drawn glass carriage must surely be the only sort worth having.

The city centre and the embankments – the Lungarni – alongside the jade-green river, I always remember as bathed in the clear, mellow light of late afternoon, even though I saw them at other times of day. The side streets – dark under medieval walls with iron grilles over the windows, heavily rusticated quoins and wide-eaved roofs above – had a very different quality of light. The pavements were so narrow that you were always in danger of toppling sideways, or falling into one of the basement workshops, whose doors – the only source of air – were permanently open.

Florence was defined not just by its centre, but also by its most famous landmark, the cathedral with Brunelleschi's dome. It used to be said of a true Florentine that he came 'from the very *cupolone* itself'. After a visit to the Uffizi, the temptation out in the streets to see modern inhabitants of the city in terms of paintings by Florentine masters is overwhelming. But this is not just a whimsy of foreigners. Only last year I heard an old Florentine friend say of an acquaintance: 'She was not very beautiful, but she looked like a portrait painted by somebody good.'

The English attitude to Florentine art could, on the other hand, be unsophisticated. One strict mother was famous for saying to her daughters whenever they were about to cross the Piazza Signoria with its statues of beautiful male nudes:

'Children, do not look at certain things!' Whatever her ambivalent feelings about sex, Aunt Janet despised such bourgeois prudery. She had, after all, been painted naked by Carlo Orsi – a picture which hung in her bedroom and not alongside the portraits of her by Watts, Lord Leighton, Prinsep and Cabanel in the *salottino*.

Before we drove back up to Poggio in the pony-trap, Aunt Janet would stop at Doney's in the via Tornabuoni to buy me one of their boxes filled with soft hazelnut-flavoured chocolate, which I ate with a spoon as if it were ice-cream. What I regretted most about going back before nightfall was missing the wandering singers, who sauntered in the streets accompanying themselves on guitars decorated with ribbons like battle honours on a French standard – only these ribbons were awarded by female admirers. A popular singer was followed by his loyal fans, ready to applaud each *stornello* or *rispetto*. The local inhabitants, on recognizing a favourite singer, would flock to their windows and balconies, from where they would shout their cries of 'bravo' if the delivery of the song merited it. But woe betide the performer who overestimated his talents. These amateur critics were merciless. A particularly bad rendering had been known to provoke a downpour of slops.

On our return to Poggio, Aunt Janet would make sure I was fed, sending up to the kitchen for my supper. Then, before it was time for Adelina to put me to bed, she would make me read, either from the stories of the Brothers Grimm and Mark Twain or the *Nonsense Songs* from Edward Lear. Needless to say, all these authors had been friends of hers.

CHAPTER SEVEN

Food and Farms at Poggio Gherardo

In spite of her public image, Aunt Janet was not a tyrant, but a benevolent autocrat. Sometimes the triangular relationship between grown-ups, children and servants could be a curious one. Although Italians were in general much more affection-ate towards children than English people, they would still frighten them with stories about the *Befana* – a witchlike counterpart to Father Christmas who punished bad children. One housemaid, however, thought she had discovered an even more effective threat. She claimed that because I had been naughty, Aunt Janet would not leave me anything in her will. But, failing to take into account my innocence, she never imagined that I would rush off to the *padrona* and ask her directly.

'*Zia*?' I said, running into Aunt Janet's study. 'Is it true that you won't leave me anything when you die?'

'Where on earth' – those famous eyebrows lifted – 'did you get that idea?'

'Catarina said that you wouldn't leave me anything because I'd been naughty.' The notion of revenging myself on the unfortunate maid had never occurred to me. I just wanted to know.

Nothing more on the subject was said. She sent me off to play, then summoned Catarina. I have no idea what Aunt Janet said to her, but I am sure that by the time the interview was over she regretted her idea of substituting the *padrona* for the *Befana*.

The *contadini* on Aunt Janet's farms were said to have held her in such awe that none of them dared to cheat on the *mezzadria* share-out. Yet her autocracy was tempered by a matriarchal indulgence. Fellow landowners considered her most eccentric to send for such a grand doctor as Giglioli when any of the *contadini* fell ill.

One story in particular illustrated her unpredictable sway over servants. In the heat of an afternoon, Aunt Janet overheard Beppe the gardener cursing angrily under the camphor tree. Beppe was a large, colourful character with a voice that always carried a little further than he intended.

'*Porca Madonna!*' he swore – pig of a Madonna.

Aunt Janet, although not religious, felt very strongly that people should respect their own faith. She summoned Beppe to the balcony and gave him a very severe lecture. His excuse that everybody used that curse was swiftly dealt with.

'Very well, then,' said Aunt Janet. 'In future you must say "*Porca padrona*" in its place. You can start by saying it now. Come on, let me hear it!'

'But signora,' Beppe quailed under her gaze, 'I could not possibly say such a thing.'

'And yet, Beppe, you can speak like that of the Madonna – you, a practising Catholic. *Never* let me hear you say it again!' And neither Beppe nor anyone else on the farms used the term again, at least not within her hearing.

Aunt Janet's establishment at Poggio Gherardo was very

grand when compared with the simplicity of life at the castle. The outdoor staff included Neno the coachman, who lived down in Ponte a Mensola just outside the property; Baldassare the cellarman; Beppe the gardener, who lived in the house at the north gate where his wife also acted as lodge keeper; Paganelli, an odd job man, who used to bring blocks of ice up in a cart for the cold-store next to the kitchen; and Pietrino the under-gardener, who brought bundles of kindling wood and small split logs for the boilers in each bathroom and the iron stoves in the bedrooms. Another of his tasks was to bring Aunt Janet's cockatoo indoors each evening to his other perch in the bird-room, where there was a huge cage of canaries.

Beppe and Pietrino had much to do in the gardens with all the watering. From the semi-circular south gate, decorated with statues of the Four Seasons, the drive, bordered by flowering fruit trees and little pink monthly roses – *rose d'ogni mese* – curved up the hill for half a mile. Even though Poggio was lucky to have its own well, no water could be wasted; circular mounds had to be dug round each shrub or plant to concentrate the irrigation.

The gardens at Poggio were not Italian, in the sense of parterres, gravelled paths, statues and vistas framed by cypresses, but neither were they that English attempt at a palette of colours in thickly stuffed borders. As well as the large terracotta pots of hydrangeas, plumbago and lemon trees, there were oleanders (called *mazzi di San Giuseppe* because they were generally in flower by St Joseph's day), syringa (*pazienza*), balsam (*bei uomini di Parigi*), tree peonies and banksia roses. The glasshouses, which still held Uncle Henry's collection of rare orchids, also required constant attention. These conservatories had long pools down the middle with water plants and more of Aunt Janet's Burmese goldfish.

The indoor staff were divided between household and kitchen: the respective domains of Davide and Agostino. Davide, a small man with a much taller wife, flattered Aunt Janet with his deference and she in turn spoiled him. Each evening he came to her sitting-room to discuss the next day's programme, and the interview would end with Aunt Janet standing up, as a signal for departure, and Davide bowing to kiss her hand.

Davide was, in his way, devoted to Aunt Janet and so was his wife Ida, who acted as her personal maid, bringing her a camomile infusion each night to bathe her eyes. Yet Aunt Janet showed herself a bad judge of character in entrusting Davide with the role of steward. The responsibility turned his head and eventually led to a rather grandiose fraud. He began bottling the special vermouth that she made to a private Medici recipe, and selling it secretly in Florence to shop-keepers, displaying a label bearing a family crest with three towers – his family name was Torrini – which he designed for himself. This extravagant deception was not discovered for some years.

My favourite was Paolina, who kept Aunt Janet's *guardaroba*. A genius with the needle, she could mend almost any tear invisibly. Tall and devout, and very kind, she took over as nanny from Adelina, whom Aunt Janet dispatched back to Aulla. Paolina was never without her grey shawl around her shoulders. It acted both as overcoat and headcovering for church. She lived with her nephew beyond Settignano and each morning, after rising at five to say her prayers, she would walk to Poggio.

*

Although the most modest of men, the presiding genius at Poggio Gherardo was Agostino. He had been the under-chef at I Tatti with the Berensons, and when Aunt Janet's old chef, Giuseppe Volpi, retired, he had advised her to appoint Agostino as his successor. She trusted Volpi's opinion without reserve. It was he who had provided all the recipes for her outstandingly successful book on Italian vegetable cookery, *Leaves from our Tuscan Kitchen*, first published in 1899 and still in print today in a version revised three quarters of a century later by my nephew Michael Waterfield. And so Agostino moved to Poggio from I Tatti, but such was his development as a master chef that the Berensons, whenever they came to dinner, regretted their loss anew.

Agostino was a man of few words and many smiles. He had the kindest eyes of any man I have ever known, but he was very firm about his work. He insisted on having his own room off the main kitchen, with a marble-topped table, in which he could work undisturbed on his specialities for grand occasions. His most famous consisted of baskets of spun sugar to hold raspberries – *fragoline nelle ceste* – or the ice-creams that he made from every imaginable fruit in season.

His first rule, both for the simple dishes and the more ornate, lay in the selection of raw materials, whether vegetables from the *orto*, olive oil from the farms or produce from the market. Tuscans distrust any food of which they do not know the provenance intimately, oil above all. At Poggio, with its three little farms, most produce – bread, eggs, milk, butter and poultry – came from the property. And Aunt Janet's menagerie added the possibility of rabbit, pheasant and even wild boar.

As at Aulla, the preliminary stage before considering any menu was to inspect the *orto*. Dante, Ramponi's son, who came over later from Aulla to replace old Beppe as gardener, still talks of the fascination of working with Agostino. He would keep Agostino informed of the progress of all vegetables in the *orto*, and Agostino would come out to examine them himself. In the case of lettuces, for example, Agostino would ask for them to be harvested young. Dante would then bring them up to him in the kitchen just before lunch. Agostino would drop them into boiling water for just an instant and then put them with butter on a dish in the oven.

Dante took any excuse to linger in the kitchen to watch the maestro. His wife, Modesta, an impressive cook in her own right, showed admirably little resentment or jealousy whenever he used to say: 'Oh, but how well Agostino does this particular dish.' It was, at least, different to the traditional nostalgia of a husband for his mother's cooking.

Agostino, to satisfy his desire for the best produce possible, began his day at five o'clock in the morning, setting off for the *mercato centrale* in Florence. The day before, he would have been told the guest list for lunch or dinner. Aunt Janet might have mentioned dishes that would please them, but the final decision was left to him when he reached the market. He carried a great cloth which, when the corners were knotted together, he slung over his shoulder as a sack to bring back all his purchases. Once he had selected all the fish and the meat, as well as any exotic vegetables or fruit not available on the property, he would meet up for a coffee and a chat with the other chefs from the great houses. He would then carry his load to the Duomo, whence he used to catch the number 9 tram for Settignano. On the way it stopped almost opposite the main gate to Poggio and he would then trudge up the hill to the house.

*

Agostino's kitchen, with all its subsidiary rooms such as the cold-store and larder, was on the first floor. A service lift to a pantry below formed the key link to the dining-room. The kitchen took up most of the north side of the house, with the square tower above used mainly as a storeroom. Kitchens were traditionally installed upstairs in Florentine villas so that the smell of cooking did not enter the reception rooms and main bedrooms on the ground floor. I often used to climb the stone staircase to Agostino's domain. On one occasion, I heard curious slithering and clattering noises coming down towards me: I looked up and saw an escaped lobster. It made me feel a little like Alice in Wonderland.

The kitchen itself, long and vast, had a large range including a hot-water tank, a fireplace and two little *fornelli*, in a row along the outside wall. The two *fornelli* were square, charcoal-fired barbecues; when the temperature needed to be raised, you made the black charcoal glow red by waving a straw fan. Beyond the cast-iron range, under a large hooded chimney, was an open fire with a spit in front of it. The spit was turned slowly by a system of cogs and gears connected to stone weights cranked up to the ceiling on the far side of the room. This Heath Robinson contraption was, in effect, similar to the mechanism of a grandfather clock. Near the spit there were always goose feathers and a saucer of olive oil to baste the roasting fowl or fish on the grill.

Above, on a high ledge round the walls, were kept the moulds for mousses. The copper saucepans hung together, invariably well polished after use. In the centre of the room was the massive kitchen table, its solid wooden top several inches thick. On a side table were separate sets of pestles and mortars, one for making the *battuto*, that preparation of onion, garlic, celery, carrot and herbs in olive oil so essential to many dishes, and a different one for crushing hazelnuts and other ingredients for *dolci*.

The *dispensa*, or làrder, was a gastronomic Aladdin's cave. Rows of jars contained preserves in every form: dried tomatoes, tomatoes in oil and artichokes in oil (*sott' olio*), pickled vegetables, capers, pine nuts, breadcrumbs, juniper berries for ground game and saffron for risotto. There was also a large terracotta jar full of olives.

It is easy to forget from such an array of ingredients that there were, in fact, few sauces in the cookery of Medicean Tuscany, which was based on the idea that, whenever possible, food should be cooked in its own juices. But peasant cooking, with staple dishes such as polenta and, more recently, pasta, was ripe for the revolution of the tomato, brought north from Sicily by Garibaldi only in the last century. The other basic sauces, *battuto* and *salsa verde*, were developed to improve or disguise poor quality meat.

On the other hand, the idea of an *agro-dolce* – sour-sweet – sauce went back long before Medicean cookery to the ancient Romans. The more modern version of this sauce used chocolate and vinegar for wild boar, venison or hare. Agostino, cooking one of Aunt Janet's domestically raised wild boar, prepared this autumn speciality with chocolate, sultanas, vinegar and pine nuts. Since it was both laborious to prepare and a very rich dish, we did not have it often. Another great delicacy was risotto of woodcock. For a grand occasion, as I mentioned earlier, Agostino would prepare one of the ornamental pheasants, roasted and delicately sliced, then served in its pelt of glorious feathers in Renaissance style. Less spectacular, but more delicious, was pheasant cooked with white truffles and cream.

On a normal day, we were far more likely to have fish,

fowl or meat cooked very simply. I particularly remember Agostino's *involtini di vitello* – little rolls of veal with thin slices of *prosciutto* or *mortadella* inside, speared with toothpicks. (My greatest cooking disaster in later life was to replicate this in England using toothpicks purchased from the chemist. They turned out to have been medicated.) Trout, basted with oil and herbs, were grilled over a very low woodfire, and chicken or rabbit on the mechanical rotisserie. Simplicity of this order was no hardship. Agostino's greatness as a chef lay in dishes that managed to be both simple and exquisite.

His antipasti, mainly vegetables fried in Poggio's purest olive oil, were so delicate and delicious that you wanted to go on eating them throughout the meal. These included the flowers of zucchini fried in a batter so light that you were hardly aware of its existence; slices of fennel in batter served with pesto or lemon; *frittate* of cardoons or artichoke; asparagus served in half a dozen ways, such as *alla Parmigiana*, grilled with cheese; *all'Italiana*, with coddled eggs and cream; and *ai gamberi*, with prawns and a lemon mayonnaise. Sometimes he served *crostini di fegatini* – minced chicken livers with herbs on fried bread, or a *risotto ai carciofi* (with artichokes), or a *risotto toscana* (with mushrooms), or a *soufflé ai piselli* made with the freshest peas from the garden.

Agostino's *dolci* reduced everyone to silent ecstasy. They included *nocciola*, pounded hazelnuts with egg and cream; *biscuit* made with amaretti, eggs and cream; chocolate mousses surrounded by boudoir biscuits dipped in brandy; and curled wafer biscuits filled with cream.

I always wished – after it was too late – that Agostino had prepared a book of pudding recipes to complement the vegetable recipes of his predecessor, Giuseppe Volpi. One recipe of his, which I later used often for parties, was *Mont*

Blanc. Sweet chestnuts were cooked and passed through a hair sieve, then mixed with chocolate and brandy and covered with whipped cream, or whipped white of egg and sugar, which is lighter. But I do not recommend this recipe for a buffet dinner. One short-sighted young man who had taken off his spectacles to impress a girl offered to serve her. He reached across to remove what he thought was a china cover and his hand disappeared into the cream.

The relationship between the house and its three dependent little farms was close, particularly for us children. John and I, roaming the property, were constantly invited into the *podere* kitchens and spoiled. There was one farmhouse on the San Martino a Mensola side, another on the Fiesole side, while the largest was beside the south gate.

Adamo Innocenti, the *contadino* who had the *podere* by the south gate, was quite a large man – what the Italians call *un bel pezzo d'uomo*. His daughter Ada, who was much older than me, was well known for the beauty of her embroidery. Adamo's wife never failed to beckon us into the kitchen, especially when we had already been enticed there by the smell of woodsmoke and baking bread.

Adamo's farmhouse was a solid, well-proportioned building. The living quarters were all on the first floor, over the storerooms and a big arched recess where farm carts were kept. Beyond were the stables, which housed a pair of beautiful white Val di Chiana oxen and the cows. The cows, as compensation for being kept inside in the Tuscan manner, were groomed each day like horses. All these buildings gave on to a large stone-flagged courtyard where we often played. It was Adelina's favourite place to sit and gossip. This courtyard also served as the centre for celebrations, most notably the dinner and dancing after the *vendemmia*, or grape harvest, in September or October. The autumn scene there was as colourful as at Aulla, with tomatoes, peaches and figs set out for drying and maize, golden pumpkins and melons left out to ripen.

Adamo's brother, Cesare, had the *podere* halfway up the hill on the Fiesole side, and amongst his farm buildings was the *frantoio* or olive press for the whole property. The olive harvest was not celebrated in the same way as the *vendemmia*, but its importance in the Tuscan agricultural calendar was, in many ways, even greater. This was partly due to the profound mistrust of 'foreign' or 'fabricated' oil bought in bottles. 'Real' oil was made from olives you had picked by hand and pressed yourself. Some of the horror stories about additives found in olive oil sold over the counter were undoubtedly true: a scandal in the trade erupted every few years. But many of the more exaggerated stories formed part of the harvest fun.

As in most of the olive groves on the Fiesole hillside, each tree at Poggio was pruned to keep it roughly in the shape of an upturned umbrella so that the sun would penetrate evenly. Manure was dug into the ground in a circle round the trunk. (Needless to say, there was a Tuscan proverb on the subject: '*Agli olivi, un pazzo sopra e un savio sotto*' – 'A madman at the top of the olive tree and a wise man at its roots.') The hillside was arranged in gentle terraces, each with a line of olive trees on the outside and a line of vines on the inside. The space in between was ploughed and sowed with grain and even rows of lettuces, while the banks of the terraces provided fodder for the oxen and cattle. With typical Tuscan thrift, no piece of ground was wasted. Haymaking, however, was slightly hampered around Florence because of the old tradition that it should never be carried out before 24 June, the feast day of San Giovanni, the city's patron saint.

The development of flower and fruit was closely watched throughout the spring, summer and autumn months. Then came the difficult decision of when to harvest. The oil content of each olive grew substantially from October to December, but it was risky to leave things too late. A balance had to be struck between picking them from the tree too early and allowing them to drop, because as windfalls they could not be considered for a virgin pressing. At Poggio the harvest usually took place in late November. And in January, any remaining olives were picked for eating.

The 'first quality' oil came entirely from hand-picked olives. Any that fell to the ground were used for 'second quality'. The distinction between the two must not be underestimated. Bencino, one of Adamo's predecessors at Poggio in the 1880s, always used to remind Aunt Janet of the old Tuscan proverb: '*La prima oliva è oro, la seconda argento, la terza non val niente*' – 'The first olive is gold, the second silver and the third is not worth anything.'

The pickers – as a child I was only allowed to collect the fallen fruit – went out with half-moon wicker baskets some nine inches deep strapped round their waists in front. I remember a day of blinding cold sunshine, the sky limpid from the north wind off the Alps, the tramontana, and the knotted, black vine stumps of winter. For some reason, the cypresses higher up the hillside looked darker than ever.

Aunt Janet would accompany us, wearing one of her broad-brimmed straw hats. Characteristically, she joined the children in the hardest task of picking up the fallen olives, even though she was well into her seventies. 'My back's tired,' I once complained after what seemed like hours of bending down.

'Nonsense, child,' she retorted. 'Mine's not, and I'm much older than you.'

The gathered olives – hand-picked and windfalls – were transferred to separate containers on the ox-carts. These carts had such heavy wheels and thick axles that they could bear almost any weight, including large blocks of marble. The beautiful white Val di Chiana oxen with their long curving horns and large, liquid dark eyes had been paired in teams since calfhood. These huge, slow, gentle beasts – Aunt Janet claimed to have seen a pair at Prato more than twenty hands high – were extremely valuable. They were also just about the only animal in Italy treated with real affection. Some people used to say that the *contadini* regarded them as almost human because their pregnancies last nine months. Certainly they used to compare oxen to their own womenfolk. A favourite Tuscan proverb strongly advised against seeking a wife or an ox from afar: '*Donne e buoi de' paesi tuoi*' – 'Women and oxen from your own neighbourhood.' Whatever the truth, one of the most touching sights in the Tuscan landscape was that of a peasant boy less than half their height, guiding his family's pair of oxen home before dusk.

The olives were then taken to the *frantoio* and the oil crusher, a sort of millstone turned by a blindfold donkey, horse or, in some cases, by an ox. Oxen, for some reason, did not get giddy and so did not need their eyes covered. The atmosphere inside the *frantoio* was warm and dank in comparison to the clean chill outside. The olives were tipped in, stones and all, and were soon ground to a green-brown mass. This was scooped up with clean wooden shovels and the pulp put into circular containers made of rope from rushes grown in the marshes near Pisa. When several of these had been filled and piled one upon another under the great press, the first extraction of the best quality oil was ready to begin. A huge screw, with a block of wood to apply the pressure on these *gabbie*, or rope cages, containing the crushed olives, was then turned by a long thick piece of wood that acted as the tourniquet. Several strong men had to exert their full force to extract the oil, which poured down through a hole in the floor into a large marble basin covered by a wooden lid to prevent any dust or dirt entering.

The heavy trickle attracted great excitement and interest. After a sample of fresh oil had been examined with great care and ceremony, we pushed forward with pieces of bread to dip in the deep green liquid. The dipped bread was known as *pan unto*. It had a delicious, slightly piquant flavour as if it contained a dash of mustard. Pressings of the fallen olives produced the second quality. The third quality, if one can use such a contradictory term, was used to make soap, and the final pulp ended up as a sort of dark brown cake, which was used either as fertilizer or fuel.

Once the oil had sat in terracotta *conche* for two to three weeks, it was ready to be taken for long-term storage. The oxen would again be harnessed, and the *conche*, containing the share due to the *padrona*, taken up the hill to the ancient cellars under the villa itself. They were reached through large double doors under the raised *piazzale* outside the main door. In the cool depths both oil and wine were stored, but a certain distance had to be maintained between them. Olive oil in earthenware containers had to be kept away from wine or its flavour could be affected. Once inside, the best quality oil was transferred to the tall terracotta jars, which were then sealed. Agostino had his supplies for the next year, but we had lost our secret hiding places in the Ali Baba jars.

*

The idyll of childhood in Tuscany was soon to be broken. In my 'me too' imitation of older brothers I was an incorrigible tomboy. For example, having watched Austrian prisoners marched past by guards during the war, we played captors and captives with the local children during one holiday in the mountains above Prato. 'At first the boys were rough to Kinta,' my mother wrote to Mary Berenson, 'but she doubled up her fists at them and met them squarely in the road while she poured forth a volley of abuse.' My Italian was fluent as well as voluble. Unfortunately, my mother never realized that, owing to the useless governess she had chosen, I could hardly read or write English. The problem of sending a girl quite so unprepared to an English boarding-school never occurred to her.

Not long after I reached the age of ten, she arranged for me to start at Downe House. Aunt Janet complained in yet another letter to Mary Berenson that Lina had never even checked to see whether I had the right clothes. And she was furious that my mother, embroiled in her work for the *Observer*, would not have time to accompany me back to England at the start of the first term or even to see me off herself.

In spite of my tomboyish behaviour, I arrived at Downe to find that I was known only for my Continental habit of dropping curtseys to grown-ups. News of this curious behaviour had unfortunately preceded me to Downe via some cousins who were already at the school. Priscilla Hayter, who was very tall and thus appeared very senior, thought it would be amusing to pretend that she was head girl and that I had to curtsy whenever I saw her. So great was my ignorance of English school-life that I believed her. For most of the first term, I used to hide in the cloisters whenever she

Kinta aged twelve (*Aubrey Waterfield*)

was around and dodge from one pillar to another to avoid the indignity of a curtsy that would send all the other girls into screams of laughter.

Although I was initially unhappy at Downe – and during some of the short holidays spent in England with fierce aunts who would not have disgraced the pages of Saki – I soon found that my mother could not have picked a better school. The headmistress, Olive Willis, had great sense and kindness and remained a friend until the end of her life. She even became a neighbour in Italy when she bought a small house between Lerici and Tellaro. Her love of Tuscany was a precious link during the term-time. All I could think of and dream about – regrettably, all too often in class – was Poggio and its farms, and the castle and its garden in the sky.

This day-dreaming redoubled with an unbearable intensity at mealtimes. As at most boarding-schools, Downe's standard fare seemed to consist of a collapsed suet pudding. One glance, one sniff at the stodgy nursery food congealing on the plate in front of me was enough. With my mouth in my mind, I would dream of Agostino's delicate *fritti misti* or Adelina's *tortelloni*. I nearly wept with longing.

CHAPTER EIGHT

Growing Up

Since travel to the Continent in those days involved lengthy journeys by Channel steamer and train, I went out to Italy to rejoin my parents only for the summer holidays. Christmas and Easter were spent with one of my aunts in Kent.

I was so impatient that the journey out with my brother John seemed filled with the slowest hours of the whole year. They were vividly memorable – the hiss of steam at Victoria Station when boarding the boat-train with my suitcase covered in fresh labels, the hard benches of the cross-Channel ferry, then, on the other side, the French porters in blue overalls and battered caps with yellow cigarettes of *papier maïs* permanently attached to their lower lips – a remarkable feat when they argued.

Everything smelled different, whether the compartments impregnated with the smoke of black tobacco or the pungent odour of hole-in-the-floor lavatories. (My headmistress, Miss Willis, once surprised me with the observation that the Continental practice of squatting provided a much better angle for expulsion.)

We were definitely abroad, but our excitement really started in the Alps at Modane, a dozen hours later. First, the

French customs made their way down the train crying 'Passeports, s'il vous plaît!' Then, a little later, the Italian customs – the *dogana* – arrived calling 'Passaporti, per favore!' We were back in Italy at last. More cries of 'cestini caldi' from vendors selling little baskets of hot food confirmed that we were indeed over the frontier. Unfortunately, since we had been sent off from England by one of the aunts with an over-generous supply of dull, solid sandwiches and hard-boiled eggs, we had no real excuse to spend our emergency money on a first taste of Italy. I have hated hard-boiled eggs ever since.

From Genoa onwards we stood in the corridor with the window open, catching glimpses of the deep-blue Ligurian Sea as the train thundered in and out of tunnels down that mountainous coast. We reeled off the names of the stations by heart. Finally, after reaching La Spezia, we took another train back up the Magra valley and, ignoring our favourite notice of È PERICOLOSO SPORGERSI, we leaned out of the window to catch our first sight of the castle on its spur.

The last couple of kilometres seemed to take for ever. Then the train slowed down, and as it came to a halt the stationmaster in his smart uniform and red cap cried 'A-ulla! A-ulla!' On the low platform below we saw our parents waiting, and Ramponi, who had come to help with the luggage, raised his hand in welcome.

Johnnie and I would insist on racing up the castle hill on foot, heedless of the hot sun and exertion. Once again there were the ilexes, the smell of baked earth and pine needles, and the monotonous rhythm of the crickets. Catching our breath, we ran over the drawbridge and then up the stone staircase to the roof. The garden in the sky had not changed. Nor had the profile of the Carrara peaks, nor the ridge of the

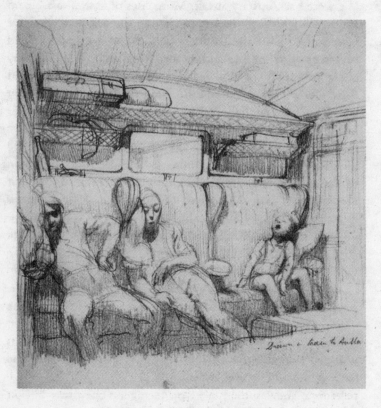

The train to Aulla (*Rex Whistler*)

Apennines. Everything was still as beautiful as ever. School had vanished behind us. Eight weeks of holiday stretched ahead: at that moment it seemed an eternity.

Usually, the family began to pack up the camping gear for Lagastrello soon after our arrival from England. In the summer of 1927, however, when I was fifteen and a half, my father took us to Bocca di Magra because it was not so far from Florence. Aunt Janet was close to death and my mother had stayed at Poggio Gherardo to look after her.

Even on her deathbed Aunt Janet did not change. She pointed to the small nude painting of her by Carlo Orsi and shocked the rather starchy nurse by revealing the identity of the subject. She was in a doubly difficult mood because her favourite doctor, Giglioli, did not come. Giglioli was in England, but nobody dared tell her this, so they said he was with a very ill patient, an old man who needed his constant attention.

'Isn't that patient of his dead *yet*?' she finally demanded in exasperation when the story was repeated once too often.

'Er, no, not yet.'

'Well he ought to be.'

On another occasion she struck the replacement doctor with the ivory handle of her fly whisk when he said something which displeased her. Fortunately, Giglioli returned: he was the only person who could talk to her firmly. 'You will die much sooner if you carry on refusing to eat,' he told her. His remark provoked her into ordering boiled eggs and Champagne. This indigestible combination certainly seemed to revive her, but the recovery was short-lived. A few days later, my mother, taking a break from the sickroom, was out walking in the vineyards when the large bell in Poggio's tower began to toll. She hurried back. Aunt Janet had died quietly in her sleep.

My mother arranged for her to lie in state so that friends, servants and the families of the *contadini* on the property could pay their respects. After they had filed out, everybody commented on how beautiful she looked. There were also many predictable remarks about it being the end of an era. The span of years was indeed impressive. Aunt Janet had arrived in Florence sixty years before, in 1867. The city was then the capital of Italy, with King Victor Emmanuel's court installed at the Palazzo Pitti.

Nobody was more conscious of her passing than my mother, who genuinely regretted the furious rows and deep wounds caused by her engagement. But the two proud Scotswomen, one Victorian and one Edwardian, were never able to admit that they had been wrong over this issue that had lingered on, affecting all our lives.

My mother prepared herself to make a final goodbye to Poggio, which had been her family home since her parents' divorce and the sale of Fyvie. But a final surprise was in store when the will was read. Aunt Janet had completely disinherited Alick Ross, her only son. Alick, whom we had never met, was apparently very gifted but hopeless; an unfortunate remittance man by then well into middle age, who must have been embittered from an early age by his mother's outspoken regret at ever having borne a child.

I will never forget my mother arriving at the little railway station near Bocca di Magra and almost collapsing into my father's arms as she stepped down from the carriage. It was a day of overpowering heat. The strain of looking after Aunt Janet for most of the summer, then the death and, finally, the confused emotions caused by the will, had exhausted her. She blurted out the news: 'The *Zia* has left Poggio to Johnnie, but with a life interest to me.'

John and I were too astonished to speak, but my father digested the implications very quickly. His wife would want to centre our lives on Florence because of her attachment to Poggio and sense of responsibility towards the place. And Florence clearly offered a much better base for her newspaper work. He saw his beloved castle relegated to a holiday home. It cannot have been easy for him to accept the sudden change to his whole way of life. Perhaps he foresaw a change in his wife as well. He must have also wondered whether Aunt Janet would continue to haunt their marriage. If she had a ghost, it would certainly be vigorous.

Davide, Aunt Janet's favoured steward who had pronounced the castle 'not fit for Christians', fought my mother at every step when she tried to reduce the wasteful and corrupt practices that had grown under his regime, especially during Aunt Janet's final years. He held a strong hand, because the Fascist labour laws forbade a foreigner to dismiss an Italian employee without huge compensation.

Just as the situation was becoming intolerable, my mother received a mysterious telephone call from an important wine merchant. He asked her to call on him in Florence. When she was shown into his office, the first thing she caught sight of was a bottle of vermouth on the desk in front of him. The bottle was the same shape as the Poggio Gherardo vermouth's and its contents had the same rich, dark colour of the Medici recipe. But an ornate label declared the contents to be the produce of Davide Torrini: it even bore a fanciful crest of three towers. The crude effrontery of this fraud provided the perfect release. After being confronted with the evidence, Davide and his family disappeared in the night.

My mother, never much of a gardener and certainly no agriculturist, found herself in charge of running the whole property on top of writing her weekly articles for the *Observer*. Her plight provided a mixed blessing. Everyone sympathized with her predicament and wanted to help, but much of the advice conflicted. She soon learned to choose just one person for each particular subject.

For wine she turned to Salvatore, the *contadino* in the middle farm at Poggio, for he had the reputation of a great wine taster. My mother was much amused by his politely condescending attitude towards the wine of the *padrona* while he praised his own, ascribing its quality to clean, well-kept vats. 'The signora's wine,' explained Salvatore, 'has fallen into a hard bed and therefore has not been able to rest well – while mine has found a good bed. It has rested well and been the most successful.'

She also persuaded Salvatore to help supervise the manufacture of the Poggio Gherardo vermouth in the cellars under the old house. And not long afterwards she was able to rely on Ramponi's eldest son, Dante.

Dante had emigrated to Montevideo to find work but, like so many from the Lunigiana, he pined for his country and returned. He was lucky to find a good job working on the power lines from the hydroelectric station in the Apennines, but he soon came under pressure from his boss to join the blackshirts. Having instinctively disliked the Fascists from the beginning, he refused and was fired. As there was no other work in Aulla at that time, my father suggested that he might like to visit Poggio Gherardo for a short stay. He could see if he liked the place and the people, with a view to becoming the gardener there and keeper of the *orto*.

Dante did like it and moved there permanently. When my mother asked whether he could also become responsible for manufacturing the Poggio Gherardo vermouth, he was at first uneasy at such responsibility, not knowing how to write or to calculate. But he went to evening classes and learned very quickly. After completing one batch of vermouth with my mother at his side, he took over the whole process. He had a good nose and palate and greatly enjoyed the work.

The basis of the vermouth was a strong white wine with a fifteen per cent alcoholic content, specially imported from Sicily in wooden casks. Once it had arrived and sat for a time, Dante prepared the blend of thirteen herbs, which were crushed and then marinated in almost pure alcohol and a mixture of three bitters, including the wormwood that gives vermouth its name. Working on two quintals at a time – a ladder was rested against the huge vats – he added first sugar to the Sicilian wine, then the herb mixture and the bitters. Altogether some six or seven quintals a year were made – less than a hundred cases.

Aunt Janet used to ship a few cases back to England to old friends like Hilaire Belloc, who loved it, but she always made a loss. My mother decided that if the vermouth-making was to continue, the produce had to be sold properly through commercial channels. Some was sold locally to Florentine wine merchants and above all to Signor Carlo, the jovial proprietor of Old England, a shop just off the via Tornabuoni, which specialized in everything from Cooper's Oxford marmalade for British expatriates to tartan rugs for Anglophile Italians. Most of the production she shipped back to England in casks and sold through the Army & Navy Stores, which had a well-known wine department.

My mother's most intimidating experience in her new guise of businesswoman and viticulturist followed a slight contamination of a batch of Poggio Gherardo vermouth bottled in England. Since she had made the complaint to the Army & Navy Stores, after hearing from friends who had bought some of these bottles, she had to go to the director's office and, in front of the wine-buyers, identify the right and wrong vermouths in a blind tasting. Three glasses were put in front of her. She picked up the first glass and sipped. 'This is quite horrible,' she said straight out, then regretted her rashness in case she had made a terrible blunder. Fortunately, it turned out to be the produce of one of the largest brands on the market.

She picked up the second glass. This time she was much more cautious. But the *profumo* and taste were unmistakable. 'This is proper Poggio Gherardo vermouth,' she said.

The third glass puzzled her deeply. She took several sips. It was similar to the second, but something was wrong. 'This must be from the batch that people have complained about.' Inquiries then showed that on reaching England the vermouth had been transferred for some reason to casks that had already been used for port.

My mother told me later that the whole experience had been terrifying, but I rather suspect that she had thoroughly enjoyed herself, especially on being proved right. When Fortnum & Mason wrote refusing to stock the vermouth on the grounds that it was too expensive, she was so angry that she wrote the following reply: 'Sir, You say you can buy vermouth at no more than three shillings a bottle. So can my cook. Yours faithfully . . .' This letter had little effect, but several years later Fortnum & Mason finally did decide to stock it because it was such a success at the Army & Navy.

★

Dante was not the only Aullese to move with the family to Poggio Gherardo. First came Vittorio, the small messenger boy who had distinguished himself at the lunch party for the admiral. On his first visit to Florence, Vittorio was so concerned about the drought back in the Lunigiana and its effect on the castle's vines that he could not resist going into watchmakers' shops down in the town to study their barometers. His future wife, Maria Balestracci, also came to Poggio. Agostino, with an amused pretence of Florentine superiority, used to tease these 'foreigners' from the Lunigiana by claiming that Aulla was not even on the map.

Another newcomer was Adelina's niece, Primina, the girl whose twin sister Secondina had died as a child in the great influenza epidemic. Primina was an endearing character, rather rotund in shape, but her mind was seldom on her work. She fell in love with Oreste, the driver of a fiacre. He used to crack his whip whenever he was in the neighbourhood and she would rush to the window and call out to him in a lovelorn wail '*O, Oreste!*'

Aspects of Aulla arrived in other guises. My father, accepting the move with good grace, brought plants from the roof-garden and set up his studio in one of the large rooms on the ground floor. He soon began to decorate the hall by painting large floral still lifes in framed recesses and above in the lunettes formed by the vaulted ceilings.

Once they were installed, my mother, who had loved the informality of Aulla, clearly started to enjoy the formality of the establishment at Poggio. She became very *signorile*, as the Italians say, and when Agostino used to go to her to discuss menus for the next day, she followed the same routine as Aunt Janet. Having warned him several days in advance that Queen Sophie of Greece and her daughter, Princess Irene, were coming to lunch, my mother summoned Agostino to the *salottino* to discuss the menu.

'Since the queen has a delicate digestion,' she began in her dignified Italian, 'I think that we might give her . . .'

'*Ma signora*,' Agostino interrupted her with one of his warm, wry smiles, '*già tutto fatto.*'

'What on earth do you mean?' my mother asked, slightly taken aback.

'It's all arranged. I met her chef in the market this morning. He gave me a list of all her favourite dishes. We discussed which ones she had not had recently, and together we came to the following menu.'

My mother accepted this gentle lesson on the way things were done and agreed to all their suggestions.

Next day, Queen Sophie duly ate her lunch with evident appreciation. Agostino had once again surpassed himself. After the final course was cleared away she turned to my father. 'I have never eaten such pure-tasting food,' she announced. 'And now, Mr Waterfield, will you show me your studio and paintings?'

My father did not like showing his studio to people and he guessed that Queen Sophie simply felt that a visit was expected of her, but the rules of politeness could not be unwound. 'Of course, ma'am,' he said, 'if that is what you wish.'

The dining-room doors were opened, and we all filed out in a procession following Queen Sophie and my father. This tour of inspection filled me with foreboding. In the studio the queen dutifully examined easel and paintbox while the rest of us stood around watching. She then turned to the canvases. The silence was most uncomfortable. No approval, let alone enthusiasm, was expressed at any of the paintings shown to her and my father's unease at such an embarrassing charade became all too clear. But as the party trooped back out of the studio, Princess Irene turned to him with a twinkle in her eye. 'You know, Mr Waterfield,' she said, 'my mother has a truly regal taste in art.'

Our new life at Poggio Gherardo was far from assured because my parents' financial state of affairs became even more precarious. Under Aunt Janet's will, Alick Ross received an inheritance of £30,000 from her marriage settlement, but he had run up huge debts on the prospect of inheriting Poggio. This was what had persuaded Aunt Janet to change her will to save the property from being sold with all its contents. She could not forget how her brother Maurice Duff Gordon, my mother's father, had frittered away his inheritance and lost Fyvie Castle.

Once Alick heard that Poggio was to go to John he launched a ruinous lawsuit to contest the will, which he lost. Following his defeat and subsequent impoverishment after another failed business venture, my mother renewed the allowance that Aunt Janet had given him and later helped the wife he abandoned. He then disappeared from England. After the Second World War we heard that he had last been seen in Budapest in 1941. Nobody knows his exact fate, whether he died in his bed or perished in a German or Russian camp.

Defending the will was an expensive process, but worse was to come. Italian law declared that leaving property to a great-nephew was to leave it outside the immediate family. This meant that the maximum inheritance tax of 40 per cent would have to be paid. And a closer inspection of the farms revealed the degree of reinvestment needed to make them viable. Some of the cows proved to be at least thirty years old.

In 1930 my mother went to Rome to negotiate with the tax department. All she achieved was an extension of the time in which the inheritance duties were to be paid. Returning in the train to Florence, she could think only of the question of raising money to save Poggio. The idea came to her of starting a school for English girls, but instead of a 'finishing school' it should be a 'beginning school' for art studies and appreciation.

My father's initial reaction was one of horror. It was bad enough, he said, to have one overexcited school-leaver in the house – I was by then eighteen and had just left Downe. To have the place filled with chattering young women struck him as intolerable. But my mother reminded him of all he had said about the teaching of art as a subject and how badly the English went about it. Here at last was his opportunity to do something. Cornered by his own past pronouncements, he soon came round to the idea and finally adopted it with enthusiasm.

Plans were made. The upstairs rooms at Poggio on the south side looking out over the gardens and farms towards the Duomo would be redecorated. The idea was to have about ten girls at a time, but at one stage their number rose to seventeen with some of them quartered in the *villino* at the south gate. Professor Scarafia, a friend from the university, taught them Italian language and literature, my mother taught Italian history, my father taught them how to draw and explained the construction of paintings (Bernard Berenson allowed us to use the library at I Tatti and his collection of photographs), and Agostino taught them cooking. I was detailed to take a driving test in preparation for acting as chauffeur for visits round Tuscany and Umbria to churches and galleries.

Learning to drive was a considerable challenge, for the Italian test was by far the stiffest in Europe. It required a long written exam on the internal-combustion engine and all other mechanical functions before you were even allowed into the driver's seat. As women drivers were a very rare breed in Italy, I found myself the only female on the course. I passed first time (to the astonishment of many) and found that the very existence of a young woman at the wheel of a huge open Fiat automobile was enough to startle Florentine pedestrians and other drivers.

Growing up in Italy was not easy in other ways too. Young Italian men in those days pursued foreign girls most vigorously, mainly because these girls were not kept on quite such a tight rein as their own Italian sisters and cousins.

One night at Aulla I was startled by noises below my bedroom window. I went out on to the little Romeo-and-Juliet balcony to find that Giovanni Borghese, whom I had met in Florence shortly before he began military service in the navy, had climbed the creeper on the castle wall to my tower bedroom to beg a goodnight kiss. The romantic aspect of this act may well have been diminished by the bet he had probably made with his fellow lieutenants at the *arsenale* of La Spezia.

Inevitably the most dangerous territory for the innocent girl abroad was where life was at its most informal, and for us that meant the seaside at Forte dei Marmi. My mother had first taken me there in 1915. It lay on the Versilia, the coastal strip north of Viareggio, covered with lovely *pinete*, or pinewoods. Behind this narrow plain, the Carraras rose steeply to the sky. In front, the Tyrrhenian Sea sparkled in the sun. The beach stretched limitlessly in both directions. Forte itself then consisted of little more than a few houses in the shade of the umbrella pines, which sighed in the midday breeze before lunch.

We were staying in a little house in the *pineta* when Italy entered the war on the Allied side. The surge of patriotism led to some ugly scenes of xenophobia. My mother and I heard the approach of a mob searching for enemy aliens – Austrians, Germans and Turks – to lynch. To our great horror they were chanting for the blood of our Turkish neighbour, Nehad Bey, the kindest and most civilized of men. Then we found that John had disappeared. Only later did we discover that upon hearing the first cry of '*Morte al Turco!*' he had slipped off to warn Nehad and his family. They managed to slip down to the shore and take a rowing-boat to safety.

John and I made friends with the children of the other families also drawn to Forte. As we played on the beach, we sometimes saw an Austrian aircraft circling overhead before descending to bomb the Italian fleet at La Spezia. In 1917 our association with the two young sons of a White Russian mother came to an abrupt halt when John abused their country for letting down the Allied side.

Only a few families, such as my mother's close friends the Pallavicini and the Rucellai, had villas at Forte. After the war we rented a little fisherman's cottage, called La Madonnina because of a small pottery medallion of a Madonna and child set in the wall. Life was very simple. We lived off pasta and vegetables, and there was no shower to wash the salt from our skin, only a tin tub which we dragged out into the little garden behind.

During the 1920s, Forte gradually became the resort of smart Florentines. A curious social game developed. As the summer emigration from the city began, they all bade each other a fond farewell during the pre-lunch *passeggiata* on the via Tornabuoni. Then a couple of days later they would all meet again on the beach at Forte with extravagant expressions of surprise.

Life, of course, changed, but luckily not too much. Villas of apricot stucco, terracotta roofs and green shutters went up. Soon the Pandolfini, the Ginori, the Casardi and the Corsini families all built or bought one. Even a hotel – the Grand – was constructed. The Madonnina disappeared to make way for its bar.

I especially remember one summer when my mother had to spend a long time in Rome and I went to stay with the Pallavicini. Their daughter, Yvonne, who first married the pianist Luigino Franchetti and later the publisher Hamish Hamilton, was slightly older than me. They were days of gossiping on the beach interspersed with energetic bouts of surfing and swimming, then a picnic lunch off tables improvised from wooden surfboards. The meal was simple but delicious – *fiaschi* of wine, both red and white; *prosciutto*, *focaccia*, tomatoes and fresh basil, then pears and succulent figs.

Afterwards the children, who were kept in the shade by their nannies, would make volcanoes and marble runs in the sand. And in the afternoon we would take out a *patino* – a sort of catamaran raft that we rowed from a bench – and use it as a diving platform. On one occasion, when we were all swimming naked, having left our costumes on the *patino*, we spotted, just in time, the head of Count Pallavicino, Yvonne's father, swimming out towards us. 'You young ones are all so idle,' he called, 'that I thought I'd come out and row the *patino* back so you'd be forced to swim for a decent distance.' Treading water round the sides of the *patino*, we were able to retrieve our costumes and struggle into them before he reached us.

Sometimes from the beach at dusk we could see the 'green flash'. The sky had to be perfectly clear, and just as the last tiny segment of the sun disappeared below the horizon, the streak of tangential light through the surface of the sea would produce this extraordinary optical effect.

There was something of a 'fast set' amongst the young at Forte, although most of the nocturnal activities were fairly innocent. After a late dinner – sometimes a picnic dinner on the beach – a group of us used to take out *patini*. We pushed them down the sand into the surf and rowed well out from the shore. On a warm, still night, the only sounds were the water gently lapping against twin hulls of the *patini* and the creak of oars.

We would stop and gaze back at the Versilian coastline and the outline of the Carrara mountains above it. The patches of white that gleamed in the moonlight were marble, not snow. Stars bright overhead and phosphorescence flashing in the water all around us made the whole scene magical and mysterious. A few hundred metres out, we all used to strip off and dive naked into the water, where we twisted and played like dolphins.

Afterwards, on the beach, the good-looking young Florentines could be very persistent. There were one or two occasions when refusal had to take a more vigorous form than words. I knew I was too young and inexperienced to consent and so had to clench my teeth against the taunts of English frigidity.

Forte's rather progressive activity in those days was influenced by the immensely tall and charming figure of Aldous Huxley. He and his tiny Belgian wife Maria used to stay at the Ginori's house, La Maietta. In retrospect, it seems as if Aldous was attempting to reinvent love at Forte dei

Marmi. Maria would permit almost anything to him on the theory that a writer continually needed new experiences: an escape from the ordinary to open up his mind to see things afresh. As a result, Aldous lent an intellectual imprimatur to sexual experimentation at Forte. His theory (and practice) that a man's potency was increased by going to bed with more than one woman at a time led to imitation amongst the bronzed youth. Indulgent mamas never imagined why their children slept so late on such beautiful mornings.

Soon afterwards, Aldous, shaking off the dust of Florence – which he described with sweeping artistic licence as 'a third-rate provincial town, colonized by English Sodomites and middle-aged Lesbians' – decamped to Rome.

CHAPTER NINE

Florence in the Thirties

Even if you left aside Florence's past and the architecture of its buildings, the city hardly merited the description of a 'third-rate provincial town'. With a population of nearly half a million, it had five theatres and two music-halls, as well as opera at the Teatro Verdi where the audience always joined in on favourite arias, and two concert-halls – the Sala Bianca at the Palazzo Pitti and the Politeama, where Yehudi Menuhin played as a twelve-year-old prodigy.

Both by day and night, Florence was fun for a young woman, but it too had its share of sexual gauntlets to run. As a fair English girl, the quantity of sometimes inspired but usually inane compliments did not encourage one to linger in the street. On one occasion, when I was hurrying because I had missed the tram and was late for lunch at Poggio, I became increasingly exasperated with a man who drove alongside the kerb, calling to me from his car, '*Vuol favorire, signorina?*' Up went my chin in lofty sang-froid and I ignored him successfully until the next corner, when he brought his car round and stopped, blocking my path. I suddenly saw that it was not a young blade propositioning me but our family lawyer offering me a lift. I apologized profusely,

explaining that I had missed the Settignano tram. He immediately offered to drive me all the way up to Poggio, and we
arrived just as the bell in the tower rang for lunch.

My expeditions down to Florence to chat with girlfriends
and boyfriends in the via Tornabuoni were usually disguised
under some other pretext. The English girls at my parents'
school were not allowed out except on accompanied visits to
churches and galleries; but if there were only one or two of
them around at the end of term, such as Camilla Russell, a
great friend who later married Christopher Sykes, then I
could take them with me.

We usually made our visits respectable by dropping in at
the British Institute, which my mother had set up in 1917.
Very conveniently, it was at the top of the via Tornabuoni,
on the first floor of the Palazzo Antinori. A tea-room in the
courtyard served as an unofficial and inexpensive club, but for
the fashionable late-morning *passeggiata* one had to go down
the street to the cafés, bars, restaurants and *confetterie*. Most of
the establishments there tried to combine all four functions.

At Doney's, famous for its caviare, foie gras and chocolate,
cavalry officers in uniform were able to show off their pale-
blue cloaks for no more than the cost of a Carpano vermouth.
Doney's was always supposed to be the smartest place, and I
sometimes used to meet up there with Emilio Pucci and his
brother Puccio, who was my special friend; but among my
contemporaries it was considered more a place for the rich
and old.

Holding off overenthusiastic old goats was a minor
drawback of Florentine life. One of the most notorious was
Violet Trefusis's father, Colonel George Keppel, a cousin of
Aunt Janet and my mother. He would appear in Doney's
wearing his panama hat and try to persuade the girls to go

for a ride in his red Lancia sports car, followed by a swim in the pool at the Ombrellino, the Keppels' villa at Bellosguardo. Once we agreed as a joke. He took photographs of us there in our Jantzen swimming-costumes, which were Joan-Hunter-Dunnishly decent. We all knew that he was longing to take more 'artistic' poses. He even kept a studio-cum-*célibataire* in the city for such purposes, but this extravagance was rather under-used. Perhaps we should have felt sorry for him. Everybody adored his wife, Alice Keppel, King Edward VII's favourite, and he must have felt left out.

Florence's version of the Bright Young Things would drift into Doney's at around midday – when the older generation tended to be leaving – for aperitifs, often a Negroni or a tomato juice. Young lions would saunter through to see who was present, eyeing the girls with a charming insolence, then go on to congregate outside Casoni, on the other side of the street. There they would discuss the party of the night before, or the one planned for that evening.

The favourite lunchtime meeting-place for the young, especially when hungry, was Procacci's, which had the most delicious *panini* imaginable. The best were filled with fresh anchovies, which had a taste totally different to the salty, metallic bite of the English tinned variety. If we were hungry in the afternoon and needed sustenance before or after a long tour of the Uffizi, we would go to the Casa dei Bombolini in the via del Corso for a doughnut. There they had an ingenious system. In the kitchen upstairs, each *bombolino* would be taken boiling hot from the pan and dropped down a herring-bone chute with slides back and forth all the way down. This removed any excess oil during the descent, which ended with the doughnuts dropping into a tray of sugar on the ground floor. They were the best I have ever tasted.

As well as providing the parish pump for Florentine gossip, the via Tornabuoni also had some of the smartest shops in Italy for those who could afford them. The newly engaged, or even those who merely contemplated the prospect, would gaze in at the windows of Parenti, which specialized in silver, jewellery and glass. Optimists had their wedding list there. Ferragamo, recently returned from America, had set up shop and become the darling of Florentine women. He did not just draw outlines and make wooden lasts, he felt the feet of each client carefully. A pair of shoes then cost 200 lire, with a reduction to 180 for new clients. Gucci in those days was still a small family firm of saddlers and luggage-makers, with their premises in a side-street, the via della Vigna.

When it came to fashion, Florentines bowed to nobody – especially not to the government in Rome. The National Fascist Federation of the Clothing Industry decreed that, for 1930, fashion must return 'from the present straight and angular lines to womanly curves'. Strenuous efforts, declared the directive, had to be made to free Italian women from their slavery to foreign styles. Inspiration was to be sought from the style of the fifteenth century. But to judge from the slim, exquisitely cut dresses shown off on the late-morning *passeggiata*, young Florentine women clearly thought that the *quattrocento* was all very well in their buildings and paintings, but not on their bodies.

As in the 1890s, when the scruffiness of English visitors had attracted strong criticism – a state of affairs that has seldom improved over the years – the area around the via Tornabuoni still provided a shopping centre for fashionable British tourists and Anglo-Florentines. For a meeting-place, the British used Giacosa's café near the Palazzo Strozzi. Vieusseux's Circulating Library provided reading matter, with everything from

Jane Austen to Ruskin and Dorothy Sayers. Roberts's British Pharmacy, still known today as the Profumeria Inglese, sold boxes of quinine pills and Dr Collis Browne's Chlorodyne for upset stomachs. And for those who disliked apricot jam for breakfast, there was of course Signor Carlo's stock of Oxford marmalade.

Florentines, as befitted such a cosmopolitan society, took their social life even more seriously than the Anglo-Florentines. Dancing lessons in the foxtrot and the tango were given once a fortnight by Maestro Riolla in the via della Vigna. In those days, white tie was still *de rigueur* for balls, as it was in England, and black tie for dinner. Dinner parties would be given before a dance, often at the Circolo Unione or, most dreaded of all, at the Florence Club, a gloomy, brown-leather imitation of St James's.

One mother would act as chaperone for a clutch of girls, but with a little determination they could easily escape. A 'misunderstanding' over who was going in which car quickly separated them from their chaperone. Soon mothers gave up and delegated escort duty to an older brother. One way or another, the great objective of slipping off to a nightclub by the end of the evening was usually achieved, and boasted about the next lunchtime at Doney's or Procacci's.

During the dances themselves, young couples would go out to see the moon; then, strolling along the *palazzo*'s gravelled paths, they would slip behind a statue for a passionate embrace. The warm night air, heavy with the scent of gardenia and box, was doubly intoxicating. Inevitably, some girls dared to break the rules and taboos in private, but the conventions were never openly challenged.

As I grew older, I naturally began to see my parents' friends on a more equal footing than I had at the Fiesole nursery parties and picnics of childhood. Nobody could accuse my mother of failing to mix. In Florence she had more Italian friends than English. At times the multi-lingual conversation at table could become baffling. My mother, when she complained during one dinner that she could not follow a crossfire of conversation, received the retort from Filippo de Filippi: 'But Lina, you've got two ears!'

Nevertheless, it was true to say that her best friends were English. Among the closest were Percy Lubbock and his wife Sybil, now on her third marriage. They asked my parents to find them a piece of land on the coast south of Aulla on which to build a 'cottage'. My father found them a promontory between Lerici and Tellaro, with its own little rocky bay and grotto. It was a stretch of coast he knew well from when the Lawrences had lived there just before the First World War.

The land was marvellously secluded. All one saw from the little road, which twisted along the precipitous hillside above, was an olive grove. The trees were not pruned in the Florentine upturned-umbrella way, but allowed to become magnificent trees. Beyond, perched on a cliff amid tall umbrella pines, Percy and Sybil decided to build their 'cottage'. When finished, this turned out to be a large villa, named Gli Scafari. It had a loggia looking down on the sea, floors of Carrara marble and walls clad in Sybil's favourite Lucca silk – altogether a palatial summer retreat overlooking the dazzling Chinese blue of the Bay of Lerici.

Sybil's hypochondria was not eased by the beauty of the place or the gentle, rhythmic echo of the waves in the grotto below. The occasional boom from warships firing at sea prostrated her. Once, when she had a headache, she forced

Percy to ring the admiral of the naval base at La Spezia. Percy had to tell him that the warships must cease their gunnery practice immediately. I cannot help wondering whether an account of this telephone call, proof either of British decadence or of an insulting disregard for Italian naval prowess, was passed on to Mussolini.

Yet Sybil's recoveries were as abrupt as her collapses. One day she would feel close to death and the next morning she would be out in her canoe, which she paddled standing upright.

The other great friends of my parents, Bernard and Mary Berenson, were not merely the best of neighbours, but guardian angels to our whole family. B.B., who had lived at Poggio Gherardo with Aunt Janet while I Tatti was rebuilt with a loan from her, repaid his debt of gratitude many times over.

During the difficult years of paying off the inheritance tax on Poggio Gherardo, the Berensons always helped in any way they could, often with presents. I adored Mary for her Quaker 'thees' and 'thous' in speech, and her face, which was very animated in a quiet way. Her generosity was compulsive. She even wrote to her sister, Alys Russell (Bertrand Russell's wife), saying that B.B. should not set aside his money to endow I Tatti, but spend it on helping my mother keep Poggio. And it was typical that she should have sent me to the best dressmaker on the via Tornabuoni, accompanied by Nicky Mariano, B.B.'s devoted organizer, to buy my first ball dress. I will never forget it. It was beautifully cut, in white satin with diamanté straps.

To say that we lived in each other's houses would have been an exaggeration, but the *va et vient* was frequent. B.B.'s bright young men often came along the hillside to Poggio for a breather from the rarefied air. The American, Johnnie Walker, was one of the most charming – and the most forgiving. I crashed his 'Tin Lizzie' Ford in the stable yard, because the accelerator device, which was on the steering column (he had suffered from polio as a child), caught when I was turning the wheel.

Kenneth Clark had been the first of B.B.'s bright young men, following his introduction to Florence, when he stayed at Poggio with Aunt Janet. But as a great friend of my brother Gordon at Oxford, K became involved in family affairs from an unexpected direction. Gordon had fallen very much in love with a fellow undergraduate called Jane Martin and they had become engaged. But my mother opposed the match strongly, mainly on the grounds that they were both too young and could not afford it. (She refused to acknowledge later that she had reacted just as Aunt Janet had towards her own engagement.)

Everything was, however, solved when Gordon went off to Egypt. He arranged a job for Jane at Downe – she was the most inspiring teacher I ever knew – and asked K to look after her in his absence. K used to come over to take Jane brass-rubbing in local churches, and I was taken along in the inappropriate role of chaperone. I did not realize that K and Jane were falling in love. Eventually K had to write to Gordon in Alexandria to explain. Yet instead of sighs of relief at Poggio, everybody seemed to feel most upset, and not just out of loyalty to Gordon. Aunt Janet refused to speak to Jane when K, who was very much a favourite of hers, returned to Florence, and the Berensons felt they had in some way been let down because they had been expecting a bachelor assistant.

I Tatti could hardly be described as a house in the usual

sense of the word. The Buddha at the end of the library corridor, perfectly positioned, suggested a mixture of artistic shrine, centre of higher learning and even something of a stage set. The impression of theatricality came mainly with B.B.'s carefully timed entrances when joining a collection of attendant guests. They were not ostentatious in any way and yet when Celestino the butler opened the door, the moment possessed a certain electrical impact. Paradoxically – or logically – B.B.'s small stature and the apparent frailty of his physique increased the effect. This was certainly not diminished by the cashmere shawl that was draped around his shoulders when he was seated outside in the *limonaia* after lunch or inside in the library late in the evening. His perfectly cut grey suits confirmed the studied elegance and, as a final touch, he often wore a gardenia in his buttonhole. The gardenia was almost the symbol of I Tatti: house guests found their breakfast tray decorated with a single flower.

Guests new to I Tatti were clearly in awe of their host. They were perhaps afraid of B.B.'s conversational reputation, yet he encouraged the gauche and put down only the pretentious. He was, however, far from perfect in other ways. High amongst his worldly pleasures was to hold the hand of a beautiful woman, preferably a silent and unopinionated one, and enjoy her expression of rapt attention as he talked. When it came to the *place-à-table*, social precedence generally gave way to the judgement of Paris. On one occasion, the rather luscious mistress of an American magnate received the accolade of being placed on B.B.'s right. Her ring finger was adorned with a solitaire diamond of conspicuous caratage. B.B. slipped his hand over hers and gave it a little squeeze. 'Tell me, my dear,' he said with his most understanding smile. 'And what did you have to do to get that?'

Berenson has often been accused of arrogance and yet in later years when I had just arrived out from England he demonstrated the opposite. Seated next to him at a lunch party, I told him that I brought greetings from a great friend in Kent, Mary van der Woude. She was the daughter of Barrett Wendell, B.B.'s professor and protector at Harvard. As soon as he heard this, B.B. lifted a hand and instantly stopped all the conversations round the table. 'Do you realize,' he announced to the company, 'I have just received a message after more than fifty years from a member of the Wendell family. I will never forget that it was in their house in Boston that I first learned which knife and fork to use.' There was no false humility in this pronouncement and the silence that followed was not one of unease. Everyone present just sat in wonder.

The stage-management of all social occasions at I Tatti was impeccable, largely due to the faultless instinct of Nicky Mariano who, when Mary retired from social life, took her seat at the other end of the table. Everything had its place and moment. After dinner the arrival of a tray of camomile tea was a signal not to be ignored. You drank your cup and left.

B.B. had been married from Poggio Gherardo in 1900 when he was living there with Aunt Janet until I Tatti was complete. So a third of a century later, when I was to be married to Jack Beevor, B.B. insisted on returning the favour by having the bridegroom and best man to stay at I Tatti and by giving the eve-of-wedding dinner.

Jack was a brilliant classicist. He had been a favourite of Professor Spooner at New College and had delighted him with a double first in Mods and Greats. Although at one stage he had dreamed of becoming an archaeologist, he

Bernard Berenson at the time of his marriage
(*James Kerr-Lawson*)

finally chose a less precarious career in the law. At the time of our wedding he was the youngest partner in the City firm of Slaughter & May. In a very indirect way, his choice of firm was to lead him back to Florence later under curious circumstances. In the early part of the war, Special Operations Executive recruited many of its officers from Hambros Bank and Slaughter & May. Jack became a colonel and the senior SOE officer on Field Marshal Alexander's staff in Italy. In August 1944 he managed to get to Florence with the leading troops. He was able to send back news of Poggio and I Tatti to the family in England and offer help to B.B. when he emerged from hiding.

The eve-of-wedding dinner at I Tatti was wonderful. Nicky had gone to every trouble to make it a success, but the conducted tour of B.B.'s art collection afterwards was marred by my father's older brother, Frank Waterfield; a tiresome snob of unshakeable views. He interrupted B.B. as he told the story of the Buddha in the library corridor, and then proceeded to recount – in the most long-winded fashion – how he had been reading a marvellous book about India. 'And what was the title of this remarkable book?' asked B.B. with admirable patience. Uncle Frank thought for a long time.

'You know, for the life of me, I can't think. But it was a very good book. I do remember that.'

The next morning, family and friends came with us to the Palazzo Vecchio for the civil marriage. Everyone was shepherded by Jack's best man, the art historian Ellis Waterhouse, who was then at the British School in Rome. The civil ceremony was conducted by the young mayor of Florence, Pifi Gomez. It felt rather strange to be married by somebody I knew from parties. Pifi, the son of an old friend of Aunt Janet, had married Joan Haslip's sister, Lalli.

The day after the civil ceremony, the religious ceremony took place at the Holy Trinity in via Lamarmora; one of the two English churches in Florence. On the way back, passers-by wished us '*tanti auguri*'.

Sadly, many Italian friends felt unable to attend because the Catholic Church still held rigidly to the view that it was a mortal sin to go to a Protestant service, but afterwards everyone returned to Poggio Gherardo, where the hall had been decorated in beribboned swags of bay leaves with several sprays of mistletoe, for it was three days after Christmas. The wedding breakfast, with twenty of us at a long table, was held at my special request in the 'Poodle Room', surrounded by the frescoes. Agostino had prepared all my favourite dishes, finishing with his famous spun-sugar baskets of ice-cream.

That afternoon Jack and I drove by way of Lucca, where we stopped to see the cathedral, to spend our wedding night at Aulla. When we reached the castle, Ramponi rushed out of his house opposite the drawbridge to say that a young signore had turned up, and was very worried that we had not yet arrived. Ramponi led us to the edge of the rock-face by his *orto* and pointed down to the piazza where a solitary and, at that distance, unrecognizable figure could be seen. He must have seen us, for he jumped up and waved and set off towards the road up the hill.

Mystified at this curious turn of events, we waited for him to arrive. With very mixed feelings, I found it was Alessio Olsouffieff; another young naval lieutenant doing his military service at La Spezia. As his duties had prevented him from attending the reception in Florence the night before and he had come all this way to wish us well, we invited him to stay for a drink. Then, since he showed no sign of moving, we felt obliged to invite him to join us for dinner. After dinner he insisted on playing the piano in the *salone* to serenade us. Finally, exhausted by the last two days of wedding celebrations, we had to eject him.

The next day we set off for a skiing honeymoon at Sestriere before returning to live in London. I could not help feeling uneasy for my parents, whom I was leaving behind in Italy. My mother had received several warnings from the Fascist government about her highly critical articles in the *Observer*. Even the British ambassador had advised her of the dangers. She risked expulsion and the confiscation of all their property in Italy, both the castle and Poggio.

In the course of the next three years Italy was to invade Abyssinia, provoking British-led sanctions, and Mussolini's blackshirt division were to leave to fight for General Franco in the Spanish Civil War. The peace of Europe had started to look precarious indeed.

CHAPTER TEN

War Clouds and Wine-making

After my return to England in 1934, I made an effort not to lose touch with what was happening in Italy. A hankering for all the ingredients of Tuscan life took me frequently to Soho. Many of the shopkeepers there came from the valleys of the Lunigiana. As they shovelled dried beans or thick grains of yellow rice from sacks ranged inside their doors, I heard some of the local gossip.

I also received long letters from my parents. Sadly, politics dominated all the news, and my mother needed to be very careful. Even private letters had to be entrusted to friends, not the post, for she was still watched the whole time. An incident which took place before my marriage will illustrate how closely. I had had to go to Milan to collect one of the girls coming to the school at Poggio. Her train was late – despite Mussolini's widely acclaimed miracle – so I rang a Florentine boyfriend who was then working in the city, and we met for an early dinner to while away the time until she arrived. The next day I said nothing of my innocent little tryst. But then members of the secret police turned up at Poggio and interrogated my mother, demanding to know the purpose of my rendezvous with this man. It would have been funnier if the implications for the future had not been quite so sinister.

In the early 1920s, before the Fascists had absolute power, politics away from the big cities had mainly consisted of wearing the colours of your party, shouting insults at your opponents and, occasionally, coming to blows. Now, traditional enmities between streets and villages had, in many cases, taken on a new form. Socialist red or Fascist black appeared more like the flag of a rival *contrada*, or district, than of an ideology. Unwilling spectators feared a more ferocious, modern version of the struggle between Guelph and Ghibelline. Some saw in this behaviour the eternal need of Italians to play at the clan vendettas of Montagues and Capulets. But well before the end of the decade Fascism had been established as the state ideology and people had to be very wary of police agents.

In the Lunigiana the Fascist leaders came not from mountain villages, but from the large coastal towns where the marble industry had long been troubled by labour disputes. For a mass movement, they did not have that many followers to lead. In the province of Massa Carrara (the Lunigiana's official denomination) there were only 5,000 *avanguardisti* and 7,000 members of the *balilla* youth movement out of a population of over 140,000. And a large proportion of these members were distinctly half-hearted. Many had been shamelessly dragooned into volunteering.

My parents were horrified to see a lawyer friend in Carrara, who had always detested the regime, wearing a Fascist badge in his lapel. 'You too?' exclaimed my father.

'What else can I do?' he said. 'They put a blackshirt at the foot of my stairs to waylay my clients and tell them their cases would not get through the courts if they employed me.'

He shrugged helplessly. 'I have an old mother, a wife and children to support.'

Perhaps a more poignant story concerned a friend in Rome who refused to wear the insignia whatever the consequences. One day his son came home and announced that he had decided to become a *balilla*. The father did not explode. He knew there must be a good reason, for his son was intelligent and sensible. '*Ma perché, figlio mio?*' he asked gently.

'*Sai, Papa.*' The boy made a face – a mixture of disgust and resignation. 'I'm the only one who hasn't joined, and I'm sick of being put at the bottom of the class each time, however well I do. To come top, one must be a *balilla*.'

Italian Fascism had a ludicrous superficiality. For me, the best example was Signor Carlo feeling obliged to change the name of his Old England shop in the via Tornabuoni to Giovane Italia. He still went on selling tartan rugs and Oxford marmalade.

The Tuscan sense of humour did not miss a trick. In 1938, shortly before Hitler arrived to meet Mussolini in Florence, a man walking along a street near the city centre saw some workmen digging a large hole in the road.

'What are you doing?' he called.

'We're trying to find the Rome–Berlin Axis!' came the reply.

'*Ah, buona fortuna!*' he answered with a laugh.

Late that afternoon, on his return home, he greeted them again: 'What, still digging? Haven't you heard?'

'Heard what?'

'They've found the Axis.'

'No! Where?'

'In the via dei Malcontenti.'

*

Except for a hard core of militant blackshirts and bureaucrats who owed everything to the Duce's regime, the vast majority of people soon despised the petty and grand corruption. They were sure that Mussolini would end up like the bullfrog in Aesop's fable. My mother warned Garvin, the editor of the *Observer*, that he was wrong to admire Mussolini and that the future was dark if only because the bombastic dictator did not feel secure in the saddle of his national charger.

The mass of the population, especially the *contadini*, were anti-militarist for good reason. Even those who could not read a newspaper still had the native sense to know instinctively that Fascism would lead to disaster, and that they and their sons would be ordered to throw away their lives for nothing. In the meantime, they had little option but to keep their heads down and stay silent. This attitude was summed up by the saying: '*Chi piscia contro il vento, si bagna i pantaloni*' – 'If you piss against the wind, you get your trousers wet.'

There was a story told about Mussolini when he was on a journey across Italy. His car broke down in a small town and, while waiting for it to be mended, he decided to imitate Napoleon's penchant for wandering in disguise among his soldiers and listening to their camp-fire conversation. So, with his collar up and a soft hat pulled well down, the Duce went into the local cinema. The newsreel showed one of his speeches from the Palazzo Venezia, and members of the audience rose to cheer, mainly in case an informer was present. Mussolini did not move, but an old peasant in the next seat gave him a dig in the ribs as he hauled himself to his feet. 'I think like you,' the peasant muttered, 'but it is better to clap.'

I heard from my mother that Vittorio was soon to be called

up for military service. He was to be drafted into the Alpini. It came at a bad moment for him. To everyone's joy, he had recently become engaged to Maria, his fellow Aullese. My mother suggested to Maria that instead of waiting for Vittorio in Italy she might like to come to England and work for Jack and me. The idea of seeing a little more of the world appealed to her, and she agreed.

Maria was dark, with deep-set eyes that were either laughing or preoccupied. Like Vittorio, she was not strongly built, but she never stopped working. She was that rare combination – a perfectionist with a sense of humour. The size of London and all its activity fascinated her, but at odd moments she longed for the Lunigiana and its smells and sounds. One day, she heard a bell ringing in the street. '*Ci sono le mucche!*' she said on rushing into my room with great excitement. She was the first to laugh when I explained that she had heard not cowbells, but the muffin-man.

Maria was the best possible reminder of Tuscan country life I could have had. We always seemed to be talking about food and how so-and-so used to cook a particular dish – and we had great fun assembling her trousseau. Yet whenever I could I went back to Italy, either with Jack in the summer or on my own to help my mother with the school. She had broken her hip badly after slipping on a stone floor and was now very lame.

It was also sad to see some of the servants, whom I had known since childhood, suffering from age. Pietrino, the under-gardener from Aunt Janet's day, had been given up for dead when I arrived once, but then he recovered temporarily. I went in to see him. He squeezed my hand. '*Eh, signora*,' he said, 'I arrived at St Peter's Gate but he didn't want me, so here I am back again for a little longer.'

Agostino had grown much older in a short time. My mother and all his family tried to persuade him to allow somebody else to go down to the market each morning, but he insisted on carrying on as before. The idea of even partial retirement held no appeal for him. Above all, he would not allow anyone else to select the food that he was going to cook. But he did accept my mother's idea of bringing in Carlo Guerrini as under-chef. Finally, in the winter of 1936, he caught bronchitis and young Carlo had to take over.

Agostino could not have been happier, however, when another marriage within the extended family of Poggio came about. Carlo Guerrini, his very promising replacement, married Agostino's daughter, and my childhood playmate, Adelcisa, in July 1937. But sadly, Agostino had little time left to live. He died six months later. It was over thirty years since he had come up the hill from I Tatti.

After the first priority of seeing friends on my return to Florence, I did not feel I was properly back until I had also paid a visit to the past. I would go down to the Duomo and stand in silence before Uccello's fresco of Sir John Hawkwood on his shire-horse. Aunt Janet's proprietorial tone as she recounted the story of the great *condottiere* and the capture of Poggio Gherardo would always come back to me and I would find myself smiling.

On one occasion, I managed to make my trip coincide with the grape harvest in late September or early October. From pagan times, the *vendemmia* has always been the favourite *festa* of the year. It is a truer festival than any of those in the religious or national calendars, for it celebrates not some distant event, but the fruition of hard work.

Vines required attention most of the year round. In March

or April, depending on the advance of spring, the rows between the vines had to be hoed. Pruning, which was the next stage, took place early in May, as soon as the danger of severe frosts had passed. The work required skill and experience. The pruner had to know which shoots to leave and which to cut. He then fastened the chosen shoots to a bamboo, or attached them to a horizontal wire running the length of the rows, with raffia or with switches cut from a pollarded willow. Afterwards the fallen clippings were picked up by peasant women, to be dried and stored for next winter's kindling.

The vines were then sprayed with copper sulphate late in May, once the leaves had sprouted. The men walked up and down with heavy brass tanks on their backs, the leather straps cutting into their shoulders. They held the spray nozzles with one hand and with the other pumped a lever at their sides. The spray left the leaves with a blue-grey wash – a colour that makes me think of France rather than Italy.

Once the fruit began to ripen, everyone discussed the right balance of sun and rain, and closely examined the dusty grey must nestling in the bunches of black grapes. But the greatest fear – so great that few dared even speak of it – was of hail. A single storm of great ferocity could, in less than a dozen minutes, decimate a year's crop.

The vines at Poggio were laid out in a different way to those at Aulla, where they grew overhead on pergolas constructed along the contours of a terraced hillside. Poggio Gherardo's vineyards had most of the vines wired out between pear trees in the ancient manner. Here we grew four varieties: the purple-black *Buon Amico*; the *Trebbiano*, which was bright yellow on the inside and went brown on the side facing the sun; the yellow-green *Uva Grassa*; and lastly, the *Occhio di*

Pernice, or partridge-eye grape, which was a pale pink with ruby veins.

The ideal moment for picking came during a long period of sun which followed rain. Too much rain would make the grapes rot on the stalk. The old men used to argue that one should also wait for the moon to be on the wane. As the day of the *vendemmia* approached, the preparations grew more intense. A sound of hammering indicated the repair and renovation of casks – the fifty-litre *barile* – and the huge vats. A woman's voice singing was probably that of a *contadina*, with a broom made of millet stalks, sweeping out the *tinaia* where the vats, or *tini*, were kept.

Early on the chosen morning – rumours of postponement often ran round the night before – we would assemble at the *tinaia* to collect boxes and secateurs. The workforce was considerable since everyone lent a hand. As well as all our family and the indoor staff, the brothers and sisters and cousins of the families on the property had also come to help, some from quite a distance. After receiving our instructions, we set off in chattering groups to work on the rows to which we had been assigned.

It was advisable to wear some sort of head protection – not because of the sun, for the October day was usually a perfect temperature – but to keep earwigs out of your hair. The beefy-armed peasant women always wore their large kerchiefs tied like nurses' caps, and I followed this sensible example. The brim of a hat got in the way when you were constantly looking up into the yellow leaves at close range, searching for the stalk to cut.

As you took hold of each bunch of black, seemingly over-ripe grapes with grey powder spreading from the stalks, it was wise to give them a slight shake to dislodge any wasps that might be feeding. Wasps were the curse of the *vendemmia*, and it was rare to get through the day without being stung. The only other discomforts were sweat stinging the eyes, hands so sticky that you were almost prepared to waste your drinking-water on them, and the weight of the basket on your shoulder as you bore it off when full – a journey during which more sticky juice would trickle down your neck and inside your shirt.

Cries and cheers in the distance announced the arrival of lunch and we all put down our boxes and secateurs and went over to the shade of an olive tree. *Fiaschi* of wine were passed round. Since there were generally not enough glasses, the previous drinker would empty the dregs with a flick of the wrist, and pass the glass to the next person. Most of the pickers had brought a bottle of wine out with them as well as a bottle of water. While working, it was surprising how much wine you could drink without feeling any effect from the alcohol. It seemed to evaporate effortlessly from your body along with the sweat.

A large round basket contained all the staple elements of Tuscan open-air eating – bread, tomatoes, a bottle of oil, a paper twist full of salt, a salami and perhaps a mortadella. But from a steaming container came the main component of the meal – beans in a tomato sauce with *pinoli*. It was a tradition of the *vendemmia* at Poggio. Afterwards we bit into heavy, ripe figs and succulent pears, and more juice dribbled down our chins. It was one of those days when, however messy you were, you never felt dirty.

With the conversation and banter came horror stories about trafficked wine – *vino sofisticato* – and accounts of the often hair-raising variety of additives sometimes used. They ranged from seaweed to ox blood. I could not help thinking

Poggio Gherardo's south gate with busts of the Four Seasons

that these stories seemed to provide another reason for referring to black wine, as the *contadini* tended to call it, rather than red.

We worked on into the afternoon, filling our baskets, then emptying them into chestnut-wood tubs called *bigonce*, placed at convenient intervals along the rows. They, in turn, were loaded on to a long farm-cart with hefty axles.

This farm-cart was drawn by Poggio's pair of stately white oxen. Their only sudden movement would be the flick of an ear to disperse flies. The Val di Chiana oxen had the dispassionate tranquillity of sacred cows in India, rather than the lazy disinterest of the European variety. But where the bovine races divided in the past is uncertain. Pio Corsini, an agriculturist with a fund of astonishing knowledge – a Communist *contadina* paid him the ultimate compliment when, after a mutually enjoyable argument, she said, 'He may be a prince, but he's a true peasant' – demonstrated by research into old paintings that the red cow of Roman times became extinct in Italy during the seventeenth century. The Roman white cow was presumably the ancestor of the two breeds of Tuscan oxen.

When the *bigonce* were all loaded, the ox-driver made his gentle beasts advance, first taking the strain, then hauling the cart up to the *tinaia*. The cavernous room was cool and dark after the sunshine outside. Its only light came from a single bulb hanging on a very dusty flex, which had been tacked along a beam. The place smelt of must and damp stone.

A ladder was set up against one of the huge vats at a shallow angle. The young *contadini*, as graceful as ballet dancers, ran up it holding tubs of grapes on their shoulders. In almost one movement, the grapes were tipped in, then the young men turned and ran down again, without ever losing their balance.

Once the vats were nearly full, the men took off their boots, rolled up their trousers and, having washed their feet in buckets of water, climbed in to tread the 'boiling' must. While they trod the grapes they sang *stornelli*, usually holding on to each other for support on this shifting Sargasso Sea from which vinous fumes had already begun to rise. There were yells of laughter whenever one of their number toppled over. Height certainly helped for, if the worst came to the worst and you were tall, you could always grab at the rim of the great vat and haul yourself up. My brothers – Gordon at six foot three, and John at six foot four – were always in demand as treaders whenever they were at Poggio during the *vendemmia*.

Although the dangers of intoxication, even of asphyxiation, from the fumes were always emphasized, the families of *contadini* used to consider the heady *profuma* of the fermentation so beneficial that they brought sick children along to the *tinaia* as if it were some sort of sulphur bath. If nothing else, they certainly should have slept well afterwards.

In true Tuscan style, little was wasted. When the wine was transferred to the *barile*, the remaining pulp of stalks, skins and pips – the *vinaccia* – was refermented with some water added to make a light wine, known as a *mezzo vino*; or else it was distilled as grappa. This task was performed by a travelling distiller who brought on a cart his own *serpente*; a tortuous form of alembic. (A grappa of much better quality, however, was made from distilling a spare cask of white wine.) Even the vine leaves lying on the ground and many of those still on the branch were picked by the women as fodder for the cows.

Meanwhile, other bunches of grapes, still attached to their branches, were carried off to be hung in the loggia of the *podere*. Once the grapes on these branches – known as *pendice* – had dried, they were added to the wine to increase its strength, flavour and colour in a second fermentation.

Some of the best white grapes, the *scelta*, would also be put aside for ripening. They were laid on cane mats known as *stoie* until they were like luscious sultanas, and then added to a white wine to make *Vin Santo*; a special celebration wine for Christmas, which was rich in taste and body like a sweet fortified wine. It was usually served as a treat with almond biscuits such as *cantuccini alla mandorla*.

Other grapes were selected for smoking – usually they were hung in a chimney, high above a woodfire. Wrapped in *pacchetti* made out of vine-leaves, they would be offered as presents at the end of the year. The *vendemmia* was traditionally a time of generosity. No *contadino* or *padrone* should refuse to give the product of the vine – itself a gift of Providence – to those in need. Wine, usually the *mezzo vino* that did not keep beyond the next spring, was given to the landless poor – *i poveri del buon Dio* – who brought empty *fiaschi* to fill. The grapes that they received as well would be fermented at home, with water added to make a thin *mezzo vino* known as *acquarello*.

The night of the *vendemmia* was reserved for celebration. Long tables covered with sheets were set up in the courtyard of Adamo's farmhouse, near the south gate. A dinner of many courses included soup; specially filled ravioli, or several sorts of *torte* made with wild mushrooms, herbs, spinach or even marrow; and another *vendemmia* speciality of white beans and *polpette* – little sausages of minced meat and rice. But the real centre-piece of the occasion was, of course, wine. The best wines — each *contadino*'s *vino vecchio* — were brought out and tasted and praised in extravagant terms.

Several of those present quarrelled good-naturedly over who was to explain to me the rules of pouring and drinking. The Tuscan *contadino* always tried to avoid drinking red and white wine on the same evening. But all the men expressed total contempt for 'baptized' wine: that was only for children and women. In a wine shop, nobody would ever dare let a drop of water pass their lips. I learned that drinks there were bought clockwise round the table. I also learned a few of the many proverbs to do with wine. The favourite, and most oft-repeated, was 'Good wine makes good blood.' To judge from the consumption of most people who uttered it, they were working towards a total transfusion — yet never have I known a more amiable evening, nor more energetic dancing when it began later.

Adamo then demonstrated the rules when pouring wine for a number of people. The vital thing to remember, he told me, was to change hands as you worked your way round from glass to glass. This was to avoid tilting the bottle back-handed; an act traditionally regarded as the sign of a traitor. In peasant society the pourer might be suspected of holding a knife in his spare hand, ready for an extended lunge. In grand circles, I subsequently discovered, the same rule applied, for a slightly different but equally archaic reason. There, to pour back-handed raised the suspicion that you might be tipping poison from a special ring, in Borgia style.

At that dinner in 1937, I sat next to Dante. We naturally talked of Aulla, and his father, Ramponi. He told me that the Fascists' attempt to control every area of life had even extended to the *vendemmia*. But their attempts to turn it into a Fascist festival did not endear them to the *contadini*, who were less than enthused by the new-fangled '*Manifestazione folkloristica della Festa dell' Uva*'.

Although I never witnessed this event myself, I later saw a photograph. The posed group included that ubiquitous presence, a pair of *carabinieri*, imposing in their huge bicorn hats; a group of pretty young girls dressed in Tyrolean style with blouse, dark bodice and skirt; and several young boys, self-conscious in shorts and socks. They were not even in *balilla* uniform. It seemed very tame stuff.

There was also an inept Fascist propaganda campaign to make the nation healthy for war by drinking less. 'Eat more grapes!' it ordered, rather baldly. Perhaps the Duce should have taken a leaf out of Hitler's book of slogans and made it 'Vitamins before alcohol!' Rude remarks were also made that evening about the new notice now displayed in all taverns on Mussolini's orders: 'For the honour of Italy do not blaspheme.'

After the plates, but not the glasses, had been cleared, an improvised little band of guitar, accordion and fiddle struck up and some songs were sung. All I ever managed was the refrain or chorus, known in Tuscany as the *passa gallo*, or cock's walk, because it struts up and down. Then the music changed, and the dancing began by the light of the fire on the open side of the courtyard. The red glow lit faces as they twirled, and our elongated shadows danced on the old walls of the farm buildings.

I did not go back to Aulla until the following year, 1938, when Jack and I went out for the summer holiday. I longed to show him Lagastrello and the *campo inglese*; to throw stones on the brigand's grave together; to meet up with the shepherds and charcoal burners again; and eat trout fresh from the lake.

I particularly wanted to introduce him to the Zunini and their daughter Yetta, who used to roam the mountains as a child with the two St Bernard dogs for guardians and bring wild spinach and herbs to our summer campsite. Yetta was not beautiful, but she had a distinctive face which showed her forceful, unconventional character – no doubt the product of her upbringing. She later became Italy's first woman racing-driver.

One summer, a number of years before I met Jack, Yetta was there with a Russian named Yuri Demchenko, whom she later married. Using virtually raw spirit and wild berries and herbs collected by Yetta, Yuri made a series of exotic vodkas. I have never been so drunk in my life as after one night of celebration by the lake.

But when we reached Aulla, ready to go up into the Apennines, it was late August in 1938 and the crisis over Czechoslovakia was approaching its climax. War appeared imminent. I made up my mind that if we did not have the time to camp up at Lagastrello, there was an alternative. I had always longed to do one great walk in the Apennines, to follow the watershed from Lago Santo, above the Cisa Pass, south-eastwards along the ridge that divides the province of Parma from Massa Carrara and then, on reaching Lagastrello, descend to Comano. This might well have been my last chance. For several days, as the international crisis see-sawed, my parents and Jack argued for postponement. Finally, I got my way.

My father warned us that the ridge was dangerous if cloud or mist came down, for there were many precipices along its flank. He insisted that we take Fiore with us. I immediately agreed, for Fiore, with his knowledge and love of these mountains, was the perfect guide. He was more than willing to come. The three of us, accompanied by Sally, my father's black-and-white spaniel, took the train up the Magra valley to Scorcetoli at four in the morning. In our rucksacks we had spare clothing and bread, in case the mists came down, trapping us on the mountainside.

After a steep climb from Scorcetoli up the valley of the Caprio, we traversed the flank of Monte Logarghena, then crossed the saddle between Monte Orsaro and Monte Marmagna. On the far side lay Lago Santo. We knew there was a mountain refuge on its shore, and we intended to spend the night there before tackling the ridge to Lagastrello, but the threat of war and the lateness of the season increased the risk that the refuge might be shut. Fortunately – the nights were already very cold – it turned out to be open. Some fishermen were there and, putting together their trout caught that afternoon with the wild mushrooms we had picked on our way and the bread we had brought, the two parties enjoyed a memorably delicious dinner round the fire. Sally, meanwhile, crunched on some dog biscuit we had included in one of the rucksacks.

After a night in the *rifugio*, on wooden bunks with palliasses, Jack, Fiore and I woke early. Breakfast was no more than a crust of bread and some spring water cold enough to chill our teeth to the roots. Then the three of us set off again before dawn broke, back up to the ridge. The sun rose above the skyline ahead of us, casting a golden glow.

The day turned out astonishingly clear. From the ridge, nearly 4,000 feet above sea level, we could see for twenty miles over valleys and hills to another range of mountains. It may even have been further; distances were deceptive. The clarity of the light made everything appear much closer.

The air was as heady as the view. We felt ourselves to be lords of all we surveyed. It was easy to understand why the Temptation of Christ took place on a high mountain. In a more humble moment, we stopped and sat on the grass to watch a golden eagle soar, then circle. Its massive wings, tipped with thick, finger-like feathers, remained still as it wheeled out over the void alongside our route. Only its head moved, turning in search of prey. This magnificent bird seemed only just beyond our reach.

The air was so invigorating that I felt I could have walked for ever. I was surprised how soon we reached Monte Bocco above Lagastrello. From that height, the Carraras beyond seemed to rise from a bed of grass-covered hills. We zigzagged down the steep slope on the far side to the Lagastrello Pass. To my great disappointment, nobody was at the Zunini's house by the lake, so we carried on, following the charcoal burners' route for the mule-train that I had come to know so well in childhood.

Altogether, we had covered over twenty-five kilometres that day, without taking into account hillsides and detours. My father later claimed that Sally had shrunk to half her size as a result. Throughout the walk, all thoughts about the international crisis had disappeared from our minds, but as we descended to Comano we quickened our pace. We entered the little square and went up to the first people we saw. 'Is it war?' we asked.

We had prepared ourselves for the worst during the last stretch, but when they told us that Signor Chamberlain had returned to London with an agreement, we found it very hard to believe. Jack had no illusions. Any respite would be short-lived. He did not imagine, however, that six years later he would find himself responsible for British support to the partisans operating in these mountains and elsewhere.

While Jack returned to London, I went on for a short visit to my mother in Florence. She was very pessimistic. Garvin had dismissed her as correspondent for the *Observer* after fourteen years because of the divergence between their views. He said that her politics were 'early Victorian', and he refused to believe that Mussolini was leading Italy into terrible danger. Garvin was far from alone in his views. The 'trains-running-on-time' school of thought in England was much larger – or at least more influential – than most people now remember. Even a considerable number of those opposed to Hitler thought that Mussolini should be supported in order to wean him away from the Axis. Equally, many Italians who despised the shoddy corruption of Fascism still convinced themselves that Mussolini would manage to keep them out of the coming war. The *contadini* knew better.

CHAPTER ELEVEN

The War Years

In the summer of 1939, my parents took the girls at the school up to Geneva to see the Spanish Exhibition. Everyone sensed that this was the last outing and probably marked the end of the school. Few parents would want to send their daughters abroad that autumn.

Soon afterwards the German armies began to mass on the Polish border. My brother Gordon telephoned the castle. He was then with Reuters in Paris, having been expelled by the Italian government not long before, on account of his reports – the Waterfields, *mère et fils*, were not popular in Rome. He begged my parents to leave before it was too late. Fortunately, I had gone out to be with them and so had John and his new wife, Daphne, so they had all the help they needed.

The whole family piled into the two cars at Aulla: a little sports Lancia towing a trailer, and an enormous 'Queen Mary' Austin with extra seats that folded out of the floor. John drove the Lancia and I drove the Austin that had been used for the school. We crossed France and reached Newhaven on 1 September 1939.

An aunt, Margaret Waterfield, lent my parents a tiny cottage at Aldington in Kent; but after three months of phoney war, and little sign of Italy entering the war on Germany's side, they decided to return to Tuscany. They were homesick and thought they would be of more use reporting the war from Italy. There was little point trying to convince them of the dangers at their age; so my father, by then close to seventy, took the wheel of the little sports Lancia, packed with books and paintbrushes, and drove back behind the Maginot line through beautifully frozen landscapes.

For several months, right into the spring of 1940, they persuaded themselves that they had done the right thing in returning to Tuscany. Although Florence was plastered with virulently anti-British posters, few Florentines seemed to take them seriously. Yet even many of the Italians who despised Fascism appeared to be out of touch with reality. I later heard from friends about one of the last great dances before the war. It was given in the Palazzo Ginori-Venturi with the king's son, the Duke of Spoleto, as the guest of honour. For days afterwards, conversation centred on the misfortune that had befallen the daughter of the house: she had broken her leg skiing and so could not open the dancing with the prince.

Everything changed with the German advance into the Low Countries and France. The threat of Italy entering the war on the Axis side suddenly became real. My mother arranged a telegraphic code with friends in the British embassy in Rome. By guarded references to the health of a fictional grandmother, they kept her abreast of the situation. During the first week of June a telegram warned that 'grandmother's health' was giving cause for concern. My mother, unable to cash any cheques, sold some silver so she could leave the household at Poggio with enough money for the immediate future.

The prospect of leaving Italy, this time very probably for good, made my father both angry and dejected. He sat down to write a letter to the Duke of Spoleto, who was stationed at La Spezia. He asked the prince, whom he knew slightly, to try to protect the castle at Aulla in the event of war. A very polite but non-committal reply came back.

My parents had already made their farewells to close Italian friends, such as Rezia Corsini, Rita Michiel and Professor Scarafia and his wife, Clementina, who had done so much to help my mother with the school. Some of them still refused to believe that Mussolini could be stupid enough to enter the war. Bernard Berenson, as an American citizen, was not at risk, but he had left for his retreat in the hills near Vallombrosa to escape an early heatwave. Mary Berenson, however, stayed at I Tatti where she was entertaining a party of musicians and Nijinsky's daughter, who danced there every night. My mother, who saw Mary frequently during the last fortnight before Mussolini's declaration of war, remarked that she had 'the faculty of pushing painful things aside'.

Percy and Sybil Lubbock were set to leave Fiesole for Switzerland. Sybil's daughter Iris Origo had arranged everything. On the eve of their departure my father, with a heavy heart, went over to the Villa Medici. Percy described later how the three of them 'sat and talked amongst the Chinese birds' (the eighteenth-century painted wallpaper) and then said goodbye. My father guessed that he would not see his old friend Sybil again, for her illness was by then undoubtedly genuine; she wasted away in Switzerland and died at the very end of 1942. Whether he thought he would survive the war to see Percy again, I do not know.

At any rate he refused to follow their example by departing. Eventually my mother, who had no illusions about the situation, persuaded him to go down into Florence to see for himself. He returned to the house in a tremendous state, having seen the slogans the Fascists were posting on the walls, demanding war against France and England. 'Lina, we must prepare to leave,' he said. 'What are you waiting for?'

Saying goodbye to everyone who worked at Poggio Gherardo was a tearful experience on both sides. Early on 9 June, the day before Mussolini declared war, the final telegram arrived from the embassy in Rome: 'Grandmother seriously ill and needs your presence.' There was no time to waste. My parents drove straight to the station. Rita Michiel and the Scarafias dashed down to say one more goodbye from the platform.

Shortly after their train left, blackshirt militia arrived at Poggio to arrest them. Finding them gone, they leaped back into their two cars and drove all the way to Aulla. There they threatened Ramponi when he said nobody was at home. He was forced to show them every room in the castle.

My parents found that they had caught the last train to cross the French frontier before war was declared. But they had hardly reached safety. The train went no further than Aix-les-Bains, so they took rooms there, in the Nouvel Hôtel des Thermes.

The spa town's tranquillity was misleading in what was supposed to be the start of its summer season. Streets were bright with flower-beds full of begonias, lime trees in leaf, and newspaper kiosks. The only reminder of war was the children building a Maginot line in the sandpit of the *jardin public*. My parents' first shock was finding that they could not cash a cheque, even at an English bank in the town. Then they found that the town had already been cut off by a German army advancing down the Rhône valley. A rumour.

Aunt Janet in her study at Poggio

Below, left: Kinta dressed as Queen of the May with John, before setting off to the Villa Medici, 1917
Below, right: Sybil Cutting's May Day party at the Villa Medici, just before raisins in flaming brandy were served to the children

The best walk was up to the old Medici hunting-lodge of Bagazzano, owned by a lame Florentine who reached the house by an ox-drawn sledge. Painting by Aubrey Waterfield

Camilla Russell painting under Aubrey Waterfield's supervision

The indoor staff at Poggio. *Left to right*: Carlo, Adele, Paolina, Primina, Maria, Anna, Agostino, Gino and Vittorio

The wedding breakfast. Nearest to the camera, turning round, is the impossible Uncle Frank. To his right is Pio Corsini. The young man on the far left is Pifi Gomez, the Mayor of Florence, who carried out the civil ceremony

Lina was rather dejected when she saw Derek Hill's portrait. She asked whether he could reduce the bulk of her silhouette. 'But Lina,' he replied in horror, 'it would spoil the triangle.'

Lina and Adela Broome under the ilex avenue on the roof at the castle in 1949

Maria arrives up from the town with the shopping

The wistaria-covered terrace outside the *portone* at the front of the castle

Vittorio, on the rampart outside the *portone*, is induced into turning from his garden to give Maria a rose for the camera. '*To!*' he said – 'take it!' in Aullese

Gli Scafari – in the middle distance – on the bay of Lerici

Antony presents a bouquet to Iris Origo on her birthday picnic

Lina in her improvised sedan chair, with Vittorio, Maria, and Andreino behind

Kinta seated in the embrasure of the castle's dining-room, looking down the Magra valley towards the sea

ran round the cafés that a whole Jewish family had committed suicide together.

The sound of artillery from the north, like summer thunder, grew steadily louder. Eventually, the first German vehicles appeared in the distance. My mother refused to come down to lunch because she was watching the enemy advance on the town. 'But Aubrey,' said the inveterate correspondent who had refused to leave behind her typewriter, 'don't you understand? This is my first battle.'

The last smattering of resistance soon collapsed, and late that afternoon they stood in the street watching German motor-cycle detachments, wearing coal-scuttle helmets and goggles, lead the occupying troops into the town. But somehow more disturbing than this martial vision was the sudden, and apparently seamless, transformation to *Kultur* that took place immediately afterwards. Within a couple of hours a German military band was playing selections from Bizet, Mozart and Beethoven in the *jardin public* as if France and Germany had never been at war.

My parents soon ran short of money: none could be sent from either England or Italy. So even after the Germans withdrew from Aix-les-Bains, leaving it as part of unoccupied France, it was impossible to carry on to Spain as they had wanted. Aix-les-Bains was hardly like the cinematic version of Casablanca, but their position was nevertheless worrying until they received a stroke of luck. Shortly after their thirty-eighth wedding anniversary on 1 July they received a letter from Percy Lubbock in Switzerland, who had heard of their plight purely by a chance conversation. He generously offered both shelter and money.

I was very relieved to receive a letter at last from my

parents, sent via Switzerland, but I was horrified when I read that they planned to seek safety there with Percy and Sybil. Only a few days before, I had found that at last I was expecting a child. So, to encourage them to make for England instead of being cut off for the duration of the war, I cabled: 'Josephine expected in February.' Nobody in the family had that name, so they understood immediately. They thanked Percy and asked only for a loan to start them on their journey. I was then able to reimburse him from England.

Several weeks later, after an enforced stay in Monte Carlo, my parents reached Barcelona. On the Ramblas they were able to buy their first copy of *The Times* for several months. They opened it and found, to their astonishment, a review of a book by Gordon about the fall of France.

Further delays followed in Madrid and Lisbon until they found berths on a small cargo ship, the *Spero*, which had just finished loading sardines and cork. My mother, lame with a completely stiff leg and crutches, had to clamber up the side from a rowing-boat, in a heavy swell. The *Spero* sailed 500 miles out into the Atlantic with a sloop as escort, then south to Gibraltar, where she joined a convoy back to England. After surviving a dramatic storm, in which the ship lost its anchor, they landed at Liverpool during an air raid, five months after leaving Poggio.

After an emotional reunion, I could not prevent an outburst of exasperation against their refusal to leave Italy earlier. They could so easily have avoided this difficult and dangerous journey. 'But my dear child,' said my mother regarding me with a look of utter surprise, 'it would have meant missing one of the great experiences of our lives. We would otherwise never have seen the Prado in Madrid.' This reply was so unexpected and yet so typical of her that it reduced me to a state of helpless laughter.

I could not tell my parents (I could not even tell Jack who had by then joined SOE) that Garvin's son-in-law, who was in the Directorate of Naval Intelligence, had suggested that I parachute into the Lunigiana to gather more information on the naval base at La Spezia. Since the idea came shortly after I found I was pregnant, I had to refuse. I was nevertheless called in for a talk, and they went through all the material they had on La Spezia and the surrounding region. At that time, when the amateurism of the war effort attracted a good deal of criticism, it was very encouraging to discover how accurate their information was. But however strongly I felt about the need to win the war, I could not help thinking of the tragedy for Italy, and for friends like Alessio Olsouffieff based at La Spezia. I heard after the war of his bravery in saving some English seamen after the sinking of a cargo ship. I also wondered about Giovanni Borghese, especially when, later on, reports arrived of a Borghese responsible for the executions of partisans – but that was his cousin, a fervent Fascist who became known as the Black Prince.

The war soon became even more personal. My beloved brother John went out to serve in the Mediterranean and was killed by a bomb in Malta. His death took place on the first birthday of his son, Garrow, whom he had never seen. Then my father, almost seventy, exhausted himself on the only war work he could find: interpreting for Italian prisoners of war. He bicycled twenty miles, sometimes up to forty miles a day during the severe winter of 1941–2. Not surprisingly, it became too much for him. He and my mother took a studio in Glebe Place off the King's Road, and there he was able to paint in tranquillity during the day. The nights were less restful. He would sit on the floor by my mother's bed and read aloud the King James version of the New Testament, as much for its language as for any spiritual comfort, while the house trembled from distant bomb explosions and heaved with the occasional near miss.

His health gave way early in 1944, sapped by the winter's bicycling of two years before. My mother found him a nursing home in Hampstead with a beautiful view, but he died two weeks later. After forty years of married life, she felt alone and adrift. All her possessions, representing their whole life together, were in enemy-occupied territory.

For four years we had no news of the castle or of Poggio. We could only guess at how hard things were for everyone we knew. Almost all the young men and *contadini* had been called up. Carlo Guerrini, Adelcisa's husband, was sent to the Dalmatian coast. Ramponi's eldest son Dante had to leave the garden at Poggio to join the *carabinieri*, but fortunately he stayed in Tuscany.

Vittorio, we knew, had been recalled for service as a signaller in the 2nd Battalion of Alpini. We feared the worst when we read that Mussolini had sent the Alpini division to fight alongside the *Wehrmacht* in Russia. It was not until 1945 that we heard the story of his war.

Maria, meanwhile, had to support her Balestracci grandmother in Aulla. She just managed to make ends meet by sewing and clog-making. The castle itself had been taken over by the Italian navy to house all their archives from La Spezia. But when Mussolini was deposed by the Fascist Grand Council and Italy sought an armistice with the Allies, the naval staff disappeared, leaving their stacks of files behind. On the day Mussolini was overthrown, Pio Corsini, while bicycling in Florence, bumped into another man and they both fell over. They were just about to have a furious row, when they looked at each other and said: 'Oh, how can one be angry on such a day as this!'

The Italian armistice of 1943 caused great rejoicing in the United States and Britain, as well as a good deal of premature rejoicing in Italy itself. Yet nobody should have underestimated the savagery of the German response. The *Wehrmacht* high command sent large bodies of troops, including SS formations, into Italy and occupied the country as enemy territory. When this happened, we feared greatly for B.B. whom we had last heard of in June 1940 when Italy entered the war and he and Nicky were up at Casa al Dono near Vallombrosa. Since his American citizenship no longer gave him any protection, we assumed that he must have gone into hiding. There had been little organized anti-Semitism in Florence since the fifteenth century (in 1439 the Signoria ordered that every member of the Jewish community should wear a yellow badge) and only a fanatical Fascist would have denounced him to the Germans; but as a Jew his fate, if he were handed over, would not have been in doubt. Only afterwards did we discover that he had benefited from quasi-diplomatic protection, for he had stayed secretly with the Minister of the Republic of San Marino to the Vatican. Mary, on the other hand, had become too ill to move. She remained at I Tatti, cared for by Nicky's sister, Alda Anrep. The books and paintings had also been hidden, most of them in the Anreps' apartment close to the Lungarno. This later turned out to have been an unlucky choice, for a number of items were irreparably damaged when, in August 1944, the Germans destroyed the bridges over the Arno to cover their retreat.

We feared above all for friends in Aulla because of its position and its railway junction. One look at the map showed this tiny town as an obvious target for attack, and so it proved. La Spezia, I later heard, was semi-deserted: the population was certain that the British Mediterranean Fleet would steam in and bombard it to ruins.

On 18 May 1943 the first heavy bombing raid on Aulla took place. When the townsfolk heard the engines, many went to their windows to gaze at the silver aircraft glinting in the sky, and a number stood in the narrow streets or the piazza to get a better look. Maria remembered it as 'a pretty sight', until the bombs began to fall.

Ferruccio Feliccini, the son of the watchmaker, who had come up the castle hill to see what was going on, was killed by a bomb fragment. He was standing by Ramponi's vegetable garden, which looked down on the town below – the very spot from which Jack and I had seen Alessio Olsouffieff on the evening of our wedding day. Ferruccio's companion, who threw himself under Ramponi's bread oven a few yards away, was saved.

Maria remembered how Agostino used to tease her by saying that Aulla was not even on the map; but for Allied bombers it seemed to form the centre of the region. That December she was caught by a raid just as she was about to ford the river – a hazardous enough journey in winter with the slippery stones and freezing water. A man on the bank, seeing the bombers approach, made a curiously timed proposal to her. Maria retorted that she would much prefer to die alone than in his arms. She threw herself into the water, diving under the surface each time the aircraft came in on a bombing run. Fortunately no bombs fell in the river. She did not know that the shock waves from the explosion would have killed her just as easily.

In retrospect she was amazed that she never caught pneumonia, considering the length of time she spent in the freezing water and in wet clothes. 'We were never so healthy as during the war,' she said later. 'We ate so little and walked so much that I was never ill.' Perhaps a more important reason was that somebody like her, who was looking after other people, could not allow herself to be ill.

Each evening she walked to the simple little hospital at Fivizzano – a seventeen-kilometre walk – to look after Adelina, my old nanny who was close to death, and Bagòn's widow. These two old women had no family nearby to nurse them. Maria paid a terrible price for her kindness. Crossing the river on one of these journeys, she slipped on a stone and fell badly. As a result of that fall, she lost the child she was carrying.

Vittorio, by the miracle of the kind colonel, had been saved from the Russian front where the colonel and nearly all his men perished: most of them from cold because the Fascist government had failed to provide them with winter clothing. Vittorio, posted back to Cuneo, managed to see Maria before being sent off to Yugoslavia. He was there when the armistice of September 1943 was announced. The German army promptly disarmed their former allies and began to use them as slave labour. Vittorio was put into a concentration camp near Belgrade. Maria had no idea of his fate at the time she slipped on the stone in the river.

The Italian armistice that led to Germans imprisoning Italian soldiers also caused Italian officers to order the release of Allied prisoners of war, often at great risk to themselves, since this was in defiance of German decrees. So many stories have been told of the bravery of Tuscan peasant families sheltering thousands of Allied servicemen from the Germans that I do not need to add to them here. They cared for prisoners and refugees alike, in the hope that some family somewhere would do the same for their own son or brother or husband. In spite of the language barrier, there was at least an affinity between the British and Tuscan sense of humour. At the simplest level, both enjoyed reversing nicknames, such as calling a large man 'Tiny'.

Perhaps the greatest generosity, when their own children were already suffering from hunger, was to take on the responsibility for feeding Allied prisoners. It was a burden which, in some cases, lasted well over a year. Partly due to the appalling mismanagement of food supplies early in the war – the Fascist government refused to introduce rationing for a long time, to Hitler's angry disbelief – shortages were acute by the time of the armistice. The destruction of bridges and the collapse of the transport system, mainly due to German confiscation of vehicles, together with German food requisitioning, soon led to a state of virtual starvation in many areas, especially the cities.

Some peasant families close to large towns made fortunes on the black market. At one stage, a litre of olive oil fetched a gram of gold. Those who still had a gold wedding ring to barter (women had been forced by the Fascists to donate theirs for the cause in exchange for a miserable iron band) could expect to receive little more than a couple of litres of oil, a small bag of flour and perhaps a few eggs. How poor people in the cities, with nothing to barter, survived is impossible to tell. Many probably didn't.

Yet most peasant families made no money at all. They were ruined by the Germans and the partisans requisitioning their produce. German troops on short rations foraged endlessly. They carted away sacks of flour, killed chickens, herded off pigs and cattle and looted wine from many a *cantina*. Fortunately, they took no interest in chestnuts, and the wooded hillsides of north Tuscany provided enough ersatz flour to make an unappetizing form of bread and tapioca for a large part of the population.

Almost every commodity was scarce or unavailable. Smokers, suffering the pangs of 'nicotine hunger', found the shortage of tobacco leaf almost harder to bear than the lack of food. The impossibility of buying soap, other than at extortionate rates on the black market, could preoccupy house-proud mothers out of all proportion. For a peasant family, the most vital necessity was salt: not just for cooking, but for the preservation of meat. There were a number of salt-pans on the Tuscan coast, but far too few to satisfy the demand. Some people went down to the sea with cauldrons and tried to make enough by boiling sea water. Many were prepared to walk seventy miles or so each way, to buy salt with money or barter it for flour: a number walked from Aulla over the mountains to Parma when it was rumoured that a consignment had arrived.

The most poignant illustration of this particular famine was a true story recounted to my son Antony by Pio Corsini. In February 1944, one of the most terrible winters in Italian history, a peasant family decided that, faced with starvation, it was time to slaughter their pig. This pig was all they had left to keep them alive until the summer harvest. To have kept it hidden from several German foraging parties was something of a miracle in itself. But now there was nothing left to give it to eat. Even the acorns from the wood had been collected by hungry families.

The youngest son was sent off before dawn with the last of their savings to buy salt from the black marketeer in the town, while the remainder of the family killed the pig and started to prepare everything in readiness for the salt. The boy reached the town. He found the black marketeer and, having purchased the block of salt, wrapped it carefully in a sheet of newspaper so that no grains would be wasted. His route home, some fifteen kilometres, was across a treeless terrain he knew well. There was little danger of ambush by deserters, and he would be able to see a German patrol far enough away to escape. He felt confident that he would not disappoint his family's trust in him. Yet there was one threat to his precious parcel that had never occurred to him before setting out.

A little after the halfway point on his return journey, black storm clouds began to appear to the west. In an alarmingly short space of time they covered the sky and, although barely midday, it became as dark as nightfall. The first heavy drops fell. There was no tree in sight under which he could find shelter, nor a wayside shrine. The main body of the rain began to pour down mercilessly. He tried to shelter the parcel by bending over it, but so great were the torrents of water running down and round his body that soon the sheet of newspaper was sodden and then the salt itself began to dissolve. By the time the storm had passed and the rain had ceased, what looked like a little sample of rock crystal was all that remained. The boy wept. He did not know how he could face his family.

Some *contadini* turned to trapping hares and rabbits and netting birds. Even if they had had a gun, shooting at a target as tempting as a wild boar was dangerous. The shot might trigger a fusillade in reply, either from a partisan group or a German patrol.

In the Lunigiana, much of the occupation force consisted not of German troops but of Fascists still loyal to the deposed Mussolini – the *Brigate Nere*, or Black Brigades. As the Allies advanced northwards up the Italian peninsula, the partisans and their helpers did all they could to pass Allied prisoners southwards. Many who had been sheltered in the valleys of the Lunigiana were led by local guides round the highest point of the Carraras – the Pizzo d'Uccello – because the Germans, believing the route too difficult, did not bother to guard it.

Groups of partisans were also active around Florence. Some landowners and peasants complained that they did little to justify their often arbitrary requisitioning of food. It is no doubt true that many were escaped deserters, or fugitives from the *Brigate Nere*, forced to live like outlaws. But when the Allied armies advanced on Florence from the south in July and August 1944, partisan groups played an important part in clearing Fascist snipers from the southern bank and disconnecting German demolition charges.

Oreste, Primina's husband the fiacre driver, fought with them and so did Vittorio's brother, Silvio. Like the rest of their companions, the nearest they could get to uniform was an armband and a cap with the name of their group written on it in indelible ink.

Life for those in Florence became intolerably difficult. The shortage of food was desperate. Throughout the spring of 1944 everyone feared that the peasants in the surrounding countryside might not have sown enough to avoid famine. In any case the Germans, still in a merciless mood towards their former ally, might take the whole crop for their own troops and for Germany.

The transport of food was erratic. Most of the lorries that had not been requisitioned were converted to run on charcoal, because so little petrol was available. Public transport was non-existent, and people relied on bicycles and tricycles to get about, or handcarts if they needed to move anything. The electricity supply failed more and more often as the fighting approached, and in the heat – on 30 June the temperature reached 39 degrees centigrade – the shortage of water made the city smell. Water had to be collected in containers; this was an accepted excuse for being out on the street during the extended curfews. As a result a demijohn became known as a 'passport'.

The greatest menace came from groups of young Fascist thugs, nervous and trigger-happy. Virtually disowned by the Germans, they acted in an unpredictable manner. Pretending to search for arms, they looted and robbed and raped whenever they thought they could get away with it. The Corsini bricked up their most valued possessions in one palace and moved family jewellery to safety in a pram, under their youngest daughter, Nerina.

Arbitrary arrests increased and suspects were shipped off to a camp near Parma. Several hundred prominent citizens were listed as hostages to be taken northwards with the retreating forces, but many managed to avoid the net when the withdrawal took place.

A slightly surreal atmosphere existed. At six o'clock each morning, flak batteries opening up on Allied aircraft acted as an alarm clock for the whole city. Yet German tourists, mainly officers on leave but also civil servants, were still arriving to see the sights. The most polite and friendly were the Austrian officers who tried to convince the Italians they met that, whatever might be said about Greater Germany and *Ein Volk, Ein Reich*, they were not like their northern counterparts.

Throughout the early summer, the only consolation was that Hitler had declared Florence an open city. The Allied advance was much slower than expected. The *contadini* and landowners who had, in fact, sown full crops were still faced with the dilemma of how to harvest them. If all was done as normal the Germans would have the opportunity to take the lot, but if the crops were left in the fields the city would starve.

By the end of June the grain was almost ripe and the Allied front line no further north than Poggibonsi, forty-five kilometres from Florence. At first some of the partisan leaders wanted to burn crops to prevent the Germans taking away the grain; but secret contacts between partisans, landowners and the semi-official authorities in the city arrived at a solution. To avoid German confiscation, no more than two days' supply for the city would be gathered at a time. Each *podere* would harvest a part of a field every week. This protracted harvest, leaving so much grain still standing in the fields, ran another risk from thunderstorms. Perhaps the prayers of Florence's clergy, led by their thin, pale prelate, Cardinal della Costa, were heard, as the weather remained fine.

The Swiss consul, Steinhauselin, who worked closely with the cardinal archbishop, thought up a more worldly tactic when the time came. To hasten the German withdrawal from the city when the Allies had reached the southern outskirts across the Arno, he organized rumours to be spread that cholera had broken out in the poorer quarters.

Hitler's assurance of making Florence an open city did not prove a cast-iron guarantee. All the bridges over the Arno, except the Ponte Vecchio, which was partially damaged, were blown up by Germans on 3 August 1944, as a prelude to their withdrawal. The greatest tragedy was the destruction of the Santa Trinità bridge. They also blew up the via dei Bardi to slow the Allied advance. The destruction would have been far worse if the partisans had not succeeded in disconnecting most of the charges.

Before their general retreat, the Germans pulled back most of their forces from the city to defensive positions along the Fiesole hillside. Field guns were dug in and concealed and strong points set up. They even mounted a heavy machine-gun post on the terrace at Poggio, under the magnolia tree.

Allied artillery shelling from south of the Arno managed to destroy nearly all the guns. There was, however, one particular field gun near Maiano still causing a great deal of damage. Allied observers could not understand why they had never managed to spot it. Pio Corsini heard about the problem from an English officer. Knowing Maiano well, Pio went up there and talked to an old *contadino* who had refused to leave his farm. 'Ah. They're very clever with that gun,' said the old man. 'You see that farm building up there. It faces in the right direction. The gun's inside. They just wheel it forwards, open the doors of the *cantina* and fire.'

Having established that there were no civilians left in the farm, Pio slipped back down into the city and crossed to the south bank of the Arno. He then identified the exact building on the map to his new English acquaintance. Immediately afterwards he had to go into hiding, for he heard that he was on a list of hostages to be taken when the Germans withdrew.

The Germans had prepared their retreat in methodical style with figures painted on the corners of buildings to direct their troops – '*à la Ariadne*' as one Florentine friend described it.

Progress was slow since the shortage of petrol meant that each lorry had to tow another one. Well ahead of the rearguard, infantry detachments herded all the cows and oxen they had managed to find in a final mass-foraging expedition. They also took two hundred hostages, although many were not those on the original list. A number were never seen again. Meanwhile, Fascist militia gangs went round in a frenzied search for hidden private cars for their own flight. But before many of them got away, the partisans entered the city ahead of Allied forces and captured the Signoria. Within a day the last isolated pockets of Fascists, usually single snipers, were rounded up or, more frequently, dispatched on the spot.

My husband Jack, who was then a lieutenant colonel and the senior SOE liaison officer at Field Marshal Alexander's headquarters, arrived in Florence from Siena on a quick official visit. He had just enough time to drive up to Poggio Gherardo. Part of the brief initial report that he sent back to us in England read: 'Poggio still standing – most windows gone; three shell holes (one through the ceiling of your bedroom, one in the top floor by the tower).' The house itself had been almost entirely stripped of its contents.

A much fuller letter followed. He described how Russian prisoners of war were camped in the little ilex wood, my childhood playground. At one stage there were nearly a thousand of them held on the property. Many had Mongolian faces. The tragedy of their conscription into a European war of which they knew nothing reached its terrible conclusion with their repatriation to an almost certain death.

On that first visit, Jack saw Dante and Modesta, and also Adelcisa who was on her own. Carlo was still trapped in

Yugoslavia. Dante had heard no news of Maria since May, nor even of his father Ramponi and the rest of his family. The Lunigiana had been completely cut off.

My mother also received a letter from Captain Enthoven. (Enthoven acted as the British army's representative on art treasures and it was he who had sat guard over the Uffizi collection hidden at the Sitwells' castle of Montegufone.) He listed the damage to Florence in detail. Santo Stefano had lost its roof, and the old parish priest had died either from shock or heartbreak. Palazzo della Parte Guelfa, Giotto's tower and San Lorenzo were slightly damaged.

Some of the damage from occupation by soldiers was less serious but very unpleasant. In the Palazzo Corsini, German soldiers guarding the Santa Trinità bridge had 'somehow managed to do both *pipi* and *pupu*' in the grand piano. As Pio's wife Elena observed with admirable restraint, it was an act that required a curious gymnastic bent.

That winter, American troops requisitioned Poggio. They took admirable care of everything, but then one of their officers decided to use the 'Poodle Room' as a cinema. To make a projection screen, he told his men to slap white paint all over the eighteenth-century fresco of Pippo. Captain Enthoven, as a favour to my mother, happened to arrive at Poggio on another tour of inspection. He was almost speechless with horror when shown into the room. The officer in charge at first could not understand. 'Oh,' he said, 'I thought the people who lived here would be wanting to redecorate anyway after the war, so it wouldn't make any difference.' Enthoven explained that one did not usually redecorate over eighteenth-century frescoes.

Once he realized what he had done, the American officer was genuinely contrite and offered to do whatever was necessary to rectify the damage. On Enthoven's suggestion, the two men walked down the hill carrying a tin of the paint in question to consult Bernard Berenson, who had just returned to I Tatti. B.B. examined the paint carefully. Finally, he looked up and gave them both a reassuring smile. It was a form of whitewash that, in fact, offered the best method of preserving frescoes. The officer was so overcome with relief and gratitude that B.B. called for some vermouth to fortify him.

B.B. did not lack visitors. It was a sad time, for Mary had just died after several years of great pain, during which they had been separated. Theirs had been a stormy marriage full of infidelities, and both of them had said many things that they regretted later, but they had remained devoted to each other to the end. Mary adored Nicky and was never jealous of her central place in B.B.'s life. In one of her last letters she urged B.B. and Nicky to marry, but Nicky saw no reason to change the basis of their relationship.

Some of the visitors in the spring of 1945 were more welcome than others, but B.B. could be very firm when necessary. Almost every war correspondent in Italy conjured up an excuse to go to I Tatti, rather as those in the liberation of Paris headed for Picasso's studio. One Italian visitor was Carlotta Orlando, daughter of the prime minister in the pre-Fascist era. She had arrived in Florence with a Red Cross Jeep and promptly drove up to I Tatti, where she had once stayed before the war.

Nicky, who met her at the door, warned her about Mary's death. She then asked her to wait downstairs while she fetched B.B., and there Carlotta Orlando silently rehearsed an emotional lamentation. She was, as a Florentine friend remarked, a true Neapolitan. B.B. eventually appeared, immaculate in smoking-jacket with a gardenia in his button-hole, and she advanced with a tragic expression on her face, her arms wide for a dramatic embrace. To her astonishment, B.B. held up a hand to stop her. '*Cara*, I know what you are going to say, but you should know that I do not like theatrical displays.'

Early in 1944, about six months before the liberation of Florence, German forces were brought in to reinforce the southern Lunigiana. Field Marshal Kesselring was constructing his Gothic line across the Alta Garfagnana, between the Carraras and Lucca.

A detachment of German *Feldgendarmerie* requisitioned the castle at Aulla. Ramponi and other friends in the town, hearing of this in advance, promptly did what they could to conceal furniture and pictures. The real looting had already been done by a local Fascist group early in the war. Curiously, the first thing they took was Ruskin's grand piano from the *salone*. (According to Aunt Janet, it had been Ruskin's wedding present to a fiancée in Florence, but he had broken off the engagement at the last moment, leaving her with the piano.) The Fascists had removed the legs and manhandled this monster down through the *galleria* to the corner tower, then over the drawbridge.

Aulla was no longer safe, so Ramponi took his family back up the Aulella valley to their village of Pomarino. SS detachments moved into Fosdinovo and Canova. In August they tried to ship out the wine stored in the village of San Terenzo, only four kilometres from Pomarino. A partisan group managed to ambush a German detachment and inflict very heavy casualties. The SS commander ordered immediate reprisals. During the round-up of hostages in the Aulella valley, Valentino Ramponi had a close escape. As the German soldiers surrounded Pomarino, he put medicines on the table beside him, and shrank into a chair in the corner with a shawl over his head and a rug over his lap, pretending to be an infirm old widow. The Germans were in such a hurry that the ruse worked.

Two hundred civilian hostages were assembled in the area and Major Walther Reder's battalion shot them in batches. One child, Luisa Cecchini, survived the massacre because she was knocked over and covered by the body of her mother in the fusillade. After this incident, it was not surprising that summary justice against Germans and Fascists sharpened. The accused were hauled in front of tribunals sitting at a table covered with the Italian flag and the trial would begin: '*Causa del popolo italiano contro . . .*'

The partisan command for the region was the Lunense Division. It included the *Diavoli Rossi*, based at Casalina in the Aulella valley, and the *Giustizia e Libertà* battalion of the Val di Vara Brigade. Blandino Blandini, who commanded the Lunense Division's 4th Battalion was a young station-master from Aulla.

Aulla itself had remained virtually abandoned ever since the first heavy bombing raids. And at the beginning of April 1945, as the US Fifth Army advanced on Massa, partisan activity began to increase against the German line of communication from Parma. On 23 April, after a mass given by the partisans' chaplain, Don Carlo Borelli, the partisans attacked and occupied the village and castle of Podenzana, overlooking Aulla from across the Magra. Their reserve company included Russian prisoners of war and German deserters.

The next day, a mortar shell fired by one of the partisan

groups on the Podenzana ridge hit an ammunition train in Aulla station. An enemy column, with German artillery and a Fascist *Brigata Nera* from La Spezia, was utterly annihilated as it retreated through the town. Over 600 Germans and Fascists were killed, as well as 150 Aullesi.

During the next few days, the fear of infection from decomposing corpses prompted anyone who wanted to cross the flattened town, or dig in the rubble for possessions, to have a clove of garlic in each cheek. Some are even said to have chewed up a couple of small cloves, then put one in each nostril to combat the stench.

Jack was able to visit Aulla very soon afterwards. He was horrified by the scene of destruction. Only odd walls still stood, with windows gaping to the sky. Streets were blocked with rubble and everything was covered in the dust of pulverized mortar. Just a handful of buildings on the far side of the town from the station still remained standing. He heard from a passer-by that Ramponi and his family had returned to Pomarino and that Maria Chiodetti was safe, but the man did not know where she was staying. In his Jeep, which could ford the Aulella river, Jack turned off to Pomarino.

Pomarino was an old hill village – a huddle of houses smelling of woodsmoke and cow dung and damp stone, set in a beautiful valley with a stream and chestnut woods on the slopes above. Part of the hillside immediately round the village was terraced with fruit trees and vines on pergolas, with pollarded willow providing the ties. Jack's Jeep was probably the first motor vehicle ever to have reached the place.

'There we found Ramponi,' he wrote to us in England, 'manufacturing copper sulphate [to spray on the vines] by pouring *acqua forte* [acid] into a cauldron containing copper salvaged from an American bomber that had crashed close to the village.' This act – the Tuscan equivalent of beating swords into ploughshares – could hardly have been a better symbol to mark the end of the war.

After an emotional embrace, Ramponi immediately asked for news of our family. When Jack told him of the deaths of Aubrey and John he took off his hat and, standing apart, wept silently. Ramponi's wife Antonietta was also sad, but more philosophical. And the other members of the family and inhabitants of the village greeted Jack in such a joyful way, with embraces and questions about the family, that there was no possibility of continuing his journey that night. Maria was indeed safe, they told him. Lina Ramponi, who had been working in the post office until just before the great explosion, had heard that she was up at Podenzana looking after somebody.

Jack gave them the coffee he had with him. It was the first real coffee they had seen after years of the Italian ersatz variety of roasted barley, known as *orzo*. After a hefty celebration dinner with much wine, they went off to prepare this luxury; but because the English style of coffee was much less roasted than the Italian and therefore far lighter in colour, they heaped it into the jug. The heady mixture of liberation and an overdose of caffeine – *'poi l'emozione, poi il caffè'* – meant that nobody slept that night.

Early next morning Jack gave Ramponi a lift back to Aulla, with some of his tools, then crossed the Magra to tackle the steep climb up the other side to Podenzana. On the way, he passed the decomposing body of a German soldier shot by partisans. He had been propped upright against a low wall and somebody had stuck a cigarette butt between his lips.

Maria was in the kitchen of her friend's house, kneeling in front of the fire making *focaccette*, when a man in khaki battledress suddenly appeared. To her utter astonishment he saluted her, then bent forward to kiss her on both cheeks. Only then did Maria recognize Jack. She began to cry and laugh with the realization that the war was truly over. Jack asked Maria if she wanted to return to the castle. She immediately agreed and packed her things together.

They drove up Monty Brown's carriage-drive in the Jeep and were greeted by the Ramponis, already re-establishing themselves in their old house opposite the drawbridge. Jack walked all round the castle to see the damage. The tower on the south-east side had been hit by an American battery based at Ponzanello, even though a radio message had been sent by a British liaison team with the partisans not to bombard Aulla any more since the Germans had left. The extraordinary mixture of nationalities fighting in the Lunigiana – Italian, British, German, Russian and American – was somehow reminiscent of the Middle Ages, when foreign *condottieri* and armies fought back and forth across this frontier region. To the surprise of locals, who had never seen anyone more foreign than a German or an Englishman, Philippine troops of the US army occupied Bibola, the fortified village above Pomarino.

That night Jack and the officer with him, the Ramponis and Maria all moved up to the castle, which was full of homeless families from the town. They all banqueted there off ration packs from the Jeep. Next day, Jack accompanied Maria down to the offices of the *commune* in the old *palazzo* of the Dukes of Modena, to ensure that she would be one of the homeless officially settled in the castle. At first, there were a dozen families quartered there. Several months after the war had finished, half of them had still found nowhere else to go.

Maria made a bed out of drawers turned upside down, then began to return the place to some sort of order. After the occupation by German *Feldgendarmerie* and Fascist *Brigate Nere*, who had defaced almost all my father's frescoes, there was a lot to do. But the worst damage had been caused by the explosion of the ammunition train. There were no windows or doors left, and Maria even found a length of railway line, blasted several hundred feet into the air, which had landed just under the stone steps of the dining-room balcony.

Maria's overriding concern was, of course, the fate of Vittorio. She still did not know whether he was alive or dead, in captivity or free. Two remarkable coincidences and the power of the grapevine – which Italians called the *radio popolo* – had brought news of him during the war. From Cuneo he was sent to Yugoslavia in 1942. In Montenegro, by an extraordinary stroke of luck, he had come across Carlo Guerrini, Agostino's son-in-law and successor at Poggio. And another chance meeting had brought news of him back to his brother Dario, who had had the good fortune to be taken prisoner by the Americans near Naples. After chatting with a fellow captive, Dario had been astonished when the man asked if he had a brother. 'Yes,' he said, 'but no one in the family knows where he is.'

'He's all right,' the stranger said. 'Or at least he was a couple of months ago before I got out of Yugoslavia.'

'But how do you know he's my brother?'

'Is your name Chiodetti?'

'Yes.'

'And your brother's called Vittorio, right? Well, you two

look so similar, and there was no doubt about it once I heard you speak.'

In August 1945, Nanda, a sister of Vittorio who was helping Maria clean up the castle, spotted a figure in the distance. The return of soldiers on foot, limping, emaciated and often marked by their terrible experiences, was a common sight at that time, but she immediately recognized her brother. She dashed back inside to call Maria.

For Vittorio, his first sight of Aulla was a shock. Having found the town almost completely flattened by the explosion, he believed that everyone he knew had been killed. After everything he had gone through – especially the starvation at the camp near Belgrade, where he had been reduced to eating grass – this disaster was almost too much to bear. He wandered up towards the castle in a daze, and that was when Nanda caught sight of him.

The destruction was truly terrible. The only buildings to survive in any recognizable form at Aulla were the church of San Caprasio and the old palace of the Dukes of Modena. The church had received a bomb through its tower, but it had failed to explode. This was regarded as divine intervention, if not a true miracle.

On 15 September one of Aulla's main religious festivals took place; the Festa della Madonna Addolorata. Great efforts were made that year to patch up the church and clear the rubble in its vicinity. The miraculous preservation of the church was attributed to the Madonna Adolorata. Throughout the war, wives and mothers had prayed to her, the traditional protector of soldiers away at the war. The statue of the Madonna bearing the body of Christ crucified across her lap was not in Aulla: it had been taken beyond Bibola to the village of Vechietto for safe-keeping. Its ceremonial return prompted a great emotional welcome from the population of the whole valley.

A boy tried to light what he thought was a Bengal light during the celebrations that followed. Just in time, it was found to have been a phosphorous flare, which would have burnt him terribly. In those days, heady with emotional relief, its refusal to ignite first time was greeted as another miracle. Everyone gave thanks for survival. That was what really mattered. A town could be rebuilt.

CHAPTER TWELVE

After the War was Over

Damage from the war took many worse forms than the shell holes in Poggio and the castle. For a long while Vittorio suffered terrible nightmares. His sleepwalking was a further worry for his family. The ravages to his stomach after having been reduced to eating grass meant that for the rest of his life he could eat only the plainest diet of boiled fish and boiled vegetables. Maria, with saintly self-denial, insisted on eating exactly the same so he would not feel awkward, and Vittorio's strength returned little by little.

The damage to the roof over the living quarters of the castle was the first thing to be patched up. Curiously, the roof-garden itself was undamaged except for the ornate trellis pavilion, which had completely disappeared. The German *Feldgendarmerie* or the *Brigate Nere* must have broken it up for firewood. The shortage of tools and materials as well as labour meant that larger schemes, such as repairing the shell holes in the tower, had to wait. So did the making of doors and windows. For several years, sacking and tarpaulins had to serve.

Household items too were in short supply. Before the war every family had a copper ewer for fetching water, but few remained. The Fascist government had requisitioned them all for melting down by the war industries. It was not an uncommon sight to see women with jerrycans on their heads making their way to the *fontana*.

Similarly, the Lunigiana's main route to the coast depended on the US army's Bailey bridges replacing those destroyed in the fighting. They remained in place well into the 1950s, and the rattling echo when crossing them in a car remains one of my strongest memories from the post-war years.

My mother, now seventy-one and very lame, doubted whether she could return to her former life and the journalistic fray. But letters from friends in Italy during the summer and autumn of 1945 began to make her think that she could perhaps do something worthwhile. Berenson especially urged her to return to work. 'I doubt,' he wrote, 'whether England just now has another writer with such insight or such capacity for interpreting Italian affairs.' B.B.'s letter so strengthened her morale that when Ian Fleming asked her to be the Italian correspondent for the *Sunday Times*, she accepted almost on the spot.

For someone of her age, and dependent on crutches, travel in the winter of 1945 was quite an adventure. The first part was relatively simple. I drove her to Croydon airfield. She flew to Zurich, then caught a train to Milan. But the train took a whole day, mainly due to war damage. A shortage of rolling-stock meant that there was no onward connection for several days, so she managed to arrange a lift in a staff car bound for Florence. Military police warned her against making the journey, because of snow storms in the Apennines and the threat of brigands, but she did not intend to turn back at that point. The journey took many hours longer than normal, but they reached Florence safely. The driver took her up to Poggio Gherardo, and thus she reached home, still carrying the same typewriter that she had taken across France and Spain in 1940, but very little else.

Everyone attached to the house – Dante and Modesta, Adelcisa and Carlo and Primina – were there to welcome her. Then, when news of her arrival had spread down the hill, all the peasant families – men, women and children – rushed up from the farms to welcome her back. The older women embraced her, weeping as they remembered Aubrey and Johnnie. My mother, who disliked any show of emotion, was both deeply touched and disconcerted. The new *fattore*, or steward, afterwards told her with some amusement that the *contadini* on the property had not allowed him to make any decisions, not even to cut down a truncated cypress, until the *padrona* had returned and seen for herself.

The detailed reports sent back to England by Jack, Captain Enthoven, Rita Michiel and other friends had given my mother a good idea of what to expect. The damage done to the house by the three artillery shells was much less than might have been feared, but all Henry Ross's orchid houses had been smashed to pieces, and use of the property as a parking area for armoured vehicles had caused much destruction. Inside, the house had been thoroughly looted. Even the curtains had been taken. Only a few beds, tables and chairs remained.

During the war, Poggio had been occupied by a prominent Fascist, Senator Morelli, who had since fled with the Germans. Almost everything of value had disappeared, including letters to my parents from D. H. Lawrence and the whole of Lucie Duff Gordon's correspondence with Heinrich Heine, who had wanted her to be his literary executor. It was, of course, hard to know what had been stolen and what had been destroyed. Tragically, a good deal of the damage had been done by British troops who, on finding a signed photograph of Mussolini dedicated 'to my devoted friend', had thought that the British owners must have been Fascist sympathizers. Adelcisa and Modesta had rushed in, begging them to stop, but they refused to believe that the 'devoted friend' in question had been Morelli, not one of my parents. In their anger, they even destroyed a number of my father's paintings.

Such unfair depredations were greatly softened by the kindness of friends. Bernard Berenson and Nicky lent or gave as much as they could spare from I Tatti to make Poggio inhabitable, and Vittorio and Maria, who came over from Aulla, helped restore things to a reasonable order.

The damage done to the farms and their outbuildings was even more serious; and the scarcity of materials meant that repairs would take a long time. Many people, however – especially those who had lived in Florence overlooking the Arno – were in a far worse position. In the city itself, army engineers had caused a good deal of damage when clearing the rubble, to the agony of conservationists. But their work was not easy. A number of houses, both in and around the city, had been booby-trapped. Iris Origo reached the Villa Medici in a Red Cross Jeep to find bomb-disposal squads at work and one of the outbuildings on fire.

Florentines were at least able to console themselves on one point. The Ponte Santa Trinità could be rebuilt exactly, even if it took a long time, because the original plans by Ammannati were safe in the Uffizi. For some time Bailey bridges connected the great stone piles in the Arno, until eventually the Santa Trinità was recreated as before.

But the most urgent need during the first months of peace was the resurrection of agriculture. At Poggio Gherardo, shell bursts during the artillery duel across the Arno valley had destroyed thirty olive trees out of seven hundred. My mother arranged for twenty-five to be planted immediately, with more later. She also arranged for electricity to be connected to the *frantoio*, and installed a generator. The new *fattore* and each *capoccia*, or head of the household, of the three families expressed great satisfaction. The vineyards were in a terrible state. Nearly all the vines had died through lack of attention during the war. My mother undertook to replant a new vineyard for each farm.

The gardens had also suffered badly from neglect in Dante's absence and they too had been despoiled. Morelli had had all the iris roots, of which there had been several thousand, dug up and sold. In Florence the iris, the symbol of the city in the form of fleurs-de-lis, provided the basis of an ancient industry. The orris root had long been a vital ingredient in scents and soap, and were even used as teething sticks for infants.

Food was still in short supply for many months after the end of the war. My mother, looked after by Modesta, lived off vegetable soups, thickened by any leftover pasta. Meat she ate only on Sundays. And her supper each evening was like a child's tea: a glass of milk and some maize bread. She had to admit that she felt much healthier on this simple diet.

Life started to look a little better during the course of 1946. The corn planted that year grew well. Farmers were allowed more freedom in selling their produce. The olive harvest for that winter looked promising, and only a kilo of oil per tree would be requisitioned by the regional *ammassi*, or stockpiles, prepared in case of natural disasters or food shortages. True to form, many *contadini* had avoided declaring the total number of their trees. In their lifelong battle against the '*burosauri*' – the bureaucratic dinosaurs – the *contadini* trusted in the patron saint of Italian tax evaders, '*La Confusione*', not to be found out.

One person who proved a great help at this time was Walter Lucas, a member of that swarthy Quaker clan, many of whom were cousins of Jack. Theoretically a journalist, Walter had returned to live near Fiesole with his very beautiful but rather talkative wife. He had one essential quality that appealed to my mother: he was a master fixer.

'Right, Lina,' he would say, arriving unannounced in her study. 'Here are some more seeds, as I promised. Now, what crops have you got for me to dispose of today?'

'Oh, Walter,' she would reply, turning from some article she was trying to type. (One of the more curious requests from Ian Fleming in London was for a piece on 'How an Italian Gets Over a Bender'. My mother was rather proud that she knew what a bender was and did not have to ask.) 'Now, give me a moment to think. As far as I remember there's not very much at the moment, I'm afraid. But wait a minute, Dante mentioned that his next lot of artichokes in the *orto* was ready. And you could always see if they want more olive oil.'

'Fine. I'll try the Grand Hotel again. I think we asked much too little for the last consignment. There's a real shortage. I'll demand double this time.'

'Oh, Walter, are you sure?'

'No,' he would reply, 'but I'll have a damned good shot at it.' And my mother's Scottish heart would beat with excited satisfaction.

The pigs too fattened up very encouragingly in the late autumn. Their 'executions' (partisan parlance seemed to have slipped into everyday speech) were planned for some time in the New Year. My mother was very keen to find someone who could smoke the meat properly, in the manner of Modena ham. After asking many people, Walter Lucas finally heard of a *contadino* over beyond Settignano who was regarded as a specialist. He visited him first, and brought back some sample slices for tasting. My mother agreed they were delicious, so Walter negotiated a barter arrangement. The man smoked all of Poggio Gherardo's produce for that year. In return he was allowed to select one ham and keep it.

Fortunately, the olive crop of 1946 at Poggio turned out to be as good as everyone had hoped. The weather provided a true tramontana for the olive harvest, with brittle sunshine and piercing cold. The newly electrified *frantoio* was pronounced a great success. The good harvest also put an end to the shortage of soap. My mother spent 900 lire on caustic soda to make soap out of the oil dregs. She boasted afterwards that, if sold, the soap would have fetched 8,000 lire. But Maria's 'passion for washing' would not allow my mother to part with any.

Christmas approached and a tree was decorated in the hall, with presents for all the children of the servants and the *contadini*. On Christmas Eve, their mothers brought them all up to the house, and great was the excitement round the candle-lit tree. None of the children had seen anything like it before. The little girls adored their stuffed animals and the little boys their carts and trains.

Finally their fathers arrived. They and the *padrona* drank *brindisi* after *brindisi* in Poggio Gherardo vermouth. They toasted the past, silently thinking of all those who had died in recent years – Pietrino, Agostino, Adelina, John and, finally,

Aubrey – and they toasted the future, no doubt with an edge of uncertainty, for Italy's turmoil did not seem to be over. Great social changes loomed over every aspect of life.

On Christmas morning, my mother went down to St Mark's, the other Anglican church in Florence where she used to go with my father. She felt very sad 'as Aubrey's spirit was there ... So many memories came back'. The combination of cold and sunshine continued. Fires blazed back at Poggio to welcome her guests at Christmas lunch: Rita Michiel and Walter Lucas and his wife. Vittorio had specially fattened a chicken with extra rations of maize for the occasion, but a complication had arisen.

In the old days of the *mezzadria*, each peasant family at Christmas was obliged to give its *padrone* a capon, but now the law had been changed by de Gasperi's government. The Communist Party's local *casa del popolo* in Settignano had even ordered peasant families not to give any Christmas presents at all to their landlords. My mother was therefore taken by surprise when all three *contadini* families, including the Martelli who were strong Communists, insisted on bringing a capon as before.

Faced with a slight dilemma, she decided to continue as planned with the chicken on which Vittorio had lavished so much care. This was followed by her own creation, what she called 'my queer plum pudding'. But the great success of the meal was Maria's *tortellini*, stuffed with cheese and wild herbs, and cooked to perfection. My mother suddenly realized that Maria was a cook of far greater talent than she had imagined possible. This came as something of a shock to somebody brought up with Aunt Janet's prejudice that only a male chef – a Giuseppe Volpi or an Agostino – could achieve culinary finesse. In fact, the delicacy of Maria's cooking was doubly impressive, given her insistence on sharing Vittorio's diet of boiled food.

It was appropriate that Rita Michiel should have been there that day. We owed so much to her, and also to Signora Scarafia, the professor's widow. Between the two of them, they had tracked down some of the furniture stolen by Morelli and his henchmen. Rita Michiel, whose wartime bravery had made her a heroine of the partisans, then procured its rapid return with a few carefully worded threats.

In the summer of 1946, when five months pregnant with my third son, I packed suitcases for myself and my two boys. Inside the cases I hid quantities of all those things still in very short supply in Florence: coffee beans, tea, razor blades, pencils and, most important of all, peppercorns. It was still quite an adventure travelling across post-war Europe by train, and I warned Nigel and Hugh, then aged five and three, that the journey would be awful – with the result that they thought it great fun. Unfortunately, I raised their hopes by promising breakfast on the train, but the corridors of the carriages were so packed that we could not get through. I then said that there was a wonderful restaurant at the Gare de Lyon, where we would be sure to find something. But the restaurant had been damaged, and at the café downstairs the breakfast plonked down on the table in front of us consisted of tin bowls of black, rather ersatz coffee and a *baguette* of bread.

'Mummy,' said Nigel rather hesitantly, 'do you think there will be any milk?'

'No, I don't think so.'

'And will there be any butter for the bread?' asked Hugh.

'No, darling. I'm afraid not,' I said, feeling awful.

'Well, at least the bread looks jolly good,' said Nigel, and they chewed away at it. Their stoic attitude filled me with admiration.

The effort of travelling proved well worthwhile. When we finally arrived at Poggio, the welcome from so many friendly faces, all those I had not seen since the summer of 1939, was overwhelming. I was, of course, fulsomely complimented on the two boys, and they, to their confusion and then exasperation, were kissed and admired and spoiled in that compulsively Italian way.

It was a moving moment for many reasons. After nearly six years of wartime dreariness in a very grey and battered London, to feel the warmth of the sun; to smell pine needles again; to see the apricot stucco of Poggio glowing in the sun; to look across olive trees and cypresses to the roofs of Florence and the Duomo; and to hear the Angelus from the *campanile* of San Martino a Mensola – all these things combined to put the fear and tense uncertainties of the Blitz behind me at last.

And then Maria bustled over, her *zoccoli* clacking on the stone flags, her hair hidden in her kerchief turban, to ask whether the boys would prefer to start with *pasta* or to have *fritto misto* like the grown-ups. She had also prepared *ripieni* with veal and, finally, as a special treat for them, *gelato di pesche*, made from peaches picked that morning. I shook my head in wonder at all I had nearly forgotten. There was not just life after spam – there was heaven.

The following year, I came back to Poggio for the whole autumn with all three sons and Nanny Waite to look after Antony, the youngest. Nanny could not have been more English, but she enjoyed adventures and did not complain about discomfort. On the other hand, she was horrified by certain Italian household practices – sheets were never properly aired, she maintained – and she had very unindulgent ideas about child-rearing, which Italians, needless to say, did not share.

Maria and the other women at Poggio strongly disapproved of the way Nanny used to leave seven-month-old Antony in a pram under the pergola on the terrace while she had her forty winks. One day Primina came rushing into the kitchen to say that Antony had been crying for a long time, left on his own. Primina, almost as fanciful as her aunt, Adelina, was afraid that a viper might fall on him from the vine above. '*Povero piccolo!*' she wailed.

Maria, outraged that Antony should have been left to cry on his own while Nanny had her rest, spoke her mind that afternoon. Nanny was not only unrepentant, she firmly expressed her view that Italians were far too soft on children. 'However much I like you, Maria,' she said, 'I would never have you as a nanny.'

'Well, even if you did,' retorted Maria, 'I wouldn't dream of coming!'

Some ideas about children, I realized, could only have been developed in the British Isles. On one occasion, Jack's mother had eyed Nigel and Hugh running around naked on the lawn, then said to me: 'I wouldn't mind so much if they were girls.'

'What do you mean?' I asked, genuinely puzzled.

'Little girls without clothes on are all right, but the trouble with little boys is that they look . . . well, you know what I mean. Little boys look so untidy.'

More of my mother's friends returned to Florence, and life

there revived a little. Concerts began once again at the Politeama. During one interval, a cousin of ours overheard two Florentines discussing the present state of affairs in Italy. 'Well, things aren't too bad,' one said to the other. 'At least we are eating quite well.'

'*Già!*' replied his companion. 'Just imagine if we had won the war! We'd have had to feed the Americans.'

Gaetano Salvemini came back to the University of Florence from the United States to reoccupy the chair in history from which he had been ejected by the Fascists. B.B.'s court at I Tatti was in full audience, and friends like Umberto Mora came to stay at Poggio. But my mother sorely missed those she had known from the beginning of the century: Sybil Lubbock who had died in Switzerland; Mary Berenson who had died soon after the liberation; and also Filippo de Filippi. Percy Lubbock, who had cared for Sybil so devotedly, said goodbye to the Villa Medici and moved permanently to Gli Scafari, near Lerici. Iris Origo then sold the Villa Medici, for she and her family now lived entirely between Rome and La Foce, the house and estate south of Siena that she and Antonio Origo had developed between the wars.

My mother was feeling rather lonely at Poggio when she received a letter from an old friend, the writer Lawrence Jones, who was known as Jonah. Jonah and his wife Evie longed to come to Florence, but they could not face a gloomy little hotel. Since he imagined that food and everything else would be as difficult to come by and as expensive as in England, he wondered if they could propose themselves as paying guests. My mother could not have been more delighted by the idea.

After Jonah and Evie returned to England, the word spread rapidly among mutual friends. In that post-war world of austerity and rationing, the thought of good wine and perfectly cooked food fresh from the farms, as well as the peace of Poggio and its views across Florence, proved irresistible. My mother never had to soil her hands with commerce. Signora Scarafia, who now worked as my mother's secretary, was happy to handle the business side after consultations with Vittorio and Maria on what should be charged.

This new life at Poggio was perfect for my mother. She could work without interruption on her articles during the day while the guests were sightseeing, and in the evening the company and the conversation were all she could have wished for. Although she did not think of it in such terms, she was being paid handsomely for holding just the sort of house parties she could not afford to give. But one day the scales fell from her eyes.

I happened to be out there on a short visit, and entered the *salottino* just after she had opened her letters. For a moment I was worried: she looked as if there had been an unexpected death in the family. But then I sensed outrage rather than tragedy. 'What on earth's the matter?' I asked.

'My dear, you won't believe it,' she said, scarcely able to control her voice. 'A woman whom I do not know has written to me saying that she wants a south-facing room with a view across to the Duomo. What *does* she think I am? An hotel keeper?'

'Yes,' I could not resist replying. 'And a very successful one.' She looked at me dumbfounded by the revelation. Sadly for all, it was too much for her to bear. In an open conflict between pride and trade, pride could never be allowed to lose.

In May 1946, seven months after she had reached Poggio, my

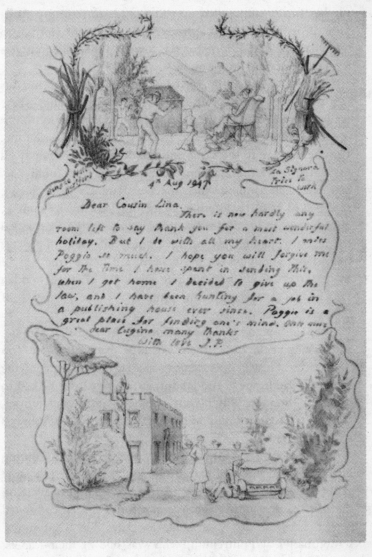

A thank-you letter from a young cousin (*J. P. Trower*)

mother finally summoned up the courage to return to Aulla with all its memories of Aubrey. She went with Gordon to see what was being done for the town by the Allied powers in their rebuilding programme.

Up at the castle, the welcome from Ramponi and his family as well as other friends – Fiore was standing there ready to present her with a large bag of dried wild mushrooms – once again embarrassed and touched her at the same time. But the damage to the castle and the destruction of nearly all my father's frescoes saddened her deeply. She could not, however, help smiling when she saw Ruskin's grand piano, returned to its place only the day before, and already shining. Shortly before his death, Ferruccio Feliccini, the man killed by a bomb splinter next to Ramponi's *orto*, had tipped off our friends about where the Fascists had hidden the legs of the piano. Nobody knew where the body of it was hidden until it was discovered in the seminary on the other side of the hill from the castle.

Gordon slept on the roof. With all the homeless families still staying at the castle, there was little space left inside, and in any case he wanted to enjoy once again the sight of the mountain landscape in moonlight. A few days later he had to return to London, leaving my mother with her memories, especially those she found in the roof-garden, where Aubrey's spirit still lived.

Soon after her return to Aulla she received a rousing welcome from the local partisan leaders, who came in a large group to the castle. The party started with *fiaschi* of wine on the roof-garden, until it grew cold up there, then continued in the *salone* in front of a blazing fire. The Communist stationmaster at Pontremoli, who was one of their leaders, turned out to be a brilliant actor and singer, and jumped from opera to opera and character to character in a bravura display which had all his colleagues cheering and roaring out the choruses. As they left, the partisan leaders suggested that my mother flew a flag from the tower of the castle to show that she was back in residence. She thoroughly enjoyed the whole evening although it went on until late. A visit from the bishop the following night proved far more tiring with its polite small talk and false departures. Each time the worthy man rose to make his farewell he thought of something else, and the conversation creaked on for another half an hour. But the bishop had the rather endearing habit of handing round caramels from his pockets as if his hostess and the other guests were all children.

My mother returned again to Aulla when she was invited to a partisan reunion at Pontremoli. Walter Lucas, who had managed to get hold of a Jeep, brought her all the way from Florence. Jeeps had become her favourite means of conveyance. They had no doors, so her stiff leg could stick out, facing forwards like a couched lance.

Bernard Berenson felt as early as November 1945 that 'the mystic cult of the USSR was on the decline'; but that did not affect the Italian Communist Party, whose popularity finally peaked in Tuscany in 1968 with 47 per cent of the vote (54 per cent in the province of Siena). Italian Communists were proud of being very different from the Russians – '*Noi, non siamo come i russi!*'

The Communists at this time were very well organized and enjoyed great popularity. For months after the end of the war they organized committees to welcome returning prisoners of war and help them, because the Allies had provided them only with rail warrants for particular railway stations.

Exhausted and often seriously ill men, otherwise faced with a long walk home, found the Communists offering food and transport.

In 1946 the imminent departure of British and American troops, and exaggerated reports that the Communists were plotting a *coup d'état*, produced an atmosphere of alarm. Italian friends begged my mother to arm herself. The idea rather appealed to her, so she wrote to Jack asking if she could borrow his heavy automatic pistol. He refused to let her have it. She would have been in far more danger from the gun than from any assailant.

One of her great friends from those days was Gordon Lett, who had served with the partisans and was now British consul in Bologna. As he was a very reliable source of information, my mother kept in constant touch with him. I will never forget one telephone conversation between them. My mother was at Poggio in the *salottino* and she was speaking to Gordon at Lerici, where he had arrived from Bologna to stay with Percy Lubbock. She was longing to hear news of the latest disturbances and I could see from her expression and tone the replies she was getting.

'Tell me, Gordon. How were things in Spezia when you passed through?'

'Oh, I didn't see anything out of the ordinary.'

'Well, what about Bologna? Weren't there riots there?'

'Oh, no. Bologna's been very quiet.'

'But isn't there any trouble *any*where?' she demanded in exasperation, her news-hound instincts thoroughly thwarted.

Although Fascism had corrupted much, the democratic anti-Fascist line taken by Benedetto Croce and other thinkers at least provided a sound base for departure after the war. The great problem was that, in typical Italian style, everyone spoke of liberty, social justice and democracy, but liberals, Catholics and Communists all had their own definitions.

The Italians, unlike the Germans, were saved from the worst effects of ideology by their own cynicism about politics and the press. My mother went to Rome to interview the prime minister, de Gasperi, for the *Sunday Times* only to find that the appointment was continually postponed. Maria, who had gone with her, finally could not contain herself any longer. 'But signora, does he want to see you or doesn't he? Why don't you just make up the interview and then we can go home?'

'*Ma, cara mia!*' exclaimed my mother in horror. 'Are you mad? I can't possibly write an interview that I haven't had.'

'But everyone expects that sort of thing,' replied Maria. 'They know that newspapers are liars, so they expect it.' My mother, who had a lofty view of her profession, was left speechless.

Yet whatever the perceptive abilities – or wily distrust – of its citizenry, any country denied democracy for a long period will have trouble finding its feet. The referendum on the monarchy, which turned Italy into a Republic, was followed by general elections. At Poggio, one of the *contadini* went to consult Vittorio, the acknowledged sage on all matters of importance. 'But Vittorio,' he said, 'what I don't understand is how we can vote without a king on the throne.'

'You don't need a king to vote!' replied Vittorio. 'Forget about them! The last king sided with Mussolini and sent me off to war. If you're for the Church, vote for the Christian Democrats.'

Vittorio was also approached for electoral advice on his return to Aulla. An old man asked if he should vote for Parri of the Republican Party. Vittorio considered Parri a dangerous demagogue. 'Vote for Parri,' he quipped, 'then we'll all be *pari* [equal]. But if we are all *pari*, and there are no *signori*, what will we do for work?'

Amidst this Don Camillo-like world of red flags and religious processions, my mother, in a thoroughly Gladstonian fashion, believed that every other country should enjoy the same parliamentary freedoms as the British. Democratic debate must be a good thing. When the Socialist Party in the Lunigiana found it impossible to find a large enough place to hold a rally in Aulla, because every suitable place was owned by Christian Democrats, she gave them permission to use the ground below the castle, where the railway company had quarried rock from the castle hill. Her Christian Democrat friends, however, were appalled when they heard.

'Lina, how could you do such a thing?' they demanded in horror.

'In England we believe in free speech.'

'But this isn't England! It's Italy. Nobody here plays by your rules.'

'Well, perhaps it might be better if you gave them a try,' she could not resist replying.

On the evening of the great meeting she sat rather nervously in the *salone* pretending to read a book, but with the windows open. They looked over the quarry and the town. She began to fear that the speeches would be inflammatory, that riots might break out, and she would be to blame for everything. But almost as soon as the loudspeakers below had crackled and whistled in adjustment, and Signor Nenni, the Socialist leader from Rome, had been introduced, the bells of San Caprasio began to ring. And they rang and they rang and they rang. The old *parroco* must have organized relay teams of all his most muscular parishioners to make the speeches inaudible.

Finally, the speakers below gave up and the meeting was abandoned. My mother breathed a sigh of relief, and just prayed that there would be no settling of accounts down in the town. But then she started in alarm when the doors of the *salone* were thrown open. The Socialist leader made a dramatic appearance flanked by two stalwarts bearing armfuls of red carnations. She was overwhelmed at the sight. But then she had to sit through a long oration in praise of English 'fair play', which, to her embarrassment, ended with an expression of the fervent desire that one day Italy would play the political game by the same rules.

CHAPTER THIRTEEN

Farewell to Poggio

My mother had been surprised when the matriarchs from each of the three farms on the property had brought her a Christmas capon in accordance with past tradition. She was even more surprised a few years later when a *capoccia* came to ask permission for his son to marry.

The purpose of this old custom was not simply to perpetuate a form of feudal tyranny. A landowner, to protect his own interests, made sure that each *podere* had a reasonably balanced workforce. If the family had too few men, then it could not farm the land effectively. If there were too many sons, there would be quarrels between their wives. And if the family had too many mouths to feed, with a host of non-productive relations living off the produce, then the *padrone* would see output fall sharply.

My mother told Ricci, the *capoccia* in question, how surprised she was that he should ask her permission now that de Gasperi's laws changing the *mezzadria* had consigned such practices to history. Ricci answered that it had always been the custom in his family to ask the permission of the *padrone*, and he was not going to change now. My mother asked him to give all her good wishes and congratulations to the young couple, and he in turn insisted that she honoured the wedding party with her presence. She asked if she might come after the wedding breakfast to raise a glass and drink the health of the *sposi*.

The wedding took place just after the olive harvest, and the weather was cold and fine. The party, forty strong, was still eating when she arrived at four in the afternoon. The Ricci were cousins of the Martelli, so almost the whole of the Poggio community was present. The effect of the food and wine had begun to show. Some of those present looked half asleep and a little bleary. She watched one old man pour his liqueur into his coffee with a far-away expression in his eyes. Every now and then the guests were suddenly galvanized into life when somebody shouted '*Evviva gli sposi!*' This cry produced deafening applause which then trailed away. Somebody then shouted '*Evviva la padrona!*' and again the applause erupted, only this time they stood up to clap. My mother, confused as usual by the public expression of emotion, went over to congratulate the bride.

Afterwards, she sat next to the bride's brother; a very good-looking and intelligent young man who farmed in the hills above Compiobbi. She asked him whether, at that time of Communist Party calls for the expropriation of land, he would like to own the land he worked. 'Oh, no,' he laughed. 'Better a good *padrone* who pays the taxes.'

He went on to say that he was against the Republic, not because he particularly regretted the departure of the king following the referendum, but because he feared it had made the aristocracy start to desert their properties, with the result that Italian agriculture was going downhill fast. My mother was interested by all he said although, for a young man especially, she knew that such views were not representative.

*

The years just after the war were much worse for the old. They saw not only political uncertainty, even the threat of a Communist takeover, but a complete social transformation. In a largely peasant society, this would affect every aspect of life.

Many have said that the end of the *mezzadria*, the crop division between landowner and peasant that formed the basis of rural life in Tuscany, was brought about by remote communities being able to listen to the wireless. The argument has much more than a grain of truth, but there were many other elements.

The hill villages of the Lunigiana provided striking examples of occupations that, having existed almost since Roman times, suddenly ended in less than a decade. The introduction of electricity and gas in *bombole*, delivered by lorry along newly built roads, meant that by the mid-1950s hardly anybody used a charcoal *fornello* any more. Our old itinerant friends the charcoal burners, up at Lagastrello, began to disappear along with their mule-trains. And, within a decade, their traditional tracks became overgrown.

The surrounding villages in those valleys suffered for a different reason. A disease of chestnut trees, which broke out just after the war, greatly accelerated the migration of the population to Milan, Turin and any Tuscan city where there was work to be found. It was not just the radio: it was also the motor cycle that allowed people to commute. Sons in hill villages, whose fathers might have ventured as far as the market in Aulla once a week or month, could now go to work each day in a factory in La Spezia; a far more profitable occupation than working a *podere* or family smallholding.

The introduction of running water meant that the village *fontana* was no longer a centre for gossip. And soon the washing-machine would change community life out of all recognition. The *bucato* was a time-consuming and laborious task for every housewife. And however friendly and picturesque the sight of village women thigh-deep in the river, slapping the water with garments as they rinsed and joked together, only the staunchest of traditionalists would have refused a machine that did all this while she got on with other work.

First the sons and daughters left the countryside, often reacting against the traditional rights of landlords, even though they had been greatly diminished by the new legislation. Radio and cinema, and then television, served only to make village society appear unbearably restrictive and boring. Fewer and fewer young women wanted to marry farmers; they wanted *cittadini*, not *contadini*. The city was smart and exciting, while the lonely beauty of the mountains suddenly seemed intolerable. So, too, did the idea of sharing a house with brothers-in-law and their wives. The new generation wanted small flats of their own. It was not just the *padrone* they were escaping: they no longer wanted to be dictated to by that peasant patriarch, the *capoccia*.

Then the disheartened and often uncomprehending parents, struggling on alone for a few years, gave up and retired to apartments in nearby towns. By the mid-1950s, between a third and a half of Tuscan *mezzadri*, or tenant farmers, had departed for the city, abandoning their *poderi*. They left behind overgrown terraces, roofless houses and unpruned olive trees. Around Florence, the agricultural population halved in just ten years.

The longer-term future became clear in one respect. The system of the *mezzadria*, which had survived in Tuscany since the late thirteenth century (some have traced its origins back to the ninth century), was doomed in spite of all the reforms that had increased the peasant's share of the crop. It might be revived later in different circumstances in the future, but politically and socially the idea of the old system was anathema to the young. And yet the Communist slogan of '*La terra ai contadini!*' did not offer any sort of solution either, as the abandoned farmhouses all over Tuscany proved. Smallholdings were doomed in an industrial age. Even larger estates could survive only if they were reorganized with fresh investment and new machinery.

My mother exhausted her capital in the attempt to re-equip the farms, replant the vineyards and renew the livestock. Her only victory had been winning a court order forcing Senator Morelli's family to hand over two cows and a horse of similar quality to those that he had sold from Adamo's *podere* during the war. Since the post-war price for a cow had soared to nearly a quarter of a million lire, Morelli's heirs were aghast.

Lame, widowed and in her late seventies, my mother lacked the will to struggle on. The biggest blow of all, following John's death, had been the fresh round of death duties. Aunt Janet's attempt to control the succession of Poggio from the grave, by leaving it to John, had proved disastrous. In 1950 my mother put Poggio Gherardo, with its three small farms, on the market.

First of all, she called in the *fattore* and the three heads of family. She told them that enough money from the sale would be given to each family on the property to buy a house and some land. They all begged her not to sell, even that staunch Communist, Martelli. Dante Ramponi, who could not bear the idea of moving away, bought a little house down by the south gate, on the road to Ponte a

Mensola. Before moving, he took cuttings from the rose by the camphor tree for his new garden.

Once my mother had made up her mind to leave, she could not bear having anything more to do with the business. Freya Stark dropped by and persuaded my mother to sell her Lucie Duff Gordon's marquetry desk for £5. If it had not been for Vittorio and Maria, who hid furniture and paintings, then dispatched them on to Aulla without telling her, she might well have sold the lot, such was her mood.

Vittorio was left to handle almost everything except the conveyancing. He showed round all the prospective purchasers, who were mostly from religious orders. When nuns came one day, he remembered the nude painting of Aunt Janet only just in time and had to flatten himself against it and stand there until they had seen enough of the room. Then, in my bathroom, which had been the Gherardi chapel, he managed to divert their attention so they never looked up at the ceiling and saw over the bath the Spirito Santo painted in the form of a dove. They would have been deeply shocked at the idea of it looking down on naked bodies.

My mother, in deference to one of Aunt Janet's wishes, refused to split Poggio Gherardo from its farms. But she was completely taken in by a speculator. He had promised to keep the whole property together, but then promptly sold the villa on its own, with the *bosco* of ilexes and the north gate, to priests who turned it into an orphanage. The three farms he earmarked as plots for future development. He made a huge profit.

Friends, too, were distressed. 'How sad for me that you have left,' wrote B.B. shortly afterwards. 'It is almost as if my skyline towards Florence already has changed. I can't tell you how much I took it for granted that you would keep watch and guard there for ever.'

The move to Aulla was organized by Vittorio. He, Maria and Primina all made the return migration to Aulla together. The only Lunigianese at that time who decided to stay in Florence was Dante. Primina, however, did not stay long at Aulla. She soon began to miss Florence and her Oreste. Everyone was very fond of her, but she had a childlike waywardness, even more so than her aunt, Adelina, and refused to take anything seriously. Maria once, when she was very busy, sent Primina to help my mother who, because of her broken hip, could not dress herself. Primina had never encountered shoes that buttoned up before, and her efforts with the button hook, both cavalier and clumsy, reduced my mother to tears of pain and exasperation.

The castle had been fully restored from its wartime dilapidation. In the autumn of 1948, new doors and windows had been made, the roof relaid and the tower repaired. The quality of the work was excellent. My mother felt deeply moved that the workmen from Aulla and its surrounding valleys took such a pride in their tasks because they felt that the *fortezza* was an important symbol and a part of the Lunigiana. She laid on a celebration banquet to mark the end of the work, and there were many stirring and emotional speeches made in the best Italian fashion.

Caring for my mother – she was by then seventy-eight and a large woman – proved even more difficult than envisaged. She had become very heavy to lift, and to get her out of the castle Vittorio and Andreino, the *contadino* who took over when Ramponi retired, had to carry her through the court-yard and along the *galleria* in an improvised sedan chair

The Fortezza della Brunella after the war

made from a high-backed carver, with poles lashed to the arms.

Life at the castle without her husband proved too lonely for her. She decided she would like to return to England to be near her family. Maria and Vittorio were to have come back with her but they had to stay in Aulla to help relations. We therefore bought a house with a large garden in East Kent. My mother was happy there, writing her autobiography. But she never quite became accustomed to the reality of English life after the war. She was a true Edwardian: a product of her age and upbringing. Like many of her contemporaries, her vision could be breathtakingly selective. The Nelsonian blind eye had changed in the course of a century. It was no longer a subterfuge for initiative, but a device to preserve oneself from painful facts. On one occasion, she complained that I did not spend much time with her. She held that convenient delusion so popular amongst men, that mundane tasks like cooking and cleaning, because they were out of sight, were somehow done by remote control. I explained that I had rather a lot to do in the house as well as look after three sons. 'But *where* are the servants?' she demanded with all the dignified unworldliness of a Spanish hidalgo.

Shortly before she died, however, she discarded the emotional armour of a lifetime and apologized for having been such a neglectful mother. I was taken aback because it was so unexpected. Apologies had never come easily to her Scottish pride. She had been like Aunt Janet in so many ways, yet nothing would ever have induced her to admit it. I could not help reflecting on the sad paradox that Aunt Janet, the mother who had rejected her own offspring, had been much the better mother to me.

★

The castle now belonged to my brother, Gordon. But he, with his work at the BBC, as head of the Arabic service, and as a biographer, could not possibly live there. The only way to keep the place going was to rent it to friends, and we would go out each year. Vittorio and Maria agreed to stay on, for they too loved the castle.

As with the paying guests at Poggio, word went around quickly. Families and groups of friends would rent it for a fortnight at a time. Some came for the peace of the roof-garden with its views, others strode across the mountain landscape in the tradition of Robert Trevelyan, though without necessarily stripping off at every pool and stream. Those with children found it conveniently close to the sea, whether the white beaches of the Versilia, the rocky bays round Lerici or the precipitous coast of the Cinqueterre, north of Portovenere. But for everybody, one of the great attractions was Maria's cooking, set off to perfection by the castle's wine.

John Sparrow, the Warden of All Souls, would bring reading parties from Oxford. Vittorio, who had a profound reverence for learning, was intrigued to know what books these great intellectuals had brought with them to read. So one day, on the roof-garden after lunch, he discreetly peered over their shoulders as he served them coffee. He returned to the kitchen, his illusions shattered. 'Just imagine,' he told Maria. 'They were all reading Agatha Christie.'

One such holiday was interrupted in dramatic fashion, when an old peasant who had a smallholding below the castle decided to burn the straw from his rabbit hutches in the middle of an August drought. The flames caught the brushwood and raced up the side of the hill. Maria, in the kitchen on the other side of the castle, had no idea what was happening until the telephone rang. It was a *carabiniere* down in the town. He asked whether she was aware that the castle was on fire. Her alarm can be imagined. But worst of all, she thought that Vittorio was up at Podenzana.

Vittorio had, in fact, returned in the nick of time. Without wasting a moment he armed Sparrow's undergraduates with staves to beat at the flames, and led the attack with a garden hose. Rushing on ahead of his troops, he disappeared into the smoke and flames like a Napoleonic hero. The under-graduates, concerned for his safety, began calling 'Vittorio! Vittorio!' Finally, he emerged, blackened but triumphant. The castle's walls were only singed.

Every year I took the boys out to Aulla. It was a curious reversal of going home to my own childhood. Their favourite place nearby was Gli Scafari, where Percy Lubbock still lived.

I would drive the whale-shaped Humber Hawk down the valley, following the stony river-bed of the Magra. We would pass favourite landmarks: the ruin of a Roman bridge, then the hill village of Caprigliola whose castle, with its central tower, gave it the profile of an ocean liner. After Sarzana, excitement would increase in the back of the car as we mounted the steep wooded hills behind Lerici. Suddenly, at a corner we knew well – just after the summit – the whole Gulf of La Spezia lay below us, with towns and islands and ships and Portovenere on the far side, hazy in the distance.

Further down the hill we branched left, away from Lerici and towards Tellaro. The little road twisted along the hillside between olive groves and stone walls cut from volcanic rock. From time to time there would be a tantalizing glimpse down through the umbrella pines to the rocks and the glistening sea.

Released from the oven of the car, I always wanted to pause a moment – to breathe in the sea breeze and the smell of the pines and listen to the sound of the waves on the rocks below. But the children were always impatient. First of all, I reminded them, we had to greet our host.

Percy had been something of a martyr to Sybil's egotism. His sight, which had by now failed entirely, was partly ruined by his wife's hatred of electric lights in their room and her asking him to read to her at night by candlelight. Thick, enormous spectacles made him look increasingly like a wise old owl.

We would find him sitting slumped in a wicker chair in the loggia, his Buddha-like belly protruding through his shirt, listening to one of his young guests reading aloud. Reading to him was no penance. Everyone who did it enjoyed both his huge knowledge of literature and his lugubrious wit.

I would stop and chat to him for a moment after the children had bowed to him as instructed. Shaking hands with each of them would have been a bore for him. They then rushed down the stone steps that led to the rocky bay and grotto. Often Iris's two daughters, Benedetta and Donata, who were the same ages as Nigel and Hugh, were already there, playing in dinghies or Sybil's old canoe, or diving from the board that stuck out over deep water. Happy screams and splashes ascended from below. Around half past four, shivering children wrapped in scratchy towel robes, their hair rubbed by Nanny, would run back up the steps for the famous Scafari refreshment: large jugs of iced tea with freshly sliced peaches accompanied by home-made almond biscuits.

On Iris's birthday there would be a treasure hunt, followed

by a picnic tea. We did the treasure hunt in bathing dresses, because there was much rushing up and down the rock steps to the sea. One year I did it with Antony, then aged four and on crutches from Perthes' disease, clinging to my back. The last clue was in a bottle attached to a buoy in the middle of the bay and, in the excitement, I dived in with him still on my back. We nearly drowned.

While we were at the castle, old friends sometimes used to come over from Florence, from Forte dei Marmi or, closer still, from Lerici if they were staying with Percy and Iris.

Pio and Elena Corsini once brought Pietro Annigoni, who had his studio in one of their houses in Florence. Dinner was served outside on the terrace under the vine-covered pergola facing the Carraras. But Annigoni, instead of admiring the view, nearly caused another conflagration by teaching my sons to fire blazing matches from their toy cannons.

B.B. also came with Nicky Mariano. They arrived in time to see the sunset on the Carraras from the roof-garden. The mountains were at their best and, since it was another fine night, we went down to have dinner on the terrace outside the *portone*. Towards the end of dinner, B.B. suddenly noticed that there was a new moon that night. He immediately rose to bow to it in oriental fashion but, to his consternation, found that he could not implement his other superstition: turning money over in the pocket. He quickly had to be lent some change, and all was well.

It was one of the last times I saw him. In 1959, following an invitation from Nicky, I took Nigel, my eldest son, to stay at I Tatti. We had been driving around Tuscany, visiting hill towns, so when we arrived at I Tatti as arranged, it was a shock to find the place besieged by television crews. Nicky had been ringing friends in an attempt to track us down and warn us of B.B.'s death. There was obviously no question of staying at such a moment, but Nicky asked us to come back in a few days' time when the journalists and camera crews had left.

The strain on Nicky during that time of loss and turmoil was terrible, but she greeted us again when we returned with all her old affection. She had invited one or two friends from the past to dinner, including Luigino Franchetti, Yvonne Hamilton's first husband. Luigino was perfect. He made Nicky laugh with tales of his visit to hospital for an operation. The nuns had tried to take some of the bunches of flowers he had received from friends to decorate their shrine to the Madonna. 'But I am the one who is ill!' Luigino had shrieked. 'Not the Madonna!'

After dinner we moved to the music room. Nicky sat in her usual place by the fire. In its light she looked like a Rembrandt portrait, with a pale chiffon scarf draped round her shoulders. 'You know, Nicky,' I suddenly said, 'I've known you since I was a child, but I have never known how it was that you came to I Tatti.'

'Well, Kinta,' she said with a far-away smile, 'it was like this.' And for two hours we sat without moving as she told us of her Baltic childhood, and the curious turns of fate that had brought her to this house.

I was so captivated by the spell of her story that next morning, when she came to my room after breakfast, I told her that she must write down everything as she had told it the night before. 'Well, I don't know,' she said. 'There are many indiscretions.'

I replied that anyone who had the understanding and compassion that she possessed could not write anything hurtful. But alas, when she did write the book, it was both discreet and factual, and lacked the magic of her story by the fire.

During these years of the Italian economic miracle – the construction of the Autostrada del Sole truly marked the end of the post-war period – I watched Aulla grow and change. From the sleepy little market town that my parents had known at the beginning of the century, it started to develop: first with a flour mill, then a jute factory, and soon (fortunately out of sight on the road to Pontremoli) some light engineering.

The natural talents of the Lunigianesi were never in doubt. And as soon as education became widely available, parents made sure that their children seized the opportunities that had been denied to them. I remember Ramponi's wife, Antonietta, rebinding her children's school-books in strong brown paper to preserve them better. The parents had to buy these school-books and, with true Tuscan thrift, they saw to it that their children made good use of them. Each day the father would ask what they had learned, and he would treat their education with great pride. In a single generation, the sons of peasants became bank managers and experts in electronics. But a son seldom spurned his background. In Tuscany the *cittadino* took a pride in his *contadino* roots. Come the *vendemmia*, he would turn up in his smart company car, take off his suit, make a face when his mother said he was not feeding himself properly, and laugh when brothers and cousins joked that he had become flabby behind his grand desk.

The *vendemmia* at Aulla always remained very much a family affair. Vittorio would be joined by his brother Dario, and Dario's wife Rina, a daughter of Ramponi. Rina's sister

Lina also came with her husband Enrico, a grandson of Montàn, Ramponi's predecessor. Maria's stalwart cousin, Anamaria, and her good-looking husband, Luigi, always lent a hand; in later years they took over the castle farm entirely.

We all gathered outside the house of the *contadino* by the drawbridge with boxes and secateurs. I would wear my kerchief, like the other women, against earwigs in the overhead vines. Then we would troop out to the terraced vineyards on the Aulella side of the castle hill and begin to work our way along the rows. The men – including any of my sons, or Gordon's son Michael, or Johnnie's son Garrow – would carry the full boxes up the hill – sweating profusely – and round over the drawbridge, through the *galleria* from the corner tower, and down into the *cantina* from the courtyard. The *cantina* was so cold after the sunshine outside that their sweat chilled them and they hurried back.

In the *cantina* Vittorio would be standing over the vat with the grape-crusher, the *follatoio*, and when the bunches of grapes were tipped into the wide funnel above, he would crank the handle round and round as if it were a barrel-organ.

Every *vendemmia* that I remember (and photographs support the memory) took place on a day of bright sunshine, with an autumnal clarity to the view across the valleys to the mountains beyond. The vine leaves formed irregular patterns of green and yellow, and the pools of the Aulella river below were a deep, silent green. Behind us the tall, straight umbrella pines from Elba along the drive, and the crooked Aleppo pines on the little hill called the Cucuzzolo, formed a background to the rough amphitheatre of the vineyard.

During the afternoons, while we hurried our work to finish the last few rows, the children would build a large fire in the house of the *contadino*. At dusk, when the heart of the fire was very hot, hollow terracotta discs known as *testi* were pushed in to heat. When all was finished, and we had gathered together in the firelight to eat and drink, the terracotta discs were put to work. First, one was pulled from the fire with tongs and filled with a mixture of dough, the sort to make unleavened bread. Then another was taken out and stacked on top of the first. It, in turn, was filled with dough, then covered with another terracotta disk, and so on. As the discs cooled, they cooked their contents, and this made *focaccette* – *fugacine* or *fugacette* in Aullese.

Once, a little girl proudly brought round the hot *focaccette*. She was very pleased with her new dress and a great chatterer. I was reminded of a peasant woman's remark to Aunt Janet when she had admired the dress and singing voice of the woman's daughter: '*Sì, signora, ma è come il cuculo, tutto voce e penne*' – 'She is like the cuckoo, all voice and feathers.'

To go with the *focaccette*, Dario and Rina, who had the best provision store in Aulla, provided every imaginable form of salami as well as *coppa* and *prosciutto di Parma*, and delicious cheeses such as a particularly good *stracchino*, which was perfect combined with the *coppa* or ham.

Yet, as at Poggio, the main point of the evening was wine rather than food. Everybody had brought the best wine from their own *cantina*, which was tasted in turn and praised in sound, rather than extravagant terms. The home-made produce of the Lunigiana was a natural wine, which did not travel. Great was the disappointment whenever one tried to bring a bottle home to prolong the memory.

The pleasure of that sort of honest, simple and completely untrafficked wine was to drink it *in situ* under your own vine and your own fig tree. It was not a wine that was *sofisticato* in either sense of the term. You knew it was clean because you could drink it in great quantities and never have a bad head the following morning. Yet, for a Tuscan, such consumption rarely happened outside a celebration. Wine was made to be drunk as an accompaniment to food.

As we sat round the fire after eating, I remembered Ramponi coming to my father all those years ago to ask for more wine, and his explanation that if one has only polenta to eat, one needs something to wash it down. Curiously, I had been reminded of the scene recently in Kent. We had lent a young Italian worker a spare room at the lodge in return for some gardening at the weekends. One evening I sensed he was homesick, and since a bottle of red Burgundy was already open, I gave him some to have with his meal. Afterwards I asked him what he thought of it. His head moved from side to side to indicate mixed feelings. It was undoubtedly a very fine wine, he said. '*Ma non pulisce la bocca*' – 'But it doesn't clean the mouth.'

The day after our celebration I went down to the *cantina* with Luigi. He listened to the must bubbling with satisfaction. '*Eh, canta bene,*' he said – it's singing nicely. It would be many more weeks before he and Vittorio would have their first taste to check that all had gone well. That came when the wine was ready for transfer to demijohns. They would be topped up with wine from which any impurities had been filtered, and then an airtight seal would be made, not with a cork, but olive oil. When it was time to decant the wine later, the olive oil would be cleaned off with tow and the neck of the container carefully wiped. Then, at last, the raffia-covered *fiaschi* could be filled, and the black wine, vermilion at the edges, could be examined and drunk.

★

Eventually the day came when Vittorio and Maria announced that they wanted to retire and build a house for their old age. It was unthinkable that the castle could continue without them. Gordon put the whole property on the market with the exception of a good-sized plot of land, which was within easy walking distance of the town and had a view of the Carraras. Here Vittorio and Maria could build their house. When they came to build it, Vittorio's eye proved faultless. His masterpiece of design was a fireplace in *pietra serena* of perfect proportions.

The sale of the castle proved a nightmare of Italian bureaucracy. Gordon started by offering it to the *commune* of Aulla at well below the asking price, but the *commune* refused. He repeated the offer later, but again it was turned down. After numerous false starts – the whole process extended over a number of years – a firm bid was eventually made by a private buyer and accepted. The buyer was warned that as the Fortezza della Brunella was an ancient monument, the Italian government could step in at any stage within sixty days of the exchange of contracts and buy the property for itself at the same price. When the sixty days had expired, both parties prepared to go ahead with the final details. But on the sixty-first day, when the buyer had the right to become the legal owner, a dispatch-rider arrived all the way from Rome with a compulsory purchase order. Gordon knew all too well that if he stood by the sale to the private buyer he would be involved in a legal tussle with the government that would last at least ten years and would ruin him. He therefore had no choice but to offer to compensate the buyer with a substantial sum, and allow the government to have its way.

Vittorio was so angry at the way the bureaucracy in Rome

had behaved that he was determined not to leave a thing behind. The compulsory purchase order specified only the fabric of the castle itself, but there was very little time left before the government became the legal owner. He organized storage and ordered a pantechnicon, but the day it arrived snow fell in enough quantity to make the carriage-drive inaccessible to a large, heavy vehicle. In the end, with only twenty-four hours to go, he organized a team of helpers from the town with a small van to act as a shuttle running up and down, filling the pantechnicon parked below. Vittorio took out everything that could be moved, even Fiore's little terra-cotta plaque with the quotation from Horace, which he had shyly presented on completing the stone balustrade below the dining-room.

It was like a retreat before an invading army. But his efforts were not wasted. If anything had been left behind, as had originally been planned, it would have been destroyed over the next few years. The bureaucratic nightmare exceeded even Vittorio's worst suspicions. The government department of fine arts, the Belle Arti, began a programme of restoration on the castle. The Fortezza della Brunella was defined as a fifteenth-century building. Anything that was not therefore of that date had to go. When word got out that they intended to remove the garden on the roof, there were sufficient protests in the town to delay the project. But nothing stopped the complete reshaping of the corner towers, reducing and rounding their parapets so that the castle became totally unrecognizable from what my father had first seen and fallen in love with. Next, they removed the terracotta-tiled roof over the living quarters on the grounds that this was not of the period. But as soon as the roof had been removed, the section of the Belle Arti in charge of the project discovered that it had spent all its budget. The castle was then left without a roof for two years.

After every storm Anamaria would rush in and work, often into the early hours, swabbing the flood water out to prevent the collapse of a ceiling. The staircase began to sag and crack and had to be shored up with scaffolding. Finally, the Belle Arti found enough money to cover the living quarters again, but this time with a roof of imitation slate tiles made of asbestos. Local conservationists struggled valiantly on the castle's behalf, writing letters of outrage to the ministry and to the newspapers in their attempts to rectify the disaster, but the '*burosauri*' could not admit to having made a mistake.

Maria was so dejected by what had happened that she could not face going up the hill again to her old home. In any case, she had far more immediate worries. Almost as soon as they moved down to their new house Vittorio had fallen desperately ill with cancer. I went out to help Maria, who was having to spend every available moment at the hospital. Before returning to England, I went to say goodbye to Vittorio. His most urgent request was that I should buy the surgeon, who had become a close friend, some China tea from Fortnum & Mason. As soon as I reached London, I went straight there and was wondering about the quickest way to send the tea out, when the customer next to me spoke to his companion in Italian. He came from La Spezia, and promised to deliver the tea within the next two days. Vittorio was able to hand over the present himself.

He died the following day. It seemed so unjust. He had had no time to enjoy his retirement and the hard work he had put into the house. I rang Maria as soon as I heard the news, and we decided that as Gordon was flying out for the funeral, it would be better if I followed soon afterwards to be with her.

Gordon and I put an announcement of Vittorio's death in *The Times,* and she received many letters from England paying homage to her husband's qualities from those who had stayed at Aulla and known them both.

One could not have blamed Maria if she had complained bitterly against the cruelty of fate, but she never did. 'Signora,' she once said to me many years later, 'you know, I go to Aulla for mass. I see others afterwards. We have a talk and I hear of their difficulties and I realize how light my cross is in comparison.'

CHAPTER FOURTEEN

Returning to the Castle

'There it is!' we both exclaimed. The car had just rounded a curve in the road that followed the river Magra up its valley. I had been anticipating that first, far-off glimpse with the same excitement as I had in my childhood seventy years before. The castle stood on its spur in the distance with the wooded hills still sloping in on each side like scenery in a toy theatre.

This time we were going up not to the castle itself, but to Maria's house built below. Maria's house backs on to the steep hill where outcrops of volcanic rock are now well concealed by the wood of ilex trees, cypresses and those umbrella pines from Elba that my father planted before the First World War. It was strange to think that I had known Maria since she was a girl. And that I could remember the day her husband, Vittorio Chiodetti, came to us in 1928, aged only thirteen, to deliver that extra loaf of bread.

Maria still lives in the house they built below the castle for their retirement. In the fifteen years since Vittorio's death, she has kept busy to survive the sorrow she never displayed to the world. Her working dress has not changed: a kerchief tied in a turban just above her pearl earrings, a blouse, cardigan, skirt, apron, socks and slippers. Her voice quavers and her hands shake a little more, but she is still the same perfectionist.

Not long before the castle was sold, when a friend of Hugh arrived at midnight having missed a train, I was horrified to find Maria bustling off to prepare a bed. 'But when the boys are here with all their friends, Maria, wouldn't it be easier to make up the beds in advance, just in case?'

'*Ma, signora!*' she said, offended at such a suggestion. '*Se faccio così il profumo del bucato sarà sparito!*' – 'If I did such a thing the scent of the wash would have disappeared.' After that, every time I smelt fresh linen when I climbed into bed, I always thought of the *profumo* which had not disappeared.

To enter Maria's house is, in many ways, like returning to the castle before it was bought by the government. She and Vittorio had saved so much of the contents during the dispersal that familiar objects from the past meet every glance: bookcases, brass bedsteads, tables, my mother's desk, cast-iron garden chairs, terracotta pots filled with hydrangeas, irises transplanted from the sentry's walk on the castle roof, even that blue enamel teapot in which my father used to make tea in his studio. This inanimate equivalent of Noah's Ark owed its survival in part to Tuscan thriftiness; a deep-rooted dislike of throwing anything away that might once again come in useful. But it also demonstrated a tenacious affection for the life that they had known there.

Tuscans are able to look back in a far more clear-sighted way than most people. They are fortunate to be free of collective complexes and, above all, of that arrogance which hides shame. They do not romanticize what has gone before, nor do they feel a need to close shutters upon it. The past is part of them and they are part of it.

Family, of course, provides the centre of loyalty. Maria's sister-in-law, Rina, lives in the basement of the house, which has been turned into a separate flat. The two widows help and support each other and work together tending Maria's beautiful garden. She has taken on Vittorio's love of plants, which developed as soon as he began to look after the roof-garden at the castle.

The evening we returned she had prepared for us a *zuppa di verdura*, followed by *scaloppine alla milanese* because they had always been Antony's favourite. A male child, however far on from childhood, is still shamelessly indulged. The wine poured from a large old *fiasco* was the castle wine, as Maria emphasized, still made by Luigi and her cousin Anamaria who continue to tend the vines. It was just as pure as in the old days. While we were cutting up the juicy pears from her garden, and selecting figs from the trayful brought by a friend, the television, that new focus of Italian life, was turned on for the news. '*Povera gente*,' said Maria shaking her head in real sympathy when the screen showed the survivors of an earthquake. Cynicism surfaced only during a subsequent item, when a government minister was deferentially asked for his opinion on the latest anti-Mafia measures. When it was over, she asked us again about our plans. Talk and revisit old haunts, we said.

As we expected, Maria would not accompany us when we went up the hill to the castle next day. The disastrous changes, and above all the ruination of Vittorio's beloved roof-garden, still made her too sad. Luigi and Anamaria, who live in Ramponi's house by the drawbridge, welcomed us. In celebration, they brought out a bottle of their delicious sparkling red wine made from black grapes dried for twenty days.

We sat in garden chairs on the brick apron where Ramponi's family used to dry the maize and we gazed balefully across the moat. Some of the repointing was garish. All those years ago, when my father first repaired the walls, Bagòn had mixed soot from the kitchen chimney in with the mortar for Ulisse. Worst of all were the rounded-down towers. They gave the castle a hunched look. The place was no longer enchanted. It had been released from its spell, but now it was dead, finished off by the modern notion of kill to save. It had been robbed of its individuality. Even its moment of death had been chosen arbitrarily by bureaucratic decision and now it was being embalmed accordingly. This new theory that an old building should be fixed in time made me furious.

Antony regarded the shrunken corner tower caged in scaffolding. 'It looks so sad,' he remarked. 'Almost like King Kong.'

'Do you want to see what they've done now?' said Anamaria eventually, jerking her head to indicate the roof.

'Yes,' I said, feeling that after everything that had already been changed – the shape of the towers, the new roof in fake slate tiles over the living quarters – nothing could shock me now.

Anamaria made a face. 'You know what they've done to the garden on the roof?'

'Yes, Maria has told us.'

She fetched the keys and we crossed the drawbridge. This time I glanced down not at that wild undergrowth believed by the Aullesi of old to be the haunt of huge serpents but on to a flat, grassed surface. We entered the corner tower, then went down the long whitewashed *galleria* to the L-shaped courtyard, which still smelt reassuringly of damp stone.

So far, little had changed from my previous visit. But when we reached the roof, word of mouth proved to be no warning for the sight that met my eyes. It was far worse than unrecognizable. The grass was gone, the borders and the vines, while some of the ilex trees in the avenue were reduced to stumps. All the earth brought up by the Spaniards to absorb the recoil of their cannons, to say nothing of the soil swung aloft by my father, Ulisse and Bagòn at the beginning of the century, had been removed. The marble side of the sunken *vasca* at the end of what had been the grass walk stood exposed, and in between lay what looked like the hole of almost any building site before foundations are laid. If this was an archaeological dig – as it was supposed to have been – then all it had revealed was a series of arches under the rampart. I nearly cried at the scene of desolation. It seemed such a pointless exercise for what it must have cost, yet I still hoped that it had been of some use to somebody, if only to mitigate the waste.

Anamaria tried to reassure us. She told us that the new director was different. There was hope. It was hard to see what she meant when confronted with this vision, but we saw him the next day and liked him immediately. He was not one of the '*burosauri*'. He admitted straight away that great errors of judgement had been made in the restoration programme, especially in the early days, and told us that the worst excesses would soon be rectified. A budget of six billion lire had now been agreed. The protests about the destruction of the roof-garden and the opinion of experts that it was a unique creation had finally convinced them.

With commendable frankness he admitted that this new phase could not bring back the old shape of the towers, but the roof-garden would be restored faithfully. It was not so much what he promised or did not promise that gave me hope, but the change in attitude. The efforts made by all those friends of the castle – local schoolmasters and librarians protesting to Rome and writing to newspapers; the Herculean work of Anamaria swabbing out after the roof had been removed – had not been wasted after all.

A couple of days later we drove to Pomarino with Rina as our guide. We could take the car right up to the little village in its hidden valley, because since the 1950s there has been a bridge across the Aulella and a road to Pomarino, which is surfaced for a good part of the way.

Rina again told us the story of Jack's appearance in his Jeep in 1945 and about the celebration with the English coffee that stopped them all from sleeping that night. Antony wondered exactly where it was that Ramponi had been making copper sulphate with bits from the crashed American bomber at the moment of Jack's arrival, but nobody was sure. The terraced vines that had later been sprayed with the mixture stood clearly in view on the slope just outside the village. It was going to be a terrible year, someone said, nodding gloomily in their direction. There had been a late frost.

Another place I wanted to see again was Equi, up at the start of the Garfagnana and just under the main peaks of the Carraras. We took swimming things so we could bathe in the sulphur baths. The drive was easy. In the old days the train did not go further than Monzone and we would get out and walk through the chestnut woods to Equi. My father would carry his painting equipment. After our picnic, while we roamed in the woods or explored mountain streams splashing over marble boulders, he would set up his easel to record one or other of the nearby villages in their dramatic scenery of tree-crowned gorges. And soon another fresco would fill one of the lunettes in the castle.

On other occasions we took bicycles up in the train, then pedalled back down the valleys to Aulla in the evening light. We also used to explore the prehistoric cave just outside Equi. The pool of mountain water inside was immobile except for the outward ripples from drips of water falling from a stalactite. I once asked a villager who was passing the cave if anybody had ever swum in any of the cold water pools nearby. 'Only one person,' he answered with a faint smile. 'An Englishman, of course, and he never surfaced.'

'What do you mean?'

'It was a very hot day and he took off his clothes and went straight in. He never imagined how cold the water could be.' He patted his chest. 'It was too much of a shock to the heart.' The teller of the tale could not conceal a slight sense of poetic justice. Robert Trevelyan was not the only Englishman famous in the Lunigiana for stripping off and diving into inviting pools of water.

We intended to return to Aulla, but first there were other places and friends to visit. We drove south to Forte dei Marmi on the *autostrada*, down along the river Magra, leaving La Spezia and Lerici and Bocca di Magra on the far side, then along the coastal plain of the Versilia under the Carraras. We passed the depots where the huge blocks of Carrara stone are still cut. They look as if they are destined for some magnificent Ozymandias-like monument. But today they are no longer carried on sturdy flat carts drawn by teams of up to twenty oxen. A crane and a heavy-duty lorry suffice.

We crossed over little rivers, milky with marble dust, and soon found the band of coastal *pinete*, the remains of that forest of umbrella pines that had once stretched from Sarzana to the other side of Pisa. At the end of the Second World War it was said to have sheltered a thousand deserters from the different armies fighting in the region.

Forte itself has, of course, changed out of all recognition from the days of La Madonnina and *patino* parties with Aldous Huxley. We went to see Anna Corsini, the sister of Pio, who still keeps the family villa as a base for nieces and great-nephews and great-nieces and all their children. They come for the day, for the week or for the month. She is the same age as I am but she continues to swim miles out to sea twice a day. An unselfconscious longevity seems to radiate out around her. Her cook, for example, is eighty-two. Only the dogs are young, but their generations turn over too rapidly to remember exactly, even though they have always been very much part of the family.

Anna still takes charitable responsibilities very seriously. But that does not mean that she takes herself in the same way. She is amusingly philosophical about the whole business. She described how applicants for charity used to buy and sell the names and addresses of benefactors in a sort of backstreet stock exchange. Even into her eighties, she thinks nothing of going off early to the market to find the right size jeans in answer to an urgent request from one of her protégés about to be released from prison.

In spite of all the changes to Forte dei Marmi – the smart shops in the centre of town, and the wide road between the sea front and the *pineta* – there was enough left to trigger memories of a more recent past: the smell of the sea and the pine trees, the sun, the gentle wind and the fine sand. The family chaos of the bathing cabin was exactly the same. One could hear ice-cream sellers who trudged along the beach with their heavy containers slung over one shoulder crying *'Gelati! Gelati!'* The sand burned the soles of our feet as we hurried to the water's edge. It reminded me of that great paradox of modern Italian life. No self-respecting peasant today will wear *zoccoli* any more; instead they have become a vital accessory for the seaside.

After our swim from a *patino*, a picnic lunch arrived from the house and we ate off salt-stained wooden surfboards in the shade of a canvas awning, which flapped in the midday breeze. Several old friends from pre-war days were there and we swapped memories of the via Tornabuoni and of people and parties in the late 1920s and early 1930s.

Our sentimental journey soon followed the same direction. We went on to Florence, and up to Poggio Gherardo. The old house, re-rendered in cement, has entirely lost that golden-apricot glow. The bleak hygiene of a modern ecclesiastical institution has taken over entirely. I am sure that the mural of the Gherardi's poodle is buried under further layers of whitewash. Even glancing up at the bell tower, which had tolled the news of Aunt Janet's death to my mother walking in the vineyards, I found it impossible to conjure up sensations of the past. We had only just passed a marble tablet in Ponte a Mensola commemorating famous foreigners of Boccaccio's parish – 'Janet Ross, John Addington Symonds, Mark Twain, Bernardo Berenson' – but Aunt Janet's ghost must have stalked away in disgust from the sight of her old home. We would perhaps find it later, on a visit to the Duomo, in front of Sir John Hawkwood's fresco.

Antony and I went back down the hill to see Dante and Modesta Ramponi in their little house by the south gate. Inside the gate, all has changed. Adamo's *podere*, where I used to play with Adelcisa, is now covered with luxury villas, their gardens defended by guard dogs.

With Dante and Modesta we talked of everyone and everything. We asked him for his memories of making the vermouth to the old Medici recipe. Then we talked of Carlo and Adelcisa, who moved to London after the war. Adelcisa's skill with her fingers, which she had displayed as a child making dolls, had led to her becoming the chief fitter in the women's department at Harrods. Carlo, until his retirement, was for many years the chef for the directors of an American bank in London. Their son Francesco runs an electronics company. We heard news of Primina and in turn told them how we had been back to Pomarino with Rina, Dante's half-sister.

Outside, he proudly showed us the enormous rose bush grown from the cuttings he had brought down the hill in 1952 when my mother sold Poggio Gherardo.

In Florence, we wandered down the via Tornabuoni, past Procacci, which still makes its delicious little sandwiches, and Parenti, where the best wedding presents come from. But most of the shops, such as Gucci and Ferragamo, even if Florentine in origin, are now glaringly international.

It was curious how first craftsmen in leatherwork, then their grand successors in fashion dynasties took over the ground floors of ancient palaces. Above the principal entrance, you can often still see the old coat of arms in corroded stone, and sometimes a heraldic lion whose sad, irritated expression seems to suggest he is suffering more from toothache than the responsibility of symbolizing noble lineage. Today the wheel has turned a little further, taking it full circle: international banks have taken over the palaces of families whose fortunes had been founded in the late Middle Ages on international banking.

Florentines, although always beautifully dressed, have succumbed a little to that creed of the last decade: luxury for its own sake. Over the last two hundred years, Tuscan parsimony meant that even in the grandest houses show was both distrusted and disliked. Simple food, although excellent because of the quality of the ingredients, was *de rigueur*. At lunch, guests were offered wine out of politeness, but the family usually drank only water. Only recently have conspicuously lavish parties become more fashionable. Yet if one judges by the responses to the great flood of November 1966, the most ancient Florentine qualities seem to have suffered little. One heard of lawyers, civil servants, dentists – even an admiral – working alongside students and artisans as everyone rose to that disastrous occasion. And the emergency restoration work proved that if you scratch a Florentine you will find a craftsman.

We returned to Aulla, to Maria's house. We asked Maria and Rina if they would like to come up with us in the car to Lagastrello. The idea greatly appealed to them, and they prepared a copious picnic with *frittate* and cold *scaloppini alla milanesi* and a *fiasco* of castle wine. On the way we would get a good view of the castle at Monti, where the present generation of Malaspinas now live, then we would go up to see Fiore's son Amadeo in the hills above Licciana.

Maria found Amadeo's little house in a steep street at the back of the village. Amadeo, who is in his eighties, has a wonderfully wrinkled face and a smile like his father's. He asked for news of friends in Aulla, and over coffee in his little kitchen he told us about his father's adventures in America in the first years of the century. But soon the talk turned to mushrooms, which had, of course, been Fiore's greatest area of expertise after his skill as a stonemason.

Contadini despair at the way townspeople come out to collect wild *funghi* in plastic bags. The funghi start to rot very quickly inside and, unlike baskets, plastic bags prevent the spore from spreading as the search continues. '*Che sono ignoranti!*' seems to be the most devastating comment anyone can make in the countryside.

Today, in most areas of Tuscany, one is not allowed to pick more than two kilos of mushrooms per person. But the owners of private land, reserved by special licence, can pick as much as they want. When there is a dry autumn, the pickings will be very meagre. But very occasionally, when the conditions are perfect, the harvest can be prodigious. Not long ago a friend of mine with three other people collected over one-and-a-half quintals – 150 kilos – between ten-thirty and twelve one morning, and then selecting only the best specimens.

After Amadeo had shown us the room for drying chestnuts and, overriding all our protests, presented us with a generously large basket of figs, he waved goodbye from the arch on to the street.

It was strange to drive to Comano and up to the Lagastrello Pass in under an hour – a journey that used to take us a whole day by horse-drawn buggy and then, on foot, acompanying the pack-mules of the charcoal burners.

The disappearance of charcoal burning up here had produced one strange effect. The unrestricted growth of shrubs and beech trees that followed had so changed the landscape and the view that I could not find the *campo inglese* where I had spent almost every summer of my childhood and youth. It may seem paradoxical to be upset by something as beneficial as the growth of vegetation, but I felt more disorientated by this than by many of the changes wrought by urban sprawl.

Once this curious sense of shock had abated, I settled down to enjoy the picnic with Antony, Rina and Maria. We ate and drank in silence in a clearing, listening to the breeze rustling the leaves above. To my joy, we also heard the hollow tinkle of sheep bells in the distance. For a moment, I half expected Parise to come galloping up on one of the racehorses 'borrowed' from a lower pasture.

I then began to think of Yetta Demchenko again, roaming these mountainsides as a child. I had last seen her in 1952 when taking the three boys home to England in the Humber Hawk. By then well-known as a racing driver, Yetta had persuaded me as a joke to take part in a car gymkhana organized to launch the new brand of Italian petrol – AGIP. It took place outside Merano in the Alps near the Swiss border, and we stayed in a nearby village. In the middle of the night we were woken up by what sounded like pistol shots. Alone with the children, I was terrified. Next morning, I asked downstairs what the disturbance had been. It turned out to have been an eve-of-wedding party, during which the local custom dictated that the bridegroom's friends should crack the linen sheets, made by the bride for her trousseau, to check that they had been properly woven. Despite my whale-shaped car I astonished everybody, Yetta above all, by coming second in the gymkhana. The prize, needless to say, was petrol coupons.

After completing the picnic with a little siesta in the shade of the beech trees, we gathered ourselves up and drove along the lake that Yetta's father had stocked with trout. Then we descended into the Taverone valley along a twisting road, which followed the bounding torrent: more or less the route that the *guardafili* had taken when carrying my father, stricken with rheumatic fever, down on a litter. That agonizing descent was hard to imagine during such a beautiful drive, with the leaves of the chestnut trees turning yellow.

Sunday was the Festa della Capra. The two Ramponi sisters, Rina and Bruna, prepared everything downstairs. We were summoned at one o'clock, to see an impressive array of bottles brought by Bruna's husband Enrico, Montàn's grandson.

The kid, prepared in the traditional way, as I described earlier, and served with polenta and the sauce, was far lighter and richer than one could possibly imagine. Conversation inevitably turned to food. Rina talked of wild herbs and salad gathered from the hillsides – *insalata di campo* – and of wild fennel, of which the flower was used at home as a favourite decoration. Maria mentioned *acquacotta* – literally, cooked water but sometimes known as charcoal burner's soup – made with wild mushrooms and some toasted bread.

Enrico recounted how the mother of his son's wife used some forty different species of wild grasses, plants and herbs in her *torte*. 'She doesn't know any of their names,' he laughed, 'but that doesn't matter at all. The point is that the result is quite delicious, more delicious than anything I have tasted.'

Whatever the hardships brought by the war and whatever the huge changes that followed in its wake, two closely linked Tuscan emotions certainly seem to have survived: a love of the land and a love of what it produces. It is important to a Tuscan to eat his own produce from his own carefully tended *orto*. And in the Lunigiana, local patriotism (as expressed by Enrico) holds that the olive oil of Magliano is infinitely superior to the more famous oil of Lucca. The truth is that you like what you know and, above all, trust.

To this day, whether one talks of subtle creations like those of Agostino, or the Lunigiana's more robust dishes, the discussion immediately involves everybody. But food is not just a conversational common denominator like the weather is in Britain. The subject, sometimes passionately debated, represents a personal philosophy of life.

Even after all the different wines – some of Luigi's red *moussant* from the castle's vines to start with, then the conventional red from the castle, and then one of Enrico's own vintages – a bottle of home-made grappa appeared. Clearly it was special: Rina fetched a set of tall flute goblets carved from wood because good grappa is said to taste much better from wood than from glass.

'*Per digerire*,' coaxed Enrico, with the bottle poised. 'It settles the stomach.' The Italians have a marvellous way of using health as the best excuse for self-indulgence. Antony needed no such argument, and agreed immediately on hearing its local provenance. After much urging, I gave in too. I did not regret it. The grappa was wonderfully pure. Maria refused with a laugh. She said she had drunk more than enough already. Like many Tuscan women, she is careful; she drinks her wine 'baptized' while eating vegetables, and at full strength only with meat.

During our time at Aulla, the memorial mass for Vittorio took place. As the Angelus sounded, Maria and Rina went off to change into smart silk dresses, and, in our hired car, we drove the two Chiodetti widows down to the old church of San Caprasio.

The service was starting when we arrived, but this did not seem to matter, nor did it stop relations of Vittorio and Maria from coming to greet us. As Vittorio's sisters reached up to embrace Antony, it was strange to think of them bouncing him on their laps over forty years ago. The rest of the congregation, made up mostly of older townsfolk and some nuns, eyed the distraction benignly.

Kneeling, then standing, then mouthing the long-forgotten responses, I followed the service automatically, with my mind wandering between memories and irrelevant impressions. A painted statue of the Virgin was crowned with a halo of electric stars, which looked incongruously like the European Community flag. Perhaps the image was not so inappropriate if one thinks of the medieval Church's supranational role.

The old priest's hands shook from Parkinson's disease. He was assisted by a slightly retarded boy of the sort the British tend to deride as a village idiot. The Italians, on the other hand, would say that 'he has not got all his Fridays' and treat him as 'a child of God' – a universal relative. While the priest went through the ritual of the mass, covering and uncovering the chalice rather like an absent-minded conjurer, the boy wandered about behind the altar, occasionally in the way, occasionally helping. Even when he imitated the priest's shaking hand and grinned at the congregation, there was no murmur of disapproval.

This engagingly informal yet moving service was typical of the Lunigiana: both uncensorious and generous. I could think of no other community where, from the beginning, my parents and their occasionally eccentric friends could have been made to feel so at home; where the poorest peasant and his wife invited you into their house as an equal, poured glasses of their own wine, then tried to press food upon you and a basket of figs, as Amadeo had done, when you left. Any suggestion of payment was liable to cause a look of pained astonishment.

They were so good-looking, these mountain people: they had the dignity of aristocracy yet none of its vices. Their bravery could never be doubted after what they had been through – including those years of emigration before the First World War, when many had tried to walk to England to find work, not knowing that there was a stretch of sea to cross on the way. But the real trial by fire came during the Second World War, when they were dragged into a conflict they did not want, by a regime they had come to detest.

My eyes strayed to a marble tablet in a side chapel, commemorating defunct citizens of Aulla. Names such as Adalberto and Ermenegilda were resonant of the Middle Ages. This frontier region was deeply marked by its strategic position and history. The Lunigiana's main valley of the Magra, with the pass over the Apennines to Parma, had been fought for by so many rivals – Genoese, Milanese, Germans, Tuscans, Guelphs, Ghibellines, French and, much later, those Spaniards who invaded the Magra valley in the eighteenth century, having captured the arsenal port of La Spezia.

As the service approached its end, I was conscious of a slight sensation of having come full circle. On the arch above the chancel were the arms of the Malaspina Count-Bishops who ruled the Lunigiana from the early thirteenth century. Their later device, that lion rampant in a thicket of thorns, as I knew of only too well, still adorned the huge fireplace of *pietra serena* in the castle. And somewhere in the church, I remembered, there had been a plaque to the memory of Adamo Centurione, the Genoese warlord who built the Fortress of Brunella in the early sixteenth century.

One memory in particular made me feel ludicrously ancient, almost part of this chain of history. Enrico's grandfather, Montàn (Ramponi's predecessor as *contadino* at the castle), could remember from his own childhood – it must have been in the 1840s – the carriage of the last Duke of Modena, Francesco Ferdinando d'Este, rattling over Aulla's cobbled streets to his summer palace by the river. The Este Palace still stands – less than two hundred metres from where we were kneeling – but today its corridors echo to the cries of schoolchildren.

It was impossible to picture Montàn himself as a child watching the carriage go past. Even my memory of him as an old man has now been superimposed by another image. I can summon up only the bewhiskered figure in a wide-brimmed hat and mountain cloak that my father had drawn. This sketch, which I watched him working on, commemorates those days when Montàn, Ulisse the Wise and Rina's father, Ramponi, helped him to create his paradise.

The castle that he found was, to me and my brothers, the most beautiful and magical place in the world. But when I look back, I can easily see why friends and relatives, especially Aunt Janet, considered my parents wildly imprudent, if not mad, to settle in such a place. Thank God for imprudence.

ACKNOWLEDGEMENTS

The very first people to deserve credit are Andrew Nurnberg, my literary agent, and Peter Carson, who together came up with the idea for this book. Eleo Gordon took on the project from the beginning, and has been a wonderful source of encouragement and good advice ever since.

Before writing anything, I went back to Italy with my son Antony Beevor, so that I could refresh my memories of Aulla and Poggio, and in some cases have them corrected, in the course of long conversations with friends from the past. The contributions from Maria Chiodetti, her sister-in-law, Rina Chiodetti, Adelcisa and Carlo Guerrini, Enrico Ricci, Luigi and Anamaria Cuffini, and Dante and Modesta Ramponi were considerable. Staying with Maria in her house just under the castle, eating her superb cooking once again, constantly talking over old times, enabled us to relive those years in a way that would have been impossible in England.

We also owe a huge debt of gratitude to Conte and Contessa Sanminiatelli for their ever-generous hospitality and suggestions during our research; and to Donna Anna Corsini who, although the same age as me, still swims huge distances out to sea each day at Forte dei Marmi. Other friends from Florence who brought back many memories were Gigliola Maltini and Gabriella de Montemayor. My nephew Michael Waterfield and his sister Harriet have also helped with their comments and corrections.

Lastly, this book would not have been possible without my

Acknowledgements

son Antony Beevor, who worked with me and helped write it all down, his wife Artemis Cooper who advised and encouraged us both, and her father, John Julius Norwich, who made invaluable comments on the manuscript.

PICTURE ACKNOWLEDGEMENTS

Almost all the photographs and illustrations come from albums and pictures in the possession of the family, but special thanks for permission to reproduce certain drawings and paintings are due to the following: Laurence Whistler, for permission to reproduce the painting and two drawings by Rex Whistler; the Trustees of the Tate Gallery for permission to reproduce *The Return from the Ride* by Charles Furse; and Derek Hill for permission to reproduce his portrait of my mother.

I am also very grateful to my great-nephew Milo Waterfield for lending me the watercolour of the castle reproduced on the jacket and Harriet Waterfield for the pencil drawings by my father of my mother in a travelling-hat, and the two sketches of my brothers when very young.

READ MORE IN PENGUIN

In every corner of the world, on every subject under the sun, Penguin represents quality and variety – the very best in publishing today.

For complete information about books available from Penguin – including Puffins, Penguin Classics and Arkana – and how to order them, write to us at the appropriate address below. Please note that for copyright reasons the selection of books varies from country to country.

In the United Kingdom: Please write to *Dept. EP, Penguin Books Ltd, Bath Road, Harmondsworth, West Drayton, Middlesex UB7 0DA*

In the United States: Please write to *Consumer Sales, Penguin USA, P.O. Box 999, Dept. 17109, Bergenfield, New Jersey 07621-0120*. VISA and MasterCard holders call 1-800-253-6476 to order Penguin titles

In Canada: Please write to *Penguin Books Canada Ltd, 10 Alcorn Avenue, Suite 300, Toronto, Ontario M4V 3B2*

In Australia: Please write to *Penguin Books Australia Ltd, P.O. Box 257, Ringwood, Victoria 3134*

In New Zealand: Please write to *Penguin Books (NZ) Ltd, Private Bag 102902, North Shore Mail Centre, Auckland 10*

In India: Please write to *Penguin Books India Pvt Ltd, 706 Eros Apartments, 56 Nehru Place, New Delhi 110 019*

In the Netherlands: Please write to *Penguin Books Netherlands bv, Postbus 3507, NL-1001 AH Amsterdam*

In Germany: Please write to *Penguin Books Deutschland GmbH, Metzlerstrasse 26, 60594 Frankfurt am Main*

In Spain: Please write to *Penguin Books S. A., Bravo Murillo 19, 1° B, 28015 Madrid*

In Italy: Please write to *Penguin Italia s.r.l., Via Felice Casati 20, I–20124 Milano*

In France: Please write to *Penguin France S. A., 17 rue Lejeune, F–31000 Toulouse*

In Japan: Please write to *Penguin Books Japan, Ishikiribashi Building, 2–5–4, Suido, Bunkyo-ku, Tokyo 112*

In South Africa: Please write to *Longman Penguin Southern Africa (Pty) Ltd, Private Bag X08, Bertsham 2013*

READ MORE IN PENGUIN

A CHOICE OF NON-FICTION

The Happy Isles of Oceania Paul Theroux

'He voyaged from the Solomons to Fiji, Tonga, Samoa, Tahiti, the Marquesas and Easter Island, stepping-stones in an odyssey of courage and toughness ... This is Paul Theroux's finest, most personal and heartfelt travel book' – *Observer*

Spoken in Darkness Ann E. Imbrie

A woman's attempt to understand how and why her childhood friend became, at twenty-five, the victim of a serial killer. 'Imbrie has created a highly original and heartbreaking narrative. The ground she covers is impressive: everything from feminist critiques of cheerleaders, the pain of mother–daughter relationships to the anomalies of the American judiciary ... awesome and inspiring' – *Time Out*

Fragments of Autobiography Graham Greene

Containing the two parts of Graham Greene's autobiography, *A Sort of Life* and *Ways of Escape*, this is an engaging, vivid and often amusing account of the author's memories of his childhood, traumatic schooldays and encounters as a writer and traveller.

The New Spaniards John Hooper

Spain has become a land of extraordinary paradoxes in which traditional attitudes and contemporary preoccupations exist side by side. The country attracts millions of visitors – yet few see beyond the hotels and resorts of its coastline. John Hooper's fascinating study brings to life the many faces of Spain in the 1990s.

The Loss of El Dorado V. S. Naipaul

Focusing on the early nineteenth century, when British occupants inflicted a reign of terror on the island's black population, V. S. Naipaul's passionate and vivid recreation of the history of Trinidad exposes the barbaric cruelties of slavery and torture and their consequences on all strata of society. 'A masterpiece' – *Sunday Telegraph*

READ MORE IN PENGUIN

A CHOICE OF NON-FICTION

The Time of My Life Denis Healey

'Denis Healey's memoirs have been rightly hailed for their intelligence, wit and charm ... *The Time of My Life* should be read, certainly for pleasure, but also for profit ... he bestrides the post war world, a Colossus of a kind' – *Independent.* 'No finer autobiography has been written by a British politician this century' – *Economist*

Far Flung Floyd Keith Floyd

Keith Floyd's latest culinary odyssey takes him to the far flung East and the exotic flavours of Malaysia, Hong Kong, Vietnam and Thailand. The irrepressible Floyd as usual spices his recipes with witty stories, wry observation and a generous pinch of gastronomic wisdom.

Genie Russ Rymer

In 1970 thirteen-year-old Genie emerged from a terrible captivity. Her entire childhood had been spent in one room, caged in a cot or strapped in a chair. Almost mute, without linguistic or social skills, Genie aroused enormous excitement among the scientists who took over her life. 'Moving and terrifying ... opens windows some might prefer kept shut on man's inhumanity' – Ruth Rendell

The Galapagos Affair John Treherne

Stories about Friedrich Ritter and Dore Strauch, settlers on the remote Galapagos island of Floreana, quickly captivated the world's press in the early thirties. Then death and disappearance took the rumours to fever pitch ... 'A tale of brilliant mystery' – Paul Theroux

1914 Lyn Macdonald

'Once again she has collected an extraordinary mass of original accounts, some by old soldiers, some in the form of diaries and journals, even by French civilians ... Lyn Macdonald's research has been vast, and in result is triumphant' – Raleigh Trevelyan in the *Tablet*. 'These poignant voices from the past conjure up a lost innocence as well as a lost generation' – *Mail on Sunday*

READ MORE IN PENGUIN

A CHOICE OF NON-FICTION

My Secret Planet Denis Healey

'This is an anthology of the prose and poetry that has provided pleasure and inspiration to Denis Healey throughout his life ... pleasurable on account of the literature selected and also for the insight it provides of Denis Healey outside the world of politics ... a thoroughly good read' – *The Times*

The Sun King Nancy Mitford

Nancy Mitford's magnificent biography of Louis XIV is also an illuminating examination of France in the late seventeenth and early eighteenth centuries. It covers the intrigues of the court and the love affairs of the king, with extensive illustrations, many in full colour.

This Time Next Week Leslie Thomas

'Mr Thomas's book is all humanity, to which is added a Welshman's mastery of words ... Some of his episodes are hilarious, some unbearably touching, but everyone, staff and children, is looked upon with compassion' – *Observer*. 'Admirably written, with clarity, realism, poignancy and humour' – *Daily Telegraph*

Against the Stranger Janine di Giovanni

'In her powerfully written book Janine di Giovanni evokes the atmosphere of the Palestinian refugee camps in the Gaza Strip ... The effect of the Palestinians' sufferings on the next generation of children is powerfully documented' – *Sunday Express*

Native Stranger Eddy L. Harris

Native Stranger is a startling chronicle of the author's search for himself in Africa, the land of his ancestors. 'Since Richard Wright's *Black Power*, there has been a dearth of travel narratives on Africa by black Americans. *Native Stranger* picks up where Wright left off, and does so with both courage and honesty' – Caryl Phillips in the *Washington Post*

READ MORE IN PENGUIN

BIOGRAPHY AND AUTOBIOGRAPHY

Freedom from Fear Aung San Suu Kyi

Aung San Suu Kyi, human-rights activist and leader of Burma's National League for Democracy, was detained in 1989 by SLORC, the ruling military junta. In July 1995 she was liberated from six years' house arrest. *Freedom From Fear* contains speeches, letters and interviews, as well as forewords by Archbishop Desmond Tutu and Václav Havel and gives a voice to Burma's 'woman of destiny'.

Memories of a Catholic Girlhood Mary McCarthy

'Many a time in the course of doing these memoirs,' Mary McCarthy says, 'I have wished that I were writing fiction.' 'Superb ... so heartbreaking that in comparison Jane Eyre seems to have got off lightly' – *Spectator*

A Short Walk from Harrods Dirk Bogarde

In this volume of memoirs, Dirk Bogarde pays tribute to the corner of Provence that was his home for over two decades, and to Forwood, his manager and friend of fifty years, whose long and wretched illness brought an end to a paradise. 'A brave and moving book' – *Daily Telegraph*

When Shrimps Learn to Whistle Denis Healey

The Time of My Life was widely acclaimed as a masterpiece. Taking up the most powerful political themes that emerge from it Denis Healey now gives us this stimulating companion volume. 'Forty-three years of ruminations ... by the greatest foreign secretary we never had' – *New Statesman & Society*

Eating Children Jill Tweedie

Jill Tweedie's second memoir, *Frightening People*, incomplete due to her tragically early death in 1993, is published here for the first time. 'Magnificent ... with wit, without a shred of self-pity, she tells the story of an unhappy middle-class suburban child with a monstrously cruel father, and a hopeless mother' – *Guardian*